EDUCATIONAL PLANNING–PROGRAMMING–BUDGETING

A Systems Approach

HARRY J. HARTLEY
New York University

PRENTICE-HALL, INC., ENGLEWOOD CLIFFS, NEW JERSEY

Library of Congress Catalog Card No.: 68-29615

Printed in the United States of America

Current printing (last digit):
10 9 8 7 6 5 4

PRENTICE-HALL INTERNATIONAL, INC., *London*
PRENTICE-HALL OF AUSTRALIA, PTY. LTD., *Sydney*
PRENTICE-HALL OF CANADA, LTD., *Toronto*
PRENTICE-HALL OF INDIA PRIVATE LTD., *New Delhi*
PRENTICE-HALL OF JAPAN, INC., *Tokyo*

PREFACE

Midway through the decade of the 1960's a revolutionary approach to administrative planning was accorded recognition by a Presidential pronouncement introducing program budgeting into the entire federal structure. The conceptual simplicity of the new planning-programming-budgeting system (PPBS) is such that it can be applied, with judicious concern, to nearly any type of human organization. As the monolithic education complex grows to become the single largest *industry* in this country, one can envisage the types of public demands that will be placed upon schools generally and upon school leaders in particular. The rationale for this book is to attempt to provide a framework for intelligent planning which is a substantial improvement over conventional educational planning procedures.

We hear about the numerous shortcomings that afflict our educational system, and critics hasten to point out alleged weaknesses. However, it cannot be emphasized too strongly that our educational system, despite its faults, has improved remarkably in recent years. Program budgeting is portrayed in this text as a means for accelerating such advancement. This technique does not compensate for insufficient funds, nor is it intended to be a cost-reduction device for hard-pressed school officials. Unfortunately for public education, American adherence to the notion of free public schools has never been as strong as our traditional reluctance to make sufficient public and private wealth available for public purposes. A planning-programming-budgeting system (PPBS) provides a more rational basis for the efficient allocation of scarce resources among competing programs. *Its basic distinction from traditional planning procedures is that the focus is upon the outputs of an organization rather than upon its inputs.* In the case of a school, the outputs are obtained from the instructional programs and curricular activities.

The need for such a book is apparent to educators who, after learning of contemporary approaches to planning and decision making that were developed in various disciplines, have attempted to trace educational applications of these techniques by means of a review of the literature. In the case of program budgeting, there is a growing body of literature describing the usage of PPBS in industry and in the federal, state, and municipal governments, but relatively little in the context of education. Thanks are due the governmental and private agencies who provided information and much of the original research on program budgeting that preceded this text. The citation of selected works is intended to aid those who wish to read more intensively on the subject.

A major concern in preparing this book was drawing a line between a technical treatise on budget theory and the mechanics of school financial administration on the one hand, and, on the other, a more generalized description of a conceptual planning process that is appropriate for all educators. If the program budgeting process is to be successfully implemented in local schools, it should be preceded by a dialogue between instructional personnel who design the curriculum, financial administrators who devise the patterns of support, operations analysts who wish to quantify both instructional and financial elements, and skeptics who believe that the problems of education are not amenable to operations analysis. Predicting the readership toward whom this text should be pointed is difficult. My hope is that the following chapters convey the subject of inquiry to both curricular and financial specialists, without shortchanging either.

In order to combine the practitioner's perspective with that of a professor, I am proud to include in the text the contributions of Sol Levin, a widely respected school business administrator of a large, suburban school district in the metropolitan New York area, and

Robert Pavese, the young and competent Budget Director of Long Island University.

Acknowledgements are due to numerous persons. The preparation of the final draft was greatly aided by the critical comments of selected professors, although the responsibility for content, organization, possible lack of clarity or other shortcomings are mine alone. Professors who reviewed critically one or two chapters and provided guidelines for revising earlier drafts include: William Ammentorp (University of Minnesota); Joseph M. Cronin (Harvard University); Terry L. Eidell (University of Oregon); Wayne K. Hoy (Oklahoma State University); Chester Kiser (State University of New York at Buffalo); Samuel A. Moore (Michigan State University); J. Alan Thomas (University of Chicago); and Donald J. Willower (Pennsylvania State University). I am indebted to each for considerable talent and time expended on behalf of the text. Eve K. Booth, Joyce Maravich, and Joseph F. Sweeney provided assistance in the preparation of the manuscript.

Thanks are due, lastly, to Professors Daniel E. Griffiths and Richard C. Lonsdale, and to my departmental colleagues at New York University for encouraging me to pursue my interests in the topic of this book and for contributing to a climate conducive to scholarship.

Harry J. Hartley

CONTENTS

LIST OF FIGURES

LIST OF TABLES

Planning is an exercise in conflict management rather than only the sober application of technical rationality.

Bertram M. Gross

Chapter One

EDUCATIONAL PLANNING AND ECONOMIC RATIONALITY

The most severe critics of American education appear to believe that local schools possess modest aspirations and even more modest achievements. Although this may be an unjust viewpoint, it serves to point up the fact that the schools generally have been provided with ineffectual devices for planning their activities and reporting to the public their program accomplishments. The problem is compounded by the lack of consensus as to what constitutes educational output. With uncertainty surrounding the notion of educational productivity, the schools have suffered because of problems in designing their programs, assessing their performance, and developing suitable allocative strategies, or means to determine how best to utilize limited human and nonhuman resources in the process of learning.

What is lacking is a general framework for educational planning that is appropriate for local school districts and other educational institutions. The framework for program design and analysis described in subsequent chapters is a product of economic rationality and is intended to be both integrative and flexible. By portraying school activities as a system, it serves to integrate curriculum planning with financial administration and depicts the concomitant effects of all of the component variables of an educational program. The framework is flexible in that it is appropriate regardless of the prevailing educational philosophy, curricular offerings, grading and organizational structure, teaching methodology, evaluation measures, and financial administration procedures. Inasmuch as schools are expanding their services in response to increased demands and expectations, there has been a great upsurge in public interest in school programs, finance, and budgets. In this social climate, educators require more powerful instruments to interpret their contributions and needs to the public and to legislators.

Planning is used in a broad sense to encompass a rational means-ends assessment of resources and objectives by all interested parties, although some cynics contend that in education, there are *only* means, no ends. This process relates inputs and outputs and directs attention to the preparation of time-phased future activities. Inasmuch as the public's goals in education seem to exceed its present reach, improved planning and reporting by the schools can reduce the gap between aspirations and scarce resources. Emphasis is upon developing long-range plans as a basis for combating the built-in tendencies toward rigidity and inertia found in school systems; such plans should be subject to review and revision as needed. A major concern of many educators is their relative lack of active involvement in the development of educational policies that affect them. The framework to be described is deemed appropriate for elementary and secondary teachers, curriculum specialists, school business administrators and finance specialists, supervisors, administrators at both building and central office levels, board of education members, and others who share in the responsibility for educational planning and policy making. In addition, there are obvious implications for other specialized areas, including higher education, vocational education, private schools and international education.

On the surface, a term such as planning seems innocent enough to use without reservation in the context of education. However, to some persons, planning conjures up the image of a totalitarian society embracing centrally planned economic objectives and activities. In this case, self-expression and human freedom may approach a kind of universal triviality. The requisite assumption for the use of economic models in education is that *some* planning is desirable; exactly how much is less clear.

For different time spans of planning, several notations are used:

1. Long-range plans: often cover more than five years;

2. Medium-range plans: concerned with three to five years;
3. Short-range plans: pertain to the nearest year.

When the time horizon is devoted to medium and long-range plans, the process is sometimes called *strategic planning;* while for short-range planning the term *tactical planning* may be used.

Short and Long-Range Planning: Incrementalism in Local Schools

The aims of educational planning are to formulate a system-wide philosophy, general goals, and instructional objectives;[1] organize relevant data; determine personnel, space, and material requirements; examine alternative procedures and establish priorities; provide for communications and information retrieval for the system; analyze financial resources; evaluate how well objectives are being met; look to the future; and review the system continually to ensure that objectives are being reformulated and that the system is dynamic and innovative rather than static and rigid. If properly conducted, systematic planning can provide educators with a more complete basis for rational choice. It is a way of attempting somewhat to control the future instead of merely reacting to it and being controlled by it.

An approach conducive to long-range planning can result in projections of multiyear programs. Long-range may mean six years, or even twelve years, if one considers a complete program for an individual from the time he enters first grade until he graduates from high school. The most widely used time span in government program budget planning is five years, and this is adequate at least for purposes of discussion. A major weakness of present school planning is the relatively little attention given to strategic, or long-term, planning. Although most school districts make pupil projections as well as building and capital-facility estimates, active teacher involvement in planning and future resource allocation is modest,

[1] The extent to which objectives are to be operationally stated is not specified. Many systems analysts believe that one does not begin with setting objectives; rather objectives will evolve, or at least be clarified, after a model is devised for the school district. This is not quite serendipity, but it relieves the systems analyst of the need to specify *all* objectives prior to his work.

at best. Local school budgets tend to be prepared in the "incremental style," which means that the primary basis for next year's budget is this year's budget. The major difference between the two is likely to be only an increase in each of the traditional categories of an object-of-expenditure, or input, type of budget.[2] Next year's budget, for example, contains the same structure as this year's. Little attempt is made to evaluate the various programs, or outputs, which are presumed to be supported by the budget. The budget is almost never reviewed by the board of education or superintendent on a completely differentiated basis each year in the sense of reconsidering the value of each existing program. In contrast, the program budget places emphasis upon the final product, or at least the programs, of the school and provides for continual evaluation and time-phased systematic planning.

The underlying premise for this approach is that it represents an improvement over existing educational planning techniques. In very simple terms, *the advantage of the proposed approach over traditional means is that in the new format, emphasis is placed upon the outputs, or programs of the school, rather than on the inputs that are necessary to support these programs.* Examples of inputs are personnel, maintenance, space, and supplies. This distinction is elementary, but the implications for educational planning are substantial. Subsequent sections portray selected variables in school planning, including the behavioral environment.

Emphasis upon curricular designs

With the focus upon instructional programs, planning and budget requirements will be directed primarily toward the educational outcomes desired by a system and secondarily to such input components as number of buses, salaries of teachers, administrative costs, debt service, and others that are reported in a conventional local school budget. It is a rare occasion indeed when one locates a school district that reports its total budget in terms of its curricular programs, yet curriculum specialists do not hesitate to define curriculum as encompassing all of the activities of a school. The raison d'etre of expenditures reported in a school budget is to sup-

[2] A format showing conventional, line-item school budget categories is contained in Appendix A.

port some unified system of curricular objectives and instructional programs. This book is not primarily a treatise on curriculum, but curriculum, however it is defined, occupies a prominent position in the framework put forth. Some curriculum revisionists exhibit a fanaticism that causes them to redouble their energies when they lose sight of their aims; thus no good purpose is served by draping the mantle of curricular specialist around one who revises only for the sake of revision. Program budgeting calls for curricular design and revision, but the format is specified. More detailed discussions of the program structure outlined above are contained in later chapters.

Systems Analysis and Program Budgeting

It is probable that educational planning in the near future will utilize, to a great extent, the concept of *program budgeting*. In this contemporary approach to organizational planning, the word "program" does not refer to computer programming, but to the more common notion of the desired achievements of an organization. Program budgeting is a subunit of a more comprehensive approach to the study of organizational activities, which, for lack of a more descriptive term, may be called systems analysis.

By providing a framework that promotes commonalities in approach, systems analysis encourages interdisciplinary dialogues and combats the myopic fractionalization of contemporary scholarship. It furnishes the general philosophical basis for the educational planning techniques of program budgeting. However, the term systems analysis has a great number of definitions and should be applied with considerable caution. It is part of the new generation of interrelated management procedures that seek to enhance organizational rationality. A description of this concept is provided in greater detail along with a portrayal of how particular behavioral disciplines and noneducational organizations have developed and implemented sophisticated procedures that have much potential value for educators.

A grouping of schools is classified as a school system, and many of the properties of rigorously defined economic-social-political-psychological-cultural and other behavioral systems can be identified in existing schools. There is a group of academic disciplines and subdisciplines, such as the social and life sciences, cybernetics, and operations research, which may be studied together under the rubric of "systems sciences." Empirical research and models from these areas may be of much help to educational planners.

In short, systems analysis provides an intellectual technique for unifying the diverse activities of a school in a logically consistent fashion. The school system may be conceived as operating a specified "mix" of programs, each of which has a determinable cost. As a means of supporting and assessing these programs, the concept of program budgeting appears to be as appropriate in education as it has been in various government agencies and industrial settings. The experiences of the Department of Defense and several municipal and state governments with systems planning may provide clues for improved educational planning. Many problems of school officials seem to be susceptible to the design, analysis and optimization methods of systems analysis, although discretion should be exercised in the adoption of models at the local level. At present, some of the analytical procedures are appreciably more elaborate than the measurement data available in education.

The interdependence of planning and the budget

An educational budget is a financial expression of the objectives, programs, and activities of a school system. It should be viewed as more than a justification or constraint for action. Under the program budget process, the ethos of budgeting becomes planning and analysis. This type of budget is characterized by its relation to some operational guidelines of the organization, and it exposes the naked truth of whether the professed values of a human group are, in fact, transformed into resource allocations. In addition, it provides a means of central control of expenditure and accountability, and contains a statement of projected needs that encourages long-range, time-phased planning.

As an executive tool, the process of program budgeting may be used to evaluate viable alternatives, and perhaps even performance. If it is a public budget, the document reflects public objectives and social philosophy. After adoption, it provides an internal work plan. The program budget is a product of political economy, combining economic and political rationality, with emphasis on the former; it is the connecting link between the program structure of a school and its available resources; and it is the focus for organizational planning, encompassing goal-setting, resource allocation, evaluative review, and revision of objectives.

Educational Planning at Three Governmental Levels

Planning in education is dependent upon intergovernmental relations, inasmuch as it takes place on national, state, regional, and local levels. Many of the programmatic activities occurring in a classroom are shaped by external forces and are complicated by intergovernmental fiscal relations.

National

At the highest level, a nation may wish to invest in education in order to achieve desired socioeconomic objectives, such as a reduction of poverty and illiteracy with an increase in both manpower capabilities and the rate of national growth. In the United States, the decade of the 1960's resulted in an increase in federal spending for public education from a negligible amount to a figure in excess of two billion dollars. One explanation is that dollars spent on education were viewed as a form of investment in human capital, and that the return, or yield, on this type of investment was relatively higher than other programs which competed for the federal dollars. It is contended by some that education never before has loomed so important in the development of any nation.[3] Projections for the 1970's indicate that this upsurge of interest in, and financial commitment to, education will continue. A growing commitment to educational planning is found among both developed and underdeveloped nations of the world.[4] Planners attempt to determine

[3] Sidney W. Tiedt, *The Role of the Federal Government in Education* (New York: Oxford University Press, 1966).

[4] A discussion of educational planning in the context of advanced, semi-advanced, underdeveloped, and partially developed countries is contained in Charles S. Benson, *The School and the Economic System* (Chicago: Science Research Associates, 1966), Chapter 9. Additional recent research into national educational planning models was conducted by several member countries of the Organization for Economic Cooperation and Development (OECD), Paris; publications will be forthcoming.

the optimum level of allocation of scarce resources by relating the potential benefits received from a specific investment to the anticipated costs. National planning models can be constructed as a means of improving coordination of a country's educational and economic systems with its manpower needs. Many of the emerging planning and allocative strategies were originally developed by research projects supported by the federal government. The employment of national resources in educational research, development, dissemination, and implementation is increasing in response to demands for educational excellence. The program budget is also a product of federal research, and exemplifies the kind of sophisticated planning aids that local school officials might not otherwise have been able to use.

In another area of concern, some experts are contending that as education assumes a higher position of national priority, the Federal Government should establish a separate Cabinet-level Department of Education. If education is, as one President contended, ". . . the most basic single prerequisite to progress in a democratic society . . . ,"[5] it should not be relegated to a second echelon status within another department. Miles, a specialist in public administration, proposed that under the present planning structure, the President's effective span of control is being exceeded, and that a separate Department of Education is necessary in a culture which finds management of knowledge a difficult task.[6]

State

In a legal sense, the Tenth Amendment to the United States Constitution indirectly makes public education a responsibility of the individual states. This may be illustrated by such state-determined controls as certification, minimum salaries, pupil transportation, and many others. In most states, in excess of 40 per cent of a local school budget is provided by state revenue, and the state is actively involved in setting objectives and engaging in educational planning. A number of states are also demonstrating leadership in planning for higher education. The number and prestige

[5] Lyndon B. Johnson's statement is cited in Rufus E. Miles, Jr., "The Case for a Federal Department of Education," *Public Administration Review,* XXVII, No. 1 (March, 1967), 3.

[6] *Ibid.,* pp. 1–9.

of junior-community colleges, state colleges, and state universities have increased substantially in the past decade. Our two largest states confirm this notion, although their traditions differ. California's ambitious goal is to provide a college education for every high school graduate who seeks one. The interrelationship of educational planning and politics was clearly demonstrated in the 1967 clash between Governor Reagan and the University of California. New York's late-blooming State University, founded in 1948, expects to have an enrollment of 260,000 by 1974. The State University of New York (SUNY) consists of more than sixty campuses and represents virtually every kind of academic community.

California is also providing leadership in installing program budgeting procedures in its system of higher education. President Charles J. Hitch of the University of California, who supervised the new program budget procedures in the Department of Defense while serving as Comptroller and Assistant Secretary of Defense, established program analysis procedures for the entire complex of California's public colleges and universities.

At the state level, education generally ranks with highways and public welfare as a major expense and planning category. The concern for improvement of state educational planning was demonstrated clearly by the initiative taken by eight state departments of education in developing a cooperative project entitled "Designing Education for the Future."[7] Long-range planning for 1980 was one of the primary concerns of this project. One of the contributors analyzed the trend toward systems planning in education and reviewed several contemporary planning technologies. Prominent among these was program budgeting, which Culbertson recommended as appropriate for state planning agencies. Strategic variables in planning were reviewed and related to the planning-programming-budgeting system (PPBS). He advocated the creation of state planning agencies that would concentrate on the total system of education from preschool through university training.[8]

[7] The Eight-State Project is a four-year undertaking and was initiated in 1965. Directed by Professor Edgar L. Morphet, it is supported by the United States Office of Education and these states: Arizona, Colorado, Idaho, Montana, Nevada, New Mexico, Utah, and Wyoming. The project office is located in Denver, Colorado.

[8] Jack A. Culbertson, "State Planning for Education," in *Planning and Effecting Needed Changes in Education,* Edgar L. Morphet and Charles O. Ryan, editors (New York: Citation, 1967), pp. 266–85.

Local

The primary focus of this book is upon planning for instruction and budgeting at the local level. The assumption is that existing planning procedures can be improved upon by the development of systematic, analytical techniques that have proven successful in other settings. Inasmuch as there are approximately 20,000 operating local public school systems with a wide range of differences in objectives, procedures, and resources, the program budget conceptual framework is presented in a manner that makes it appropriate for each of these relatively autonomous, locally controlled systems. To improve the overall quality of education is the broad objective of system-oriented program budgeting. More specifically, this technique is designed to help educators and boards of education make better decisions on the allocation of scarce resources by assessing viable alternative ways of accomplishing desired objectives. It is not intended as a cost-reduction restraint upon teachers or upon other personnel or programs. On the contrary, it may be used to justify additional expenditures for specific programs or salaries. Too often, analytical tools are not provided to illustrate in objective terms what benefits are received from public investment in education. If the measurable benefits are substantial, it seems reasonable to assume that additional expenditures for education will be justified on this benefit-cost basis. A budget is seldom adequate to meet all educational needs, but with a program budget, value priorities are more objectively determined and expressed.

In addition to national, state and local levels, the emergence of consortia, along with county and regional organizations, will also have an impact on educational planning procedures. Scarcity of funds restricts the long-range planning opportunities for many local systems, particularly those in troubled urban areas. James examined the budgetary process of fourteen large city school districts and observed that most budget decisions in these systems are made "at the margin." That is to say, inherent in the basic structure of budget decisions in big city school systems is the assumption that existing activities and programs will continue. Thus, the analysis of the budget centers around proposed increments in, or modifications of, existing activities and programs. In the same study, James predicted that the use of program budgeting will increase in large city school systems during the decade of the 1970's.[9]

Participatory Planning

There are at least a half dozen categories of people who should be represented in some aspect of local school planning and budget preparation:

1. Students: the clients served by a school;
2. Teachers: the major element of the professional staff;
3. Building administrators: principals and supervisors;
4. Central office administrators: superintendent and assistants;
5. Board of education: representing the public; and
6. Paraprofessionals and other employees: supporting services.

Participatory planning maximizes the contributions of all personnel who express interest and possess specialized areas of expertise. It provides a way to avoid complete "top-down" direction in which policies are executed at the central administration level with little or no active involvement of teachers and others who are affected by the policies. The program budget framework allows for a delineation of responsibilities so that each of the participant groups mentioned above clearly understands its role in policy development and planning. If there is ambiguity of directions and noninvolvement in policy by most members of the organization, the consequences may be very dysfunctional for the school system. Alienation, apathy, dislike, and ambivalent feelings toward the school might result. Such factors may suggest the need for fresh modes of organization and presage the creation of new administrative ideologies. Organizational theorists, using interdisciplinary modes of inquiry, are directing greater attention not only to an improved formal structure of human groups, but to the ways in

[9] H. Thomas James, James A. Kelly, and Walter I. Garms, *Determinants of Educational Expenditures in Large Cities of the United States*, Research Project No. 2389 (Stanford, Calif.: School of Education, Stanford University, USOE Cooperative, 1966), p. 89. This study also contains a concise description of conceptual approaches to budgeting, such as the program budget format.

which members can most effectively interact and contribute to the leadership of the organization.

Teachers should be, and it is apparent that they are, seeking a more active role in shaping educational policy. Only a board of education has the legal authority to enact policy, but students, teachers and building-level administrators should have the opportunity to participate in the formulation of decisions that will become official policy. It appears that this is a crucial issue, for as many local districts have grown and increased their complexities with data banks, information centers, and other computerized administration devices, decision making has become much more centralized within a tightly defined chain of command. The deputy superintendent of the nation's largest school district analyzed the issue succinctly in a statement describing one danger of this centralizing tendency:

> If democratic government is to be preserved, a way must be found to protect the individual's rights of decision, dissent, and deviation. How to balance the advantages of centralized decision making against the human survival values of individual decision making at the "point of stress" is a basic problem of management and government in our time.[10]

Both the National Education Association and the United Federation of Teachers support increased participation by teachers in policy development. One outgrowth of this activism is the trend toward more sophisticated collective negotiations procedures in education. The impact upon school administration is great and a possible effect has been to reduce unilateral decision making.[11] Teachers are looking to their own resources to improve their conditions of employment and to increase their involvement in planning. The program budget provides a potential means for improving the organization of schools by relating economic resources to an ordering of instructional objectives.

[10] Letter from Frederick W. Hill, Deputy Superintendent of Schools, Board of Education, The City of New York, November 3, 1966.

[11] A detailed discussion of professional negotiations and collective bargaining in public education is provided in Myron Lieberman and Michael H. Moskow, *Collective Negotiations for Education* (Chicago: Rand McNally, 1966). Much more literature in this field is available, and it seems to be increasing at an accelerating rate.

Economics of Education in Planning and Administration

Economics is contributing systems procedures and models to educators who participate in policy recommendations, decision making, evaluation, and general educational planning. This growing analytical content, virtually nonexistent in the conventional wisdom of school finance specialists of the recent past, is addressed to some form of optimal educational choices in the environments of uncertainty and resource scarcity. It does not ensure instant success, but does promise a better way of "muddling through."

As a science of values, economics is devoted to the study of rational choices made by man in his attempt to utilize scarce resources to satisfy identifiable basic needs. As an aid to educational decision makers, the fabric of economics is woven to yield conceptual means for reducing uncertainty and increasing rationality in the exercise of human judgment. Precision, orderliness, and procedures governed by logic can be used in the expression of educational preferences and in the execution of policies. Economics is thus viewed as a logic of choice rather than simply a study of those things that can be related with the measuring rod of money. The program budget is derived from the economic theory of choice over time, or capital theory.

There is strong skepticism among educators who believe that economic analysis is simply a means for making decisions on the sole basis of quantitative analysis. These critics point out that since the end-product of education cannot be quantifiably measured sufficiently, the use of economic models of the school should be minimized. This thoughtful point is well made, but the purpose of economic analysis is not to serve as a constraint. Rather, it is to provide a broad framework within which the desired educational objectives can be expressed and accomplished in the most reasonable and efficient manner. The fundamental contribution of economic analysis is its dispassionate consideration of relative valuations, even though many of these valued items cannot be expressed in quantitative terms. Economics is *not* restricted to quantified value dimensions, although much of the current economic research involves mathematical models.

Participation by economists in educational planning is not new, although the degree of involvement at the present time probably is at an all-time high. In a recent study, Bowman traced the growth in human-resource-development planning, beginning with Nassau Senior in nineteenth century England and ending with Chester Bowles' planning models for the efficient allocation of educational resources. She concluded, "Bowles' work is especially interesting because he presses further into educational systems than has any other economist model-builder. This brings us to where educators and educational administrators in particular might well take over." [12]

A number of educators have already taken over.[13] Many of the university preparation programs for educational administrators have been bolstered by the addition of a greater amount of formal study in economics and other social sciences.[14] The economics of education is a rapidly expanding field of specialization. Recent bibliographies and reviews of research in this area prepared by Blaug, Phi Delta Kappa, and the American Educational Research Association are listed at the end of this chapter. The number of professors who are making substantial contributions to the economics of education is great, and many of their works are cited in the bibliographies.

As an indication of the potential economic growth of education-related fields, the so-called "knowledge industry" may well account for half the nation's gross national product by the year 2000. The knowledge industry is a broad range of activities spanning publishing, research and development, instructional media, and other areas, and it is growing at approximately twice the rate of the rest of the economy. Human knowledge is doubling every ten years instead of every two thousand years. Thus planners are faced with the problem of how to manage the mounting volume of knowledge.

One leading spokesman for this industry claimed that new elec-

[12] Mary Jean Bowman, "The Human Investment Revolution in Economic Thought," *Sociology of Education,* XXXIX, No. 2 (Spring, 1966), 137.

[13] Professor Charles S. Benson provided the major impetus for the involvement of economists in education with his book *The Economics of Public Education* (Boston: Houghton Mifflin, 1961, rev. ed., 1968).

[14] An example of this is contained in Harry J. Hartley, "Criteria for Selection of Economics Content in Educational Administration Preparation Programs," paper presented at a University Council for Educational Administration social science conference at Columbus, Ohio, March 14, 1967.

tronic instruments offer solutions and open the way to a return to the classic concepts of education as a continual process of learning and living. The president of the Radio Corporation of America pointed out that computer assisted instruction ". . . converses with equal fluency in the numbers of science, the letters of literature or the images of art and will enable us to continue the broad and balanced learning that begins with formal education and must extend beyond it."[15] The implications for educational planners are great and the opportunities unlimited. With systematic planning strategies such as the program budget, educators can become the authors of their own thoughts and actions rather than readers and followers of mandated programs.

The growing partnership between education, business, and government is reflected by the increasing number of conferences which are attended by representatives of each area. In one such recent conference, the American Management Association addressed itself to the topics of learning systems and the learning process, business' stake in education, negotiations, new information technology and software, measures of educational effectiveness and the economics of education, national assessment, and financial planning for education.[16] The impact of this corporate alliance upon educational planning strategists has not yet been fully realized, but one can only hope that it will be to the mutual advantage of the nation's private and public interests. At stake is how Americans of the next century will think and live.

Economic Rationality vs. Political Feasibility

Inasmuch as education is publicly funded by taxes, it is to be expected that it must enter the arena of politics in order to gain support. An entire new field of specialization, labeled the politics of education, evolved in order for specialists to examine the growing

[15] Robert W. Sarnoff, speech delivered at Florida Atlantic University, Boca Raton, April 17, 1967.

[16] American Management Association, Third Annual Conference and Exhibit on Education and Training, Americana Hotel, New York City, August 8–11, 1967.

interdependence of political procedures and educational processes at the federal, state and local levels. Some knowledge of recent theory and research on the politics of education, and of the budgetary process itself, is essential for those who are interested in the behavioral environment in which educational planning takes place.[17] The union of "politics and pedagogy" is such that the means for achieving ultimate improvement of schools are as likely to have political roots as economic roots. Reading deficiencies, for example, in urban schools are manifest as part of a broader problem of power that can only have a political solution. Politics and education are inseparable.

Economics and political science gradually parted company from their original union as political economy, and they retain their distinct conceptual boundaries in the context of education.[18] Economics serves as a consultative discipline to an educational decision maker, but the actual policies and decisions are likely to be made on a political basis. Program budgeting is an economic tool which provides a somewhat scientific basis for determining priorities, but the budgetary process itself in local schools continues to be a political process. Program analysis was devised by economists and thus is an encroachment upon politics by economics, but educational budgeting will remain a political process inasmuch as it reflects the desires of individual citizens and interest groups for certain educational services. Economic analysis provides supporting data with which to make more intelligent decisions. Some economists may suffer from "illusions of adequacy," but on the whole, they appear to realize that their role is more devoted to advisement for policy than with the act of policy making. Desirability based upon economic theory prescriptions must frequently give way to political feasibility. For example, economic analysis may justify an increase

[17] Several excellent works on the state level include: Stephen K. Bailey, *et al.*, *Schoolmen in Politics* (Syracuse: Syracuse University Press, 1962); Nicholas A. Masters, *et al.*, *State Politics and the Public Schools* (New York: Knopf, 1964); and Laurence Iannaccone, *Politics in Education* (New York: Center for Applied Research in Education, Library of Education, 1967). The politics of education is the theme for the entire issue of *Phi Delta Kappan,* XLIX, No. 6 (February, 1968).

[18] The economic process in budgeting is described by Jesse Burkhead, *Government Budgeting* (New York: Wiley, 1965). The political process is contained in Aaron Wildavsky, *The Politics of the Budgetary Process* (Boston: Little, Brown, 1964).

in taxes of a specified amount and time, but the policy maker may decide that this proposal is not feasible.

The political dimension of planning is described by Gross in terms that seem to be quite applicable to a superintendent of schools:

> Planning is an exercise in conflict management rather than only the sober application of technical rationality. Any real life planning process may be characterized as a stream of successive compromises punctuated by frequent occasions of deadlock or avoidance and occasional victories, defeats and integrations.[19]

Another definition of planning, provided by Morphet, restricts the scope in education:

> Planning is *not* a process of speculating on probable developments and preparing a theoretical blueprint for meeting needs. Rather it is a process of attempting to determine appropriate goals and objectives, obtaining and analyzing pertinent information that will bring into focus present and emergent problems and needs, and obtaining agreement on steps and procedures that are designed to meet those needs so that objectives can be attained.[20]

A major task of both the economic and political system specialists of any organization is to specify objectives and goals, even though the environment imposes constraints on their actions. The program budget can help to accomplish this. This technique will be adopted by local schools when it can be shown that program analysis and budgeting will tend to make better that which is already best.[21]

Behavioral Perspectives in Education

Behavioral scientists are participating in education with increasing intensity. The premise is that nearly all of the problems of the

[19] Bertram M. Gross, "What Are Your Organization's Objectives?" *Human Relations,* XVIII, No. 3 (August, 1965), 197.

[20] Edgar L. Morphet and Charles O. Ryan, editors, *Planning and Effecting Needed Changes in Education, op. cit.,* p. xiii.

[21] A comprehensive review of studies pertaining to school budgets was made recently by Leon Ovsiew, William B. Castetter, and Adolph J. Koenig, "Budgeting," in *The Theory and Practice of School Finance,* Warren E. Gauerke and Jack R. Childress, editors (Chicago: Rand McNally, 1967), Chapter 8. In the discussion of contemporary concepts of budgeting, no mention was made of program budgeting or PPBS, indicating both the newness of this approach and the lack of implementation in local schools.

school center directly or indirectly upon behavioral issues. Each school problem pertains to something that we need to know about human behavior. Educational planners, and ideally all educators should be planners, need to study formally some of the more notable behavioral science contributions to diverse areas in education, with topics ranging from learning theory, computer assisted instruction, group dynamics, personality explorations, and cultural differences among children to community analyses, political power structures, economic returns from educational investment in human capital, and organizational behavior. The list is brief but representative of current topics of concern.

Educational administrators in the past decade attempted to incorporate new scientific bases for their profession by deriving concepts, theories, and related research from the behavioral sciences.[22] Educators engage in the study of behavioral science literature, collaborate with resource personnel from the various disciplines, and endeavor to relate their new knowledge effectively to a school setting. Many implications exist for educational planning, but progress is commonly impeded by time lags that separate the acquisition of new knowledge by academic scholars and the implementation of this knowledge by those occupying positions of educational leadership. The techniques of systems analysis and the program budget facilitate the incorporation of contemporary behavioral research contributions in school planning.

Implications of planning in other fields for education

The planning techniques of varying levels of sophistication that have been employed in noneducational settings may suggest some useful carryover for education. To cite one, urban-regional planning is a highly specialized professional field, the leaders of which must cope with some of the problems faced by educators, for

[22] To illustrate, see Daniel E. Griffiths, editor, *Behavioral Science for the Study of Education,* Part II (Chicago: University of Chicago Press, 1964). Also, the United States Office of Education awarded a five-year grant through 1970 to the Center for the Advanced Study of Educational Administration (CASEA), Eugene, Oregon. The purpose of CASEA is to provide research and dissemination pertaining to the sociobehavioral dimensions of educational leadership.

instance, optimum designs constrained by economic cost considerations, innovative practices impeded by political factors such as zoning regulations, and widespread public disagreement over and perpetual criticism of the end product.

Planning is an important requisite for nearly every phase of rational human experience, and educators can benefit from some of the planning models developed in noneducational contexts. At the philosophic level, planning is the embodiment of the "life of reason." It entails a consideration of means in relation to ends, and the mode of inquiry chosen is dependent upon the general school of philosophy that one upholds. The development of new informational and planning technologies expands the applicability of objective analysis to policy determination by providing a framework for action. Educational systems planning can promote human distinction and uniqueness, without curbing self-definition of the creative young whom it serves. It should not suppress individuality, human privacy, or intuitive judgment.

Toward a Systems Syndrome

If current interest in the topic of systems procedures and "computer-assisted everything" is a fair indication, there is reason to believe that schools may be analyzed as systems. The question that remains unanswered is as follows: Will this be simply another fad in educational administration, or will it prove its worth as an economic planning device? In fairness to those who are a bit skeptical of economic rationality, American schools in this century have already undergone and survived an unfortunate period in which a "cult of efficiency" placed dollar concerns ahead of conscience and instructional goals. This mistake must not be repeated under the guise of systems analysis. Economic efficiency is not synonymous with time-and-motion studies or the more rigid restrictions that scientific management imposed a few decades ago. It is intended to promote better usage of all of the scarce resources that contribute to the instructional program; selective use of systems procedures in schools is one potential way to avoid financial crises and to regain educators' confidence in economic reason. The romantic age is giving way to an age of reason, albeit slowly.

Without deliberation, the schools should not accept devices founded upon an economic calculus. Critics of past economic policies point to current urban wastelands of our "postindustrial society" as examples of how humane concerns often gave way to commercial expediency with disastrous results. Perhaps, as one observer suggested, the need exists for occasional "uneconomic" allocations of resources.[23] Democratic planning institutions, such as the schools, may benefit from money being "wasted" on noncommercial values that reflect our social conscience.

Conclusion

The term educational planning is used to describe the activities in a local school system that lead to the following goals: establishment of end-means relations; ranking of alternative strategies; allocation of personnel, materials, space, and other resources; design of a supportive information system; construction of time and cost schedules; development of scenarios to portray future environmental conditions; analysis of performance; and continual revision of objectives, programming, and allocation on the basis of evaluative criteria. Planning encompasses two major components: instructional programs and the resources needed to support them. The program budget, as a component of the planning-programming-budgeting system (PPBS), provides a carefully conceived framework for systematically relating the expenditure of funds to the accomplishment of planned goals and programs. Demands for more and better educational services have placed tremendous burdens upon the schools, and the program budget may serve as the vehicle for transforming public demands into school programs. The planning procedure described in subsequent chapters is appropriate for making policy decisions at every level of education. Its main advantage over existing practices is that it enables educators to plan and to construct a budget on a curricular program basis instead of with a traditional line-item, object-of-expenditure format.

Major points of this chapter are summarized as follows:

[23] Michael Harrington, "The Social-Industrial Complex," *Harper's Magazine*, CCXXXV, No. 1410 (November, 1967), 55 ff.

1. The word program in the term program budget refers to performance objectives and curricular programs of the school;

2. Systems analysis, in a broad sense, provides a rational framework for educational planning and the workaday activities of a school;

3. Public educational planning takes place at three levels of government, but the emphasis here is at the local school level;

4. Program budgeting encourages long-range planning and is *not* limited to quantified end-products of the school. It shows how activities are distributed among schools and the priorities assigned to the various programs;

5. Participatory planning is desirable, inasmuch as it enables teachers and others to share in the development of policies which affect them;

6. The economics of education is contributing numerous analytical tools that should prove valuable to educators;

7. Program budgeting should not be confused with efforts to reduce public spending for education. It is not a cost reduction device, and may result in even greater financial support for schools;

8. Program budgeting represents a significant improvement over conventional, incremental, line-item, input budgets now used by local schools. Even so, the budgetary process is subject primarily to political feasibility, and secondarily to economic objectivity;

9. Planners in education should incorporate behavioral science contributions in new designs for schools that are more conducive to human betterment. Implications for school planning also exist in other fields such as regional planning, national defense, municipal government; ecology, sociology, and others; and

10. An educational budget is a financial expression of the purposes of an organization, and it consists of the stages of preparation, presentation, adoption, execution, and evaluation.

In a narrow sense, a hard-headed definitive treatment of any technique of analysis would probably reject the inclusion of a discussion of nonquantified, behavioral dimensions on the grounds it is superfluous. However, if program budgeting is to succeed in schools, it should be defined in a broader perspective and not restricted solely to the mathematical precision of operations-research procedures. As greater attention is given to finding ways in which the computer can simulate human behavior, we sometimes forget that human beings can simulate computer behavior. It is not clear to what extent education is quantifiable; thus the systems environment in which program budgeting is presently described is quite open and, at this stage of development in education, somewhat broadly defined.

Suggestion for Discussion

Analyze in some detail the elements of planning in education, in terms of existing practices, shortcomings, participants, usage of behavioral science knowledge, possible future developments, and relate this discussion to contemporary approaches to planning in government and industry.

Selected References

Benson, Charles S., "Economics and Education," *Review of Educational Research.* XXXVII, No. 1 (February, 1967). Chapter 8.

Blaug, Mark, *The Economics of Education: A Selected Annotated Bibliography.* New York: Pergamon Press, 1966, 200 pp.

Daedalus, XCVI, No. 3 (Summer, 1967). The entire issue is devoted to planning for the year 2000.

Deitch, Kenneth M., and Eugene P. McLoone, *The Economics of Education: A Bibliography.* Bloomington, Ind.: Phi Delta Kappa, 1966, 67 pp.

Financing of Education for Economic Growth, Organization for Economic Cooperation and Development. Paris, 1966, 421 pp.

Hartley, Harry J., *Program Budgeting and Cost-Effectiveness in Local Schools.* Paris: Organization for Economic Cooperation and Development, April 3-5, 1968, 30 pp. (Paper presented to the OECD Directorate for Scientific Affairs at a conference on Systems Analysis Techniques in Educational Planning.)

Morphet, Edgar L., and Charles O. Ryan, editors, *Planning and Effecting Needed Changes in Education.* New York: Citation, 1967, 317 pp.

Novick, David, editor, *Program Budgeting: Program Analysis and the Federal Government.* Cambridge, Mass.: Harvard University Press, 1965, Chapter 7.

Samuelson, Paul A., *Economics: An Introductory Analysis,* 7th ed. New York: McGraw-Hill Book Company, 1967, 821 pp.

Saturday Review (January 13, 1968). The special issue is devoted to "American Forecast," an analysis by the Committee for Economic Development of the crucial socioeconomic problems of the next 25 years.

Woodhall, Maureen, "The Economics of Education," *Review of Educational Research,* XXXVII, No. 4 (1967), Chapter 2.

To be is to be related.

Alfred North Whitehead

Chapter Two

OVERVIEW OF SYSTEMS ANALYSIS PROCEDURES

The concept of systems analysis may be defined as an orderly way of identifying and ordering the differentiated components, relationships, processes, and other properties of anything that may be conceived as an integrative whole. It provides a basis for the intensive study of complex phenomena that are in some way related within the defined boundaries of a unified *system.* The system may be physical or nonphysical, open or closed, dynamic or static, simple or complex, stochastic or deterministic, contain a suprasystem and subsystems, be adaptive or not, achieve homeostasis, exist in time and space, be empirical or symbolic, and possess numerous other rigorously defined attributes. Thus in a system two or more parts and their relations form a single, identifiable entity. Analysis provides glimpses into its parts and its operations.[1]

The Roles of Systems Analysis

Systems analysis has become quite fashionable as a research technique because scholars in many disciplines are increasingly

[1] The flourishing literature on systems analysis contains numerous definitions of a system. A simple and fairly widely accepted definition is of value: "A system is a set of objects together with relationships between the objects and between their attributes." See A. D. Hall and R. E. Fagen, "Definition of System," *General Systems,* Yearbook of the Society for General Systems Research, Vol. 1 (1956), 18.

choosing to regard intricate topics of human concern as systems. They are searching for forms of order and patterns of regularity that make their objects of study more comprehensible. There are at least two distinct vantages from which one might examine the literature of systems analysis. The first pertains to viewing it as a body of subject matter to be taught in its own right. The second is the use of it conceptually as an analytical tool to facilitate understanding of the essential structure of social science and other disciplines that contribute to education. Both approaches are of value to planners. A review of recent research that combines these approaches is presented in subsequent paragraphs. This overview and the more direct application to education contained in Chapter Three suggest how educators can develop systematic approaches to planning.

It is fairly apparent that the term systems analysis possesses nearly as many definitions as there are persons who advocate its use. It is a prestigious term used by many in a casual fashion, but it contributed much to various areas of human concern and promises even greater achievement in educational and other institutional settings.

In the complex process of planning, it might seem obvious that the first step would be to begin with the stated objectives of an organization. In actual practice, however, a systems analyst may discover that the objectives of an organization are not, in fact, clearly specified or even agreed upon. Even in those cases where the objectives are provided, they may be only "fronts" or "public goals" that do not truly reflect the internal thrust of the organization. The analyst's task is to use existing resources, or generate additional ones, to create new means-ends patterns and resolve conflict over problems of choice. It is not an easy mission to construct a map of the means-ends hierarchy in an organization.[2] The systems expert first decides what questions are relevant to his inquiry, attempts to operationalize vaguely stated objectives, eliminates certain imprecise factors, ascertains quantifiable variables, specifies his assumptions, and selects the appropriate models and analytical tools for the specific problem. In educational planning,

[2] For a brief discussion of this difficulty, see James G. March and Herbert A. Simon, *Organizations* (New York: Wiley, 1958), pp. 31–32.

the systems consultant assists the policy makers by increasing the information and assigning some probability priorities to relevant alternatives. He may provide data on competing strategies with estimates of the costs, risks, gains, and time required for each course of action. The major value of systems analysis as a planning tool is to organize human thinking within a framework of reason. It is possible for thoughts to be organized, but irrational. The essence of this approach is ". . . the effort to compare alternatives systematically, in quantitative terms when possible, using a logical sequence of steps that can be retraced and verified by others." [3] The contrast to this approach is represented by intuition, sophistry, illogical judgment, and irrational thought and action.

From Undifferentiated to Differentiated

Human progress has taken place in developmental stages. This tenet may be illustrated by several examples. The progression begins with an undifferentiated global mass that can be differentiated gradually in terms of distinct parts. The differentiated parts are then analyzed as contributing elements of some integrated system. Thus, the original mass can be observed as a whole comprising complex, interrelated components. The structure of knowledge is illustrative. Philosophy may be arbitrarily conceived as the originally universal, relatively undifferentiated topic of study that gave birth to discrete disciplines. Human inquiry continues to produce highly specialized new disciplines that seek to differentiate the world of knowledge to an even greater extent. The justification is that the human mind can convert these elements of study into a unified system of understanding. Reason, itself, is a unified system, or "harmony of impulses," according to the philosopher Santayana.

The study of organisms, whether they be biological, physical, social or whatever, reveals the same developmental stages. Progressing from the relatively undifferentiated to the differentiated, the human body possesses distinct, but interrelated, parts or organs. These are formed from tissues, the tissues from cells, and the cells

[3] E. S. Quade, *Systems Analysis Techniques for Planning-Programming-Budgeting*, P-3322 (Santa Monica, Calif.: RAND Corporation, March, 1966), p. 18.

from subsystems that proceed from nucleus to cell membrane, to microsomes, and so on.

In a theoretical article, Jones traced the movement from nondifferentiation to differentiation, or the "organic" process, in different academic fields. He suggested that Herbert Spencer applied the organic pattern to evolution in order to explain the origin of societies. The history of social theory reflects the belief that societies evolve in the same fashion as do organisms. In psychology, the notion of personality development includes a differentiation of complex elements that are integrated into a whole system. Biologists such as Gardner Murphy are viewed by Jones as proposing that human tissue systems possess similar developmental stages in which a final stage is reached where ". . . functional relations between the differentiated parts are established so as to constitute a system."[4] Systems analysis provides a framework for a basic conceptual organization and reclassification of the differentiated parts of any system.

General Systems Theory

General systems theory provides an organized means for studying phenomena found in many kinds of systems. As a doctrine of wholeness, it makes use of the concept of a system in the search for common properties among diverse kinds of complex systems. From the general-systems level, one may proceed to the more specific techniques developed in areas ranging from operations research in industry to program budgeting in education.

As a result of a growing interest in general systems theory, an organization was launched in 1954 by specialists from many disciplines who shared a concern for the development of theoretical systems that are applicable to more than one of the traditional departments of knowledge. The Society for General Systems Research, under the leadership of Kenneth E. Boulding, Ludwig von Bertalanffy, Anatol Rapoport, and others, presented its first annual yearbook, *General Systems*, in 1956. Subsequent issues of the yearbook

[4] Ronald G. Jones, "Towards the Integration of the Foundations of Education," *Educational Theory*, XIII, No. 2 (April, 1963), 83.

contained significant contributions to the literature of systems analysis and research. The yearbook serves to accelerate the convergence of interdisciplinary contributions and to promote a greater synthesis of systems information; it emphasizes the original aim of the Society, the investigation of like forms of systems in various fields.

The rapid accumulation of new knowledge makes it imperative that a framework be developed for its incorporation. With the fragmentation of specialization by persons with dissimilar interests, it seems that a general approach to the analysis of systems and structures would help to integrate individual contributions. The goal is to formulate a system of general principles and procedures for examining structural aspects of specific entities. General systems theory furnishes a holistic approach that encourages logicomethodological investigations of the empirical world. Systems analysis advances the construction of models that abstract from reality but represent the crucial (necessary and sufficient) relationships of the empirical world.

Systems research can provide conceptual and methodological strategies for an even greater number of areas of human concern. In education, for example, a "school system" has complex properties and subsystems, an environment, outputs, and feedback that are similar conceptually to those found in biological organisms, social systems, and architectural systems. Systems analysts are not seeking to define all of the parameters of knowledge; rather, they are concerned with drawing upon knowledge to develop general frameworks for solving particularistic problems of practitioners.

Rapoport stated, "General systems theory subsumes an outlook or a methodology rather than theory in the sense ascribed to this term in science." He contended that the salient feature of this approach is ". . . an emphasis on those aspects of objects or events which derive from general properties of systems rather than from the specific content." [5] A system is more than a mere totality of discrete units. It is organized, complex, and characterized by interactions among related parts. General systems theory performs an integrative function in its fusion of contributions from disciplines in the social, biological, and physical science—disciplines that would

[5] Anatol Rapoport, "Mathematical Aspects of General Systems Analysis," *General Systems,* Yearbook of the Society for General Systems Research, Vol. 11 (1966), 3.

otherwise share few common concerns. The umbrella of the systems approach covers facets of systems theory, research, and analysis; it can be used to counter the trend toward myopic fractionalization of knowledge that renders the generalist obsolete.

One of the most obvious systems that is a part of everyone's experience is the living organism. Our body is an organized, complex system of interrelated parts that may be studied by scientists with many specialties. The contributions of medical researchers, psychologists, anthropologists and others focus upon highly technical aspects of a very narrow segment of the human body. Systems analysis furnishes a linkage for our knowledge of the system as a whole. A framework is provided. In a similar fashion, a linguist can study the language system while other experts examine communication systems, economic systems, personality systems, and school systems. The systems approach is conducive to bringing order, unity, and the potential for manageability to our knowledge of complex topics.

Interdisciplinary Social Science Research in Systems Analysis

There is a lack of consensus as to specific definitions and models of analysis. In fact, some argue that everything is a system. The possible universality of system as a concept is put forth by Easton, who stated, ". . . it might be argued that since everything and anything, in isolation or combination, may be considered a system by definition there can be no set of variables that does not form such a position." His viewpoint is summed up as follows, "Since all things fall into the class of systems, there can be no class of nonsystem. If nothing is omitted, the concept 'system' can itself have little meaning." [6] A few may interpret this to mean that definition is useless; most will probably construe it as reaffirming the critical importance of assumptions.

In the next chapter, definitions of the properties and processes of an educational system are provided as a preliminary, but necessary,

[6] David Easton, *A Framework for Political Analysis* (Englewood Cliffs, N.J.: Prentice-Hall, 1965), p. 33. See also Easton, *A Systems Analysis of Political Life* (New York: Wiley, 1965).

condition for program budgeting procedures. A summary of recent applications of systems analysis is presented below to illustrate how selected disciplines developed systems procedures. The discussion of each discipline is brief and the references cited are illustrative of the technique, although their number is small. One concept, benefit-cost analysis, is described in greater detail as an indication of how all of these concepts may have educational applicability. The singling out of authors as proponents of views does not impute priority. Emphasis is placed upon the social-behavioral sciences, because these have made important contributions to educational, organizational and administrative theory. Systems theory enables researchers to describe, predict, and conceptualize a wide range of behavior, human and otherwise. To approximate a full account of organizational behavior in education, one can analyze it with the models developed for a social system, political system, economic system, and others. In the early consideration of systems, specifications cannot be defined with exactness. The disciplines selected vary in approaches to usage of the concept of a system, but they share a common concern for an orderly, analytic approach to methodological designs.

Political systems

Contemporary political scientists have developed methods for analyzing the processes by which complex political systems seek to adapt and prevail as systems of behavior. Easton constructed a framework for what can be termed a systems analysis of political behavior as an intellectual tendency containing eight characteristics that might also be used in a description of systems analysis procedures:

1. regularities in behavior (generalizations or theories);
2. verification (validity of theories);
3. techniques for analysis of behavior and data;
4. quantification;
5. values (ethical evaluation);
6. systematization (coherent theoretical research);
7. pure science; and
8. integration (relate findings to other social sciences).[7]

[7] *Ibid.*, p. 7.

Easton's systemic framework is a dynamic representation of political activities. He constructed a response model of a political system that includes demands and support from the intrasocietal and extrasocietal environments as inputs. Information feedback by authorities accelerates the conversion of demands into outputs that return either to the political system itself or to the systems in the environment.

Almond also developed an analytical framework to describe the process by which the political system converts inputs into outputs for the larger society. In addition to input-output analysis, his model emphasizes conversion functions (the political and governmental process), communication functions, and the boundaries of political systems.[8]

Economic systems

The concept of system is extremely prominent in the discipline of economics. Economics provides an organized system of concepts and quantitative measures in a way which prompts some to claim that it is the most precise of the social sciences, although the precision of quantification may not even approach that of symbolic logic.

Maximization methods such as linear programming, simulation, game theory, and other techniques that include operations research, planning-programming-budgeting systems (PPBS), and cost-effectiveness analysis have been developed to help assess the efficiency of alternative input combinations for achieving output goals. Three economic concepts are outlined below.

Input-output analysis. Leontief developed this technique in order to determine how various industries in the United States economy are related to one another and how changes in variables, such as demand for consumer products, will affect each of them. The model, which has predictive value for corporate and government officials, assumes that every industry in our economic system is related in some measurable degree to every other industry. An inverse-coefficient matrix and a commodity-flow table are computed from a system of simultaneous equations in order to relate nearly a hundred sectors of the economy by means of dollar totals and technological

[8] Gabriel Almond, "A Developmental Approach to Political Systems," *World Politics,* XVII, No. 1 (January, 1965), 183–214.

interactions.[9] A major drawback of this approach is that projections must be made from data that are not current. Input-output tables serve as a useful guide for corporate strategy, particularly in the realm of market planning.

Econometric models. Illustrative of the extent to which systems analysis may be applied to large abstract entities, an econometric model for the United States economy has been developed by the Brookings Institution. The model, under development since 1962, uses more than four hundred equations to provide a mathematical simulation of the economy under various conditions. Quantitative measures for the many sectors are sought.[10]

Benefit-Cost Analysis. As a practical way of assessing the desirability of ventures, the aim is to compare benefits of a particular project with the costs, subject to specified constraints. Allowance is provided for individual as well as social benefits and costs and for spill-over benefits that may accrue. Prest and Turvey employed this technique in several fields, including education, and claim that it encourages decision makers ". . . to quantify costs and benefits as far as possible rather than rest content with vague qualitative judgments or personal hunches."[11] The benefits of a project should exceed its costs, or to illustrate it another way, $B/C > 1$.

An example of the application of this approach to education might be in the assessment of certain federally funded projects, such as for compensatory school programs. Trade-offs between alternative Elementary and Secondary Education Act (ESEA)-Title I proposals might be made on the basis of calculations of some benefit-cost ratios. Of course, evaluating the long range economic benefits to society of compensatory school programs is an even more formidable task than dealing with such short-term measures as test scores. Benefits of government services are sometimes divided into tangible (related in terms of dollars) and intangible categories, with the latter being most difficult to quantify, by definition.

[9] Wassily W. Leontief, *Input-Output Economics* (New York: Oxford University Press, 1966).

[10] *The Brookings Bulletin,* V, No. 2 (Fall, 1966), 3.

[11] A. R. Prest and R. Turvey, "Cost-Benefit Analysis: A Survey," *The Economic Journal,* LXXV (December, 1965), 730. An excellent bibliography of ninety references is provided by the authors. They outline the development and scope of the subject; provide general principles; apply the technique to education, transportation, health, research, land usage and other fields; and summarize the values and limitations of benefit-cost analysis.

Examples of intangible benefits to compensatory educational projects are reduction of civil strife, greater social harmony between persons of diverse ethnic and racial backgrounds, less capacity for the political process to be seriously influenced by extremist groups, etc. The problem is that such benefits, while impossible to quantify, are nonetheless of crucial importance relative to the basic justification of the program.

Only one writer has thus far made any attempt to quantify educational benefits from compensatory educational programs on the elementary and secondary level in economic terms. This is Thomas Ribich in his forthcoming book which will be published by the Brookings Institution. To do this Ribich has had to make a series of assumptions which are by his admission heroic of necessity at this stage of the arts.[12]

Ribich calculated numerical ratios on a benefit-cost basis by grade level for selected programs. Kiesling is conducting somewhat similar research using variables such as size of district, competency of administrators (as judged by evaluators),[13] and socioeconomic background of pupils. Burkhead and associates examined input-output relationships in large city schools of Atlanta, Chicago, and the Project Talent high school sample, and these published studies indicate that the socioeconomic nature of the school is of overwhelming importance in predicting school performance. This is in line with the major findings of the well-known Coleman Report.[14]

Benefit-cost analysis is more than merely an interesting concept; it may be of great value to educational policy makers who are seeking some means of quantifying the benefits of schooling and appraising the returns on capital invested.

[12] Herbert J. Kiesling, "Title I of ESEA: Some Program Analysis," unpublished paper, Bloomington, Ind.: Department of Economics, Indiana University, 1967, Mimeograph, pp. 55–56. The author was formerly a staff member of the Assistant Secretary for Program Coordination, United States Department of Health, Education, and Welfare.

[13] *Ibid.*, p. 55. Kiesling examined a Pennsylvania State University study of Title I programs in selected school districts of that state (gains were related to competency of administrative personnel) and he suggested, very tentatively, that ". . . funds given to school districts with poor administration fall upon barren soil. Such funds would be better spent toward raising the level of administrative acumen in such districts."

[14] James E. Coleman, *Equality of Educational Opportunity*, FS 5-238: 38001 (Washington, D.C.: U.S. Department of Health, Education, and Welfare, Office of Education, 1966).

Social systems

Sociology contributes sophisticated conceptual models of social behavior by theorists such as Talcott Parsons, Pitirim Sorokin, Robert Merton, George Homans, Charles Loomis, and many others. Parsons is perhaps most often associated with the concept of social system. He focused upon the interactions of human individuals who constitute "concrete collectivities with determinate membership." He analyzed the structure of complex social relationships in a systemic frame of reference as did other social theorists. Parsons conceived behavioral organisms, personalities, and social systems as "action systems," and he proposed a general theory of action in a systems framework.[15]

Although there are divergent approaches to social theory, Parsons suggested that the major trends in the theory of social systems have been convergent rather than divergent and that varied approaches can enrich a common conceptual scheme.

Social relations are examined in the context of a system, comprising two or more interacting persons. At the global, macro level is the system of society, which contains such component subsystems as community and family. Loomis proposed that society and its parts are constructed similarly, because ". . . persistent elements and processes appear at all levels of orderly interaction. As a consequence, these elements are conceived as general components of social systems and these processes are seen as general articulators; both are important for the analysis of social action in general." [16]

Homans approached the study of social systems as "a complex of

[15] Parsons' general conceptual scheme was presented in his book, *The Social System* (Glencoe: Free Press, 1951); much of this prolific writer's subsequent work involved a refinement of the theory and an analysis of problems in the interpretation of structural phenomena and types of process in this area. One example is his concern with the theory of formal organization based on Max Weber's work. For a 1500-page, single-volume reference that contains a comprehensive collection of essays on many aspects of a social system, the reader is advised to examine Talcott Parsons, Edward Shils, K. D. Naegele, and Jesse R. Pitts, editors, *Theories of Society: Foundations of Modern Sociological Theory* (New York: Free Press, 1965). See also Parsons, *Social Structure and Personality* (New York: Free Press, 1964), and an earlier work by Parsons and Edward A. Shils, editors, *Toward a General Theory of Action* (Cambridge, Mass.: Harvard University Press, 1951).

[16] Charles P. Loomis, *Social Systems* (Princeton: Van Nostrand, 1960), p. 5.

mutually dependent elements," by examining the social organization of small groups. He applied his conceptual scheme to a number of field studies of small groups.[17] A system of interpersonal relations is described with technical concepts such as internal and external systems, sentiments, and norms, personality and social ranking. Merton and Sorokin also contributed major works that deserve mention.[18]

Finally, the concept of formal organization, of which a school is one type, evolved from the analytical point of reference of social organizations and social systems. As with any social system, a formal organization is viewed as having a describable, analytical structure. Systems analysis is an attempt to duplicate in analytical form, those variables that comprise school systems or other formal organizations. There is growing evidence that ". . . the concepts, models, and laws of other fields are applicable to the study of formal organizations. Concepts such as wholeness, interdependence, open system, order, and steady state seem especially applicable to formal organizations." [19]

Other Systems Sciences: The Exact and Inexact Sciences

Credit for the term general systems theory is given to von Bertalanffy, who also helped to define the properties of biological systems. Any discipline can be considered a systems science, although not all lend themselves to this form of analysis as easily as biology. Physicochemical systems and the computer sciences typify the exact sciences, but education is more likely to emulate the approaches of

[17] George C. Homans, *The Human Group* (New York: Harcourt, Brace & World, 1950).

[18] Robert K. Merton, *Social Theory and Social Structure* (Glencoe: Free Press, 1957); Pitirim A. Sorokin, *Sociological Theories of Today* (New York: Harper and Row, 1966). The latter book covers the main currents of sociological thought and critically examines recent theories.

[19] Rocco Carzo, Jr., and John N. Yanouzas, *Formal Organization: A Systems Approach* (Homewood, Ill.: Irwin, and Dorsey, 1967), p. 19. In a similar vein, another noteworthy massive volume that synthesizes most of the important interdisciplinary research on human organizations is by James G. March, editor, *Handbook of Organizations* (Chicago: Rand McNally, 1965). A critical review of March's book that emphasizes the concepts most relevant to education is presented by Donald J. Willower, *Educational Administration Quarterly*, III, No. 1 (Winter, 1967), 89–99.

the inexact social sciences that only recently developed rigorous analytic procedures and models. Excursions into specialized, abstruse realms are not intended, but many examples of systems approaches are available. Cultural systems from anthropology and systems of behavior in a sociopsychological dimension can be thought of as subsystem components of a complex school system, inasmuch as a school has these cultural, social, and other subsystems as part of its structure.

Cybernetics is a prototype of a discipline that cuts across the established specialties of science and provides a basis for cooperative research among many scholars. As a science of communications and control, cybernetics relates information theory to goal-seeking systems, for example, information systems, by means of such processes as coding, storage, transmission, and feedback. The three points of a cybernetic system are as follows: a *detector* to provide information about the environment; a *selector* to reflect the goal of the system; and an *effector* to carry out the action selected. The relevant literature is enormous; the problem of its interpretation formidable; and any attempt to provide more than brief mention of several disciplines by one not especially trained in each would be premature and inappropriate. Exact and inexact systems sciences portray all forms of animate and inanimate matter, human and nonhuman behavior, as systems. It is striking to discover the number of times the same principles have been independently discovered by specialists engaged in different fields. Many of these are reported by organizations such as The Society for General Systems Research.

In a technical paper prepared for the Department of the Army, Marney and Smith described the convergence of behavioral theory upon management science, defined an iterative process of inquiry, and presented a classification of decision systems. They showed how it is possible to assimilate a vast range of systems: a) rudimentary quality-control devices; b) servocontrolled guidance systems; c) automated machine complexes; d) programmed computers; e) simple organisms; f) "higher" organisms, such as man; and g) human social organizations. Furthermore, they cite that a system may be organic, inorganic, conceptual, or synthetic.[20]

[20] Milton C. Marney and Nicholas C. Smith, *The Domain of Adaptive Systems: A Rudimentary Taxonomy,* RAC-TP-92 (Washington, D.C.: Research Analysis Corp., September, 1963), pp. 12–14.

Analytical Techniques for Planning

Systems approaches to planning are not blessed with clear terminology. Different writers and policy makers use terms interchangeably. In addition to general systems theory and such economic concepts as input-output and cost-benefit analyses, several other analytical techniques from management science deserve mention. One writer found forty different code names and acronyms for management controls or approaches such as PERT and OR, which are described next.[21]

Operations Research (OR)

OR is a form of systems theory that furnishes extremely precise, mathematical measures for planning and decision making. It came into use before and during World War II, when scientists applied quantitative analysis to complex military problems. OR is widely used in commercial, military, government, and industrial planning and today is largely identified with techniques such as linear programming, probability theory, gaming theory, Monte Carlo randomizing methods, and queuing theory. To some extent, systems analysis was derived from OR, particularly if systems analysis is viewed in a restricted sense as an economic concept. Although problems of overlapping terminology and lack of clear distinctions between OR and systems analysis exist, the latter approach appears more generally applicable to situations in which crucial variables cannot be reduced to quantification. "The less that is known about objectives, the more they conflict, the larger the number of elements to be considered, the more uncertain the environment, the more likely that it will be called a systems analysis."[22] Wildavsky distinguished between the two approaches rather simply, "In systems analysis there is more judgment and intuition and less reliance on quantitative methods than in operations research."[23] Systems analy-

[21] Robert W. Miller, "How to Plan and Control with PERT," *Harvard Business Review,* XL, No. 2 (March–April, 1964), 93–104.

[22] Aaron Wildavsky, "The Political Economy of Efficiency: Cost-Benefit Analysis, Systems Analysis, and Program Budgeting," *Public Administration Review,* XXVI, No. 4 (December, 1966), 299.

[23] *Ibid.*

sis tends to be more heuristic in approach, whereas OR is algorithmic (based on computation).

There are at least six essential steps to be followed in the "quantitative common sense" of OR methodology; 1) formulate the logical representation of a problem; 2) construct a mathematical model; 3) derive a solution from the model; 4) test the model; 5) provide controls for the model and solution; and 6) put the solution into effect. An alternative to this procedure is to make choices on the basis of pure chance. Between the extremes of pure reason and pure chance, there are many "degrees of rationality." OR often entails the application of computational techniques to efficiency problems in which one can maximize some "pay-off" function that clearly portrays what one is trying to accomplish. An optimum solution is achieved by relating quantitative analysis to some generic model that is usually constructed to represent a wide variety of operations. By contrast, systems analysis is more appropriate for the kinds of problems and situations which may elude quantification, such as education. The literature describing OR and its applications is extensive,[24] but OR is not yet completely appropriate for educational program budgeting and planning.[25] The state of the art presently restricts OR to low order problems, or so-called "mini-analyses."

Management Information Systems (MIS)

Any formal system of procedures established to provide useful symbolic information in the planning and decision making processes

[24] A representation of man-machine systems in OR terms is provided by S. S. Sengupta and Russell L. Ackoff, "Systems Theory from an Operations Research Point of View," *General Systems,* Yearbook of the Society for General Systems Research, Vol. 10 (1965), 43. Another representative reference is: David S. Stoller, *Operations Research: Progress and Strategy* (Berkeley, Calif.: University of California Press, 1964).

[25] Decision problems associated with program budgeting in education, urban planning, and similar areas are not well suited for OR. "Studies to help with these problems are systems analyses rather than operations research." For an elaboration of this distinction, see E. S. Quade, *Systems Analysis Techniques for Planning-Programming-Budgeting,* P-3322 (Santa Monica, Calif.: RAND Corporation, March, 1966), p. 4. This does not imply that OR is not applicable to any educational problems. Indicative of the eventual value of OR is recent research by Martin Stankard, Jr., and Roger L. Sisson, *Operations Research and Improved Planning for an Urban School District: Definitions and a Simulation Model,* Technical Memo #11667 (Philadelphia: University of Pennsylvania, 1967). The Office of Education is also promoting operations analysis.

of management is an MIS. Educational planning requires the selection of an action from among alternatives, and the greater the number of alternatives made available through the information system, the greater the probability of improving the quality of the decision. Direction, analysis, and control for general administrative purposes are provided for by the three basic functions of any MIS: collection, processing, and distribution of data. Solicited from many sources, the data are transmitted to a central point where they are processed and transformed into useful information. This is distributed and integrated into the cycle of the system. MIS is not a distinct, single process. It is any type of control system that provides informational assistance to administrators, and it can be used to supplement the program budgeting process. One such example is a government unit, Nassau County, New York, which developed a computer-based MIS with multiple-purpose management reports prepared in four areas: program development and control; performance analysis and control; financial planning and control; and resource utilization and control.[26] Program budgeting is the key to the entire information system for the county unit. Chapter Eight includes a discussion of the application of MIS to local schools.

Program Evaluation and Review Techniques (PERT)

As a specific application of the critical-path method (CPM), PERT is a device for planning, controlling, monitoring, and evaluating complex projects that have been structured into component parts, time elements, and cost factors. While providing a network of activities for a project, PERT furnishes several alternative estimates for each activity. After the activity estimates are recorded on the network, a "critical path" is constructed in order to list the activities that have no slack time and will require the greatest expected time to accomplish. PERT/Time is used by planners to estimate the time to complete each event of a rigorously defined sequence of activities and to identify critical areas and corrective action for potential bottlenecks. Associated with each activity are three time estimates: optimistic, most likely, and pessimistic. PERT/Cost provides a means of comparing the cost of the alternative courses of action listed on the PERT network. In evaluating the

[26] Eugene H. Nickerson, *Management Information System* (Nassau County, New York, Office of the County Executive, June 17, 1966), p. 3.

progress of a project such as a school building program, the sum of actual costs to date can be compared directly with funds authorized and the estimated cost of completion of the project.[27] PERT relates time schedules to activity costing, and it has been used in several phases of educational research and planning.[28] The critical path approach has been applied to curriculum-development projects, school-construction programs, and instructional-media planning. The fundamental premise is that if an ordered sequence of events is to be achieved, this order must be created.

Cost-effectiveness analysis

Analytic attempts that relate the cost of a particular activity or project to the effective performance or goal-attainment fall under the rubric of cost-effectiveness analysis. These differ from general systems analysis, not on principle, but on their emphasis upon cost factors. In systems analysis, the dollar cost of a project may assume a less important role than other considerations such as time, qualitative factors, stated objectives, professed values, human resources, risks, and available alternatives. Created as a means of solving problems of choice, cost-effectiveness analysis enables a decision maker to choose from among feasible alternatives on the basis of least cost and greatest effectiveness. Usually this technique consists of ". . . an attempt to minimize dollar costs subject to some mission requirement, or conversely, to maximize some physical measure of output subject to a budget constraint." [29] Comparisons are made systematically in numerical terms using a logical sequence of steps that can be retraced and verified by others. The final stage in this process, after the construction of a model to represent the various choices available, is ranking the alternatives in order of preference.

[27] PERT was originated to coordinate the work of a large number of subcontractors engaged in the development of the Navy's Polaris Missile. For a critical review and description of its application and possible future usage, see Peter P. Schoderbek, "PERT/COST: Its Values and Limitations," *Management Services,* Vol. 3, No. 1 (January–February, 1966), 29–34.

[28] Desmond L. Cook, *Program Evaluation and Review Technique: Applications in Education* (Washington, D.C.: United States Department of Health, Education and Welfare, 1966); John E. Justus, "PERT: What is it?" *School Management,* XI, No. 12 (December, 1967), 24–29.

[29] E. S. Quade, *Cost-Effectiveness: An Introduction and Overview,* P-3134 (Santa Monica, Calif.: RAND Corp., May, 1965), p. 2. Some of the gains and pitfalls of C-E Analysis are described by E. S. Quade in *Some Comments on Cost Effectiveness,* P-3091 (Santa Monica, Calif.: RAND Corp., March, 1965).

The criterion for preference is estimated cost in relation to anticipated performance for each alternative. An implicit assumption is that the system to be costed can be described adequately for costing purposes.[30] The distinction between benefit-cost analysis and cost-effectiveness analysis is that the former is concerned with the *economic* benefits of projects, whereas the latter necessarily takes into account a variety of noneconomic objectives.

Definitions, Properties, and Propositions for Systems Analysis

Numerous scholars are contributing to the literature of systems analysis. The objective is to apply both general systems theory and operations analysis to education, so that one may define a school system as a set of entities possessing specified properties and relationships. A system is analytic and it depicts abstractions from reality that constitute only a portion of the phenomenal world. It can be empirical in nature, because observed interactions may be viewed as a system.

A portion of the research of educational theorist George S. Maccia is used below as the definitional basis for an analysis of the characteristics and properties of systems.[31] Other recent research

[30] The origins of C-E Analysis are found in problems of choice for military planners, such as those encountered in the development of future military systems. Refinements have expanded the applicability of this approach. There exist subtle distinctions between the various economic concepts defined in this chapter, but there exist between them almost no distinctions in principle. The differences are matters of emphasis, degree, or specific context. For example, benefit-cost analysis may yield a single, decisive ratio, whereas cost-effectiveness analysis may result in a number of criteria on different definitions of the objectives of a project. Users of cost estimates should find value in procedures outlined by J. D. McCullough, *Cost-Effectiveness: Estimating Systems Costs,* P-3229 (Santa Monica, Calif.: RAND Corp., September, 1965).

[31] Adaptation with permission of Professor George S. Maccia from his study, "An Educational Theory Model: General Systems Theory," *Construction of Educational Theory Models,* Cooperative Research Project No. 1632. (Washington, D.C.: United States Office of Education, 1963). Refinements of this work are contained in a subsequent report by George S. and Elizabeth S. Maccia, *Development of Educational Theory Derived from Three Educational Theory Models,* Project No. 5-0638 (Washington, D.C.: United States Office of Education, December, 1966). In this latter study, general systems theory provided the basis for usage of set theory, information theory, and graph theory in education.

contributions in this area are described in the next chapter and listed in the bibliography.

Characterization of a System

1. A system is a set of entities together with their properties and the relationships between the entities.
2. The entities that make up a system may be viewed as given to man or constructed by man.
3. The entities of a system are a variety of parts.
4. Properties of entities are their specifications.
5. Relationships of entities are connections between entities.
   a. In static relationships, the properties of entities do not change with time.
   b. In dynamic relationships, the properties of entities change with time.
   c. Environment is a set of all entities that surround the system and whose action may affect and be affected by the system. It is also referred to as the suprasystem.
   d. The boundaries of a system are the regions that differentiate the system from the environment.

Properties of Systems

1. A system is a multisystem, if it has other systems (subsystems) as its entities.
2. A system is open, if it has input and output.
   a. Input is the sending of entities from the environment into the system.
   b. Output is the sending of entities from the system into the environment.
3. A system is regulated, if it has feedback.
   a. Feedback is the return of output to the system.
4. A system is adaptive if exchanges between the system and its environment lead to continuance of the system.
5. A system is stable if change in certain system variables remains within definite limits.
6. A system is compatible with its environment, if it survives.
7. A system has wholeness if a change in any entity of the system

affects changes in all other entities and affects a change in system action.

8. A system has independence if a change in at least one entity of a system affects that entity alone and does not affect change in system action.
9. A system is degenerate if it has independence in relation to all its entities.
10. A system has hierarchical ordering if it contains a gradation of entities and entity relationships.
11. A system is centralized if an entity or a set of the entities dominates the actions of the system.
12. A system is in progressive segregation if, in time, changes in the system tend toward independence of the system.
13. A system is in progressive systemization if, in time, independence tends toward wholeness.
14. A system is state-determined if its uniquely determined path is independent of the way in which the system arrived at its initial state.
15. A system is in steady state if progressive segregation and progressive systemization occur simultaneously and continue through time.
    a. Steady-state systems are adaptive and state-determined.
    b. In a steady-state system, the entities appear constant because the entities are being formed and destroyed at the same time.
16. A system contains randomness if the variables that affect a given property are so numerous or so inaccessible that the action of the system is considered to be subject to change.

In many cases, mathematical models can be developed for systems, including human organizations, in order to analyze properties and predict behavioral relationships more precisely. There is a proclivity for human beings to order their relationships. This tendency toward order, called steady-state behavior, serves to distinguish the living from the nonliving world. No attempt is made here to represent the interdependent elements of a school system mathematically, but the properties, process, and formal design of educational systems are presented schematically in the next chapter, using the preceding definitions as a foundation.

Summary of the Systems Approach

Systems analysis is a prerequisite to the successful development of the program budget in school systems. In order to assign meaningful budgetary allocations to educational programs, it is imperative to analyze the entire system. Beginning with a lucid educational philosophy and explicit, operational objectives, the planner should stress the human use of human beings, with whatever disciplinary tools are deemed appropriate. The overview in this chapter on the systemic approach to planning began with general systems theory and concluded with definitions of systems properties. A less rigorous way of defining the concept is to say that systems analysis is what systems analysts do.

Educators who prefer the operations research approach with its heavy reliance upon mathematical formulations may disagree with the selection in this chapter of the broader behavioral approach of systems analysis. Until more precise measures of educational productivity are developed by analysts or educational economists, OR probably will have only limited utility. Teachers and other educators are justified in their skepticism of and resistance to measures designed to quantify human elements that appear to defy measurement. Those who wish to develop mathematical models of a school might heed the advice of a general systems theorist who noted the limitations of the OR approach:

> Too strong confidence in mathematical general system theory therefore, may have one of two unfortunate consequences. First, far from adequate models may be taken too seriously, for want of better models which remain tractable. Second, effort may be wasted in trying to subject to mathematical analysis systems so complex that they cannot possibly yield to such analysis, with the consequent neglect of other approaches, for example, the purely organismic approach which, after all, has been considerably successful in classical biology. It would be wise, therefore, to consider an important addition to the conceptual repertoire of the scientist rather than a method destined to drive all the older methods into obscurity.[32]

[32] Anatol Rapoport, "Mathematical Aspects of General Systems Analysis," *General Systems*, Yearbook of the Society for General Systems Research, Vol. XI (1966), 10.

Systems analysis is a subject matter in its own right, and is also a tool for examining many kinds of phenomena. It enables one to raise probing questions in a universal language. By cutting across academic fields of specialization with general systems theory, much needed interdisciplinary dialogue on problems, including those pertaining to schools, is encouraged. Systemic thinking is logical thinking. By expanding the options and reducing uncertainties, the systems analyst increases the probability in his favor. The range of potential application of this concept is nearly unlimited, extending even to theology.[33] Its major virtue is the enhancement of human judgment.

[33] Professor Alfred Kuhn, of the University of Cincinnati, left the boundaries of his discipline of economics to apply systems analysis to theology. He asked why could we not define God as the system of which all other systems are subsystems and which in itself is not a subsystem of any other system. In a humorous vein, he suggested trying out this notion first on the Unitarians.

Suggestion for Discussion

Define the systems approach in your own words, and describe how specific concepts can be used to assist planners occupying various positions in the educational complex. Discuss the importance of conceptual specification in educational model building.

Selected References

Buckley, Walter, *Sociology and Modern Systems Theory.* Englewood Cliffs, N.J.: Prentice-Hall, Inc., 1967, 227 pp.

Carzo, Rocco, Jr., and John N. Yanouzas, *Formal Organizations: A Systems Approach.* Homewood, Ill.: R. D. Irwin, Inc., 1967, 591 pp.

General Systems, Yearbook of the Society for General Systems Research. Bedford, Mass.: SGSR, published annually.

Hare, Van Court, Jr., *Systems Analysis: A Diagnostic Approach.* New York: Harcourt, Brace and World, Inc., 1967, 544 pp.

Hitch, Charles J., and Roland N. McKean, *The Economics of Defense in the Nuclear Age.* Cambridge: Harvard University Press, 1960, 422 pp.

Johnson, Richard, Fremont Kast, and James Rosenzweig, *The Theory and Management of Systems.* New York: McGraw-Hill Book Company, 1967, 513 pp.

Katz, Daniel, and Robert L. Kahn, *The Social Psychology of Organizations*. New York: John Wiley & Sons, Inc., 1966, 498 pp.

McMillan, Claude, and Richard F. Gonzalez, *Systems Analysis: A Computer Approach to Decision Models*. Homewood, Ill.: R. D. Irwin, 1965, 336 pp.

Seiler, John A., *Systems Analysis in Organizational Behavior*. Homewood, Ill.: R. D. Irwin, 1967, 219 pp.

Simon, Herbert A., *New Science of Management Decision*. New York: Harper & Row, Publishers, 1966, 50 pp.

Systems analysis should be looked upon not as the antithesis of judgment but as a framework which permits the judgment of experts in numerous subfields to be utilized—to yield results which transcend any individual judgment. This is its aim and opportunity.

Charles J. Hitch

Chapter Three

SYSTEMS ANALYSIS IN EDUCATION

Educational life is a system of behavioral interaction, the objectives of which are appropriate for a program budget format. It is a system comprising interlocking human and nonhuman resources that are organized to accomplish desired outcomes. In accepting this tenet, planners may examine the phenomena of school life with the conceptual frame of reference of systems analysis. In the preceding chapter I outlined the contributions to systems analysis made by disciplines representing both exact and inexact sciences. My objective was to delineate structural and process similarities that can be of value to professional educators engaged in planning, policy making, financial administration, and instructional-curricular-supervisory leadership. The recognition that there are such isomorphies among different fields of study is what led to the development of general systems theory.[1] The purposes of this chapter are as follows: 1) to trace the roots of the current *systems approach* in administration and analyze behavioral science contributions; 2) to describe a wide range of projects pertaining to educational systems analysis; 3) to depict the process and properties of systems analysis; and 4) to lay the groundwork for a PPB system in education.

[1] The term *isomorphic* is used to describe two things that are different in ancestry but alike in form or appearance. If X is a model for Y, it is because X is isomorphic to Y.

Evolution of the Systems Approach in Education

The leadership of public school systems for the past century has been characterized by contrasting doctrines and approaches. At the outset, the superintendent, or chief school officer, was likely to be a master teacher whose prime objective was to help improve instruction through demonstrated pedagogical excellence. Advancing the movement toward more technical doctrines of administration were many forces both inside and outside the profession. The increase in size and complexity of schools and public demands for more services with limited resources led administration through a scientific management era with undue emphasis upon efficiency and cost reductions. The limitations of this approach were evident to those who observed that modern factory efficiency measures were not altogether applicable to school systems. Educational goals frequently were sacrificed in favor of the demands of business procedures.

Educational administration underwent a transformation in the past fifteen or twenty years, moving toward a much more theoretical-substantive field of study and practice. Preparation programs for school administrators retain conventional courses in school finance, business administration, law, and facilities planning; but in addition, leading universities include intensive study in the newer, specialized areas of political theory, social organizations, group dynamics, economic theory, and others that have relevance to educational leadership.

Major administrative doctrines and budgetary orientations

By analyzing the evolving nature of school administration, we can see that a number of contrasting dominant doctrines, or ideologies, that may be conceived as distinct eras have influenced this field. The current interest in PPBS and other systems approaches is indicative of the general management orientation of the times. It provides a guiding rationale for what administrators should be and do, and why. At the risk of oversimplification, three budget orientations and six doctrines of administration are portrayed in historical sequence in Table 1. I have drawn upon the work of the educational historian, H. Warren Button, and the public administration specialist, Allen Schick, in constructing this classification scheme.[2] Considerable ambiguity exists among the doctrines; and not all are indigenous to education. Their value lies in the portrayal of common themes, or shared beliefs, for educational administration at a given period in our history. The budget used by local schools evolved as a consequence of the general governmental reform movement over the past fifty years or so. Thus, it is not surprising that the distinct stages of educational budget reform are nearly parallel to those of national budget reform in the United States. It is possible that the three stages are additive rather than discrete, and that the program budget combines elements of control, management, and planning.

The era of administrative science and human relations has not been abandoned, but rather modified in the direction of systems procedures; it was committed to incorporating relevant knowledge from the behavioral sciences and developing theoretical bases for education. Some might question whether administrative science has been superseded by a systems era. After thoroughly reviewing most of the major contemporary research germane to educational organization, administration, and finance, the 1967 committee chairman for this area of specialization for the American Educational Research Association concluded:

> . . . the field is very much in flux. The erstwhile search for "administrative theory," for example, seems virtually abandoned today, though a few scholars still attempt to explain important events in terms of what The Leader is or does. There seems to be a growing tendency to assume that administrative procedures, instructional approaches, schools, and fiscal structures must be analyzed as *systems* or system components (in the broad sense) and that these systems may be extraordinarily open.[3]

Systems analysis furnishes a simple conceptual framework that may be quite fruitful in integrating the expanding sphere of

[2] H. Warren Button, "Doctrines of Administration: A Brief History," *Educational Administration Quarterly,* II, No. 3 (Autumn, 1966), 216–224; Allen Schick, "The Road to PPB: The Stages of Budget Reform," *Public Administration Review,* XXVI, No. 4 (December, 1966), 243–258.

[3] Donald A. Erickson, "Foreword," *Review of Educational Research,* XXXVII, No. 4 (October, 1967), 376.

TABLE 1

COMPARISON OF THE STAGES OF BUDGETARY REFORM IN THE FEDERAL GOVERNMENT OF THE UNITED STATES WITH THE DOMINANT ADMINISTRATIVE DOCTRINES AND BUDGET FORMATS USED BY LOCAL SCHOOL DISTRICTS

FEDERAL GOVERNMENT BUDGET REFORM			LOCAL SCHOOL ADMINSTRATION-BUDGET REFORM			
Major Orientation	Approximate Period	Budgetary Intent	Dominant Doctrine of Administration	Approximate Period	Budget Format	Budgetary Intent
			1. Teaching teachers	1870-1885	Underdeveloped	N/A
1. Control	1920-1935	Central control of spending; Prevent administrative abuses	2. Applied Philosophy	1886-1905	Nonstandardized	N/A
			3. Business Management	1906-1935	Object-of-expense	Fiscal accountability; Focus upon things purchased
2. Management	1936-1965	Assess work efficiency; Emphasize performance measurement	4. Technical Expertise	1936-1950	Function-object	Apply industrial management concepts to school finance; provide broad functional categories; unit cost analyses
			5. Administrative Science	1951-1967	Function-object	Apply industrial management concepts to school finance; provide broad functional categories; unit cost analyses
3. Planning	1966-	Use budget for policy formulation; Teletic; Extend time horizon; Emphasize programmatic outcomes	6. Systems Analysis	1968	Program	Focus upon instructional programs and objectives; long-range emphasis; specify assumptions; explicit evaluative criteria

theoretically oriented behavioral knowledge. The potential danger referred to throughout this text is that systems analysis should be viewed, not in a narrow context, but in a broad sense as a planning procedure for relating curricular objectives to human and material resources. It is not a restraint device that mandates decisions strictly on a cost basis with the quantitative measures of economic calculus. If it were, education would revert, as mentioned earlier, to the scientific management era with its "cult of efficiency." Callahan described the mania that produced efficiency measures in the 1920's and 1930's,[4] and if anything can be learned from our past, it is that we should not make educational decisions solely on the basis of minimum cost and maximum financial efficiency. A danger exists that quantitative analysts may encourage this cult at the expense of educationally desirable, but not measurable, objectives, and procedures.

Probably many school administrators are using the systems approach without knowing it, employing it by a different name. The value of a systems concept like PPBS is that it formalizes what takes place in the framework of the management decision process at any jurisdictional level.

Behavioral dimensions of school systems

No one sufficient, all-inclusive systems theory exists in education, but in relating the available systems research to this context, the educational planner might take an eclectic approach and maximize selected contributions from many sources. In studying the properties of a contemporary school system, for example, he would probably make extensive use of social science perspectives. Education has been defined as a change in behavior, so it appears that behavioral understandings are a prerequisite for systematic program analysis of schools before one attempts to improve budget narratives.

Illustrative school problems

By way of practical illustration, twenty representative problem areas facing teachers and administrators are listed in Table 2 and classified under four behavioral science categories. Systems analysis

[4] Raymond E. Callahan, *Education and the Cult of Efficiency* (Chicago: University of Chicago Press, 1962), Chapter 5.

TABLE 2

ILLUSTRATIVE EDUCATIONAL PROBLEM AREAS CLASSIFIED IN BEHAVIORAL TERMS

DISCIPLINES	PROBLEM AREAS
A.	1. Social class, stratification, and mobility
Sociology	2. Integration, social justice, and urban riots
and	3. Cultural biases, trend toward secularization
Anthropology	4. Obsolescence of knowledge, humanism vs. scientism
	5. Societal dynamics of automation and occupational changes
B.	1. Alienation, apathy, detachment among faculty and students
Psychology	2. Role-personality conflicts
and	3. Organizational health and climate
Social	4. Learning theory, testing, measures of intelligence and creativity
Psychology	5. Styles of leadership-followership in complex organizations
C.	1. Financial support for education, welfare economic theory
Economics	2. Teacher activism, collective negotiations
and	3. Power structure, political factors in educational policy
Political	4. Rates of return from investment in human capital
Science	5. Reorganization, consolidation, centralization of school districts
D.	1. Academic freedom of faculty and students
Multi-	2. Optimum curriculum, media, teaching methodology
Disciplinary	3. Educational innovation, the process of change
	4. Use of drugs for learning and expansion of mental capabilities
	5. Liberal-conservative conflicts over educational means and ends

encourages the translation of these specific problems into theoretical, more generalized terms in order for experts to propose possible solutions for practitioners. There is a body of accumulated social science knowledge, summarized as theoretical principles, which ". . . is superior to our common sense notion about human behavior. Many educational practitioners are not consciously and systematically using this body of knowledge in their professional activities." [5]

[5] Harry J. Hartley, "Towards a General Economic Theory of Educational Value," *Educational Administration Quarterly*, II, No. 2 (Spring, 1966), 153. The statement is based upon research in applied social theory adapted from Hans L. Zetterberg, *Social Theory and Social Practice* (New York: Bedminster, 1962), p. 15.

Each of the problem areas has been the object of considerable study.

After classifying urgent problem areas for a particular school system, a planner must review critically the relevant references and resources. In this manner, he can restate a specific problem of the schools in the terminology of a discipline and can draw on existing research. After plotting alternative courses of action, the educator should be in a better position to make a decision. Rational judgment replaces the less defensible "fly by the seat of the pants" approach. A means is provided for defining the parameters and social universes within which educational planning takes place. The behavioral systems approach does not ensure success, but by reducing ambiguity and increasing the number of options, the probability of success is improved. Human judgment is, like education, an inexact process with unlimited possibilities of error and a recurring element of emotionality.

To illustrate the procedures suggested by this classification, suppose that a school system is particularly concerned with the problem of how to eliminate local barriers to educational innovation and change (Problem Area D-3). Research literature devoted to this topic may be found in psychology, social psychology, and sociology, among other disciplines. The names of Miles and Bennis are prominent in this area. However, the planner may decide, for example, that Carlson's identification of three major causes of retardation of innovation is most appropriate for his unique school system. After critically reviewing the adoption rates of educational innovation of local schools, Carlson described three general barriers to change: 1) the absence of a *change agent* in schools; 2) weak research and development procedures for proposed new educational practices; and 3) the *domestication* of public schools, which reduces the desire for innovation.[6]

If educational management is to exploit the type of rich resource from behavioral research that has become available in recent years, it must provide a vehicle for inclusion in the planning process. The

[6] Richard O. Carlson, *et al., Change Processes in the Public Schools* (Eugene, Ore.: University of Oregon, Center for the Advanced Study of Educational Administration, 1965), Chapter 1. Research on this topic is reported in Carlson, *Adoption of Educational Innovations* (Eugene: University of Oregon, CASEA, 1965).

impact of the behavioral sciences upon education was clearly demonstrated in a review of the ten most significant research studies in education during the past decade. Griffiths undertook the task of identifying research that had the greatest impact; his selections were nearly all behavioral in nature, ranging from the contributions of Piaget, Bloom, Coleman, Skinner, and Bruner to the biochemical studies of the futuristic use of drugs and acids in learning and memory functions.[7] It is not the mission of the discipline to impose a solution to a particular problem. Rather, it is to provide tools to analyze in a dispassionate, objective, systematic manner both the problem and the resulting alternative approaches proposed to resolve the conflict. There exist perhaps as many diverse viewpoints toward a problem in any given discipline as there are toward a given problem in education, and so the educator should choose what he believes to be the most justifiable and feasible strategy for action. In a practical sense, for the schools this strategy is often concerned with the discovery and selection of a *satisfactory* alternative, not an *optimal* one.

Thrust of administrative science toward a systemic view

Several other important contributions to the administrative science era include the following: the influence of the University Council for Educational Administration (UCEA), composed of nearly sixty universities, in improving preparation programs for school officials; the Center for Advanced Study of Educational Administration (CASEA), established in 1964 at the University of Oregon with federal funds to examine the social context of educational administration and school organization; and the Sixty-third Yearbook of the National Society for the Study of Education, which is among the most notable publications of the behavioral aspects of educational leadership.[8] Ultimately, because of the large number of be-

[7] Daniel E. Griffiths, *Executive Action Letter,* Croft Educational Services, VI, No. 10 (May, 1967). This paper was also delivered to the annual convention of the American Association of School Administrators, Atlantic City, New Jersey, February 13, 1967.

[8] Daniel E. Griffiths, editor, *Behavioral Science and Educational Administration,* Sixty-third Yearbook of the National Society for the Study of Education, Part II (Chicago: University of Chicago Press, 1964).

havioral issues that the program budget should elucidate, planners will want to construct multidimensional matrices.

Schools may serve as laboratories for behavioral systems research

Focusing on a comparison of alternative means of conducting some activity, systems analysis offers a basis for choosing the most appropriate course of action in a problematic situation. Such a basis implies two things: 1) there exists a set of criteria, for comparing *all* alternatives; and 2) the alternative selected is preferred, by these criteria, over all other alternatives. The anticipated consequences for the entire system must be considered, and the optimistic expectation is that educators will view the whole structure with all its subsystems, rather than engage in subsystem overemphasis and a selfish kind of optimizing of particular segments. In many respects, the modern school has become a research laboratory for behavioral scientists. Persons with specialized training in anthropology, economics, political science, psychology, social psychology, sociology, and other members of this interrelated family of disciplines are converting the local school into a kind of workshop, or laboratory, in which research is directed toward an improved understanding of human behavior. Schools are faced with residual human problems that other social institutions could not resolve and that appear to defy resolution of any sort. Private foundations, corporations, universities, and the federal government are underwriting greater support for research on socioeducational problems, and such research has produced a better dialogue between behavioral scientists and professional educators. Systems analysis furnishes a common framework for integrating the vast amount of research data that is being brought to bear upon school problems.

It can provide two major services. First, it may help to reduce the dysfunctional time lag that frequently separates new knowledge from its implementation by educational practitioners: the familiar theory-practice dualism. Second, it brings order to an otherwise chaotic mass of fragmented data by offering a conceptual framework within which highly specialized data can be integrated and used as needed by educational specialists. Such synthesizing of knowledge requires a modest expenditure of effort by schoolmen.

These rather theoretical approaches have direct application to program analysis in a school in which objectives can be defined operationally and curricular programs specified. The school system is a truly complex open system possessing each of the kinds of subsystems with multiple feedbacks described earlier. As a social system, the school has certain objectives, courses of study, rules of behavior, norms and roles that influence the social participation of both students and teachers. As a political system, a school is directly dependent upon the shaping of public policy, state legislatures, and general political behavior that can determine who serves on a board of education or whether a school budget or bond referendum is approved. A school is each of these subsystems, plus many more, and when one wishes to examine an educational institution as a total system, each of these contributing approaches and behavioral perspectives is relevant.

Systems Conceptualization: Exemplary Educational Projects

The variety of ways in which systems procedures have been applied to schools is illustrated by the following projects. The overview of systems procedures in education begins with the work of RAND specialists in the late 1950s and concludes with a national symposium on operations analysis in education, the results of which were published in 1968.

Quantitative comparisons of school systems

One of the first exploratory studies of educational systems analysis was a 1959 study sponsored by Ford Foundation for RAND Corporation. The objective was to determine the extent to which quantitative analysis could contribute to better decisions in education. Admitting the difficulties encountered in measuring educational output, the authors took the position that ". . . achievement in basic subjects is the most widely accepted and the most important dimension of educational output."[9]

[9] J. A. Kershaw and R. N. McKean, *Systems Analysis and Education,* RM-2473-FF (Santa Monica, Calif.: RAND Corporation, October 30, 1959), p. 9.

A somewhat controversial choice in this study was the use of scores on standardized achievement tests as one of the major measures of output. Teachers usually hasten to point out that much of the educational output cannot as yet be measured in these quantified terms. The product of the school is more than scholastic achievement. The greatest value of the RAND study was to show that a new methodology was feasible in the solution of old problems. It pointed the way for subsequent research and refinement.

Taxonomy of systems theory in education

A later and more detailed example of the general systems approach in education was provided by Immegart. He developed a scheme for studying organizational outcomes, or outputs, which was part of a detailed taxonomic inquiry into organizational behavior in education.[10] Immegart revealed four distinct approaches toward conceptualizing systems, and he utilized each in his own research. They are as follows:

1. comprehensive systems theories, or "theories of the whole";
2. process, or subsystem theories;
3. theories of system properties; and
4. output theories, or output analysis.

In addition to using behavioral units as objects of classification and instructing taxonomic groupings, he provided operational definitions that are of value to systems analysts in education. In a related study, Immegart suggested that there are four general categories, or kinds of outcomes, for any formal organization such as a school. The first is *productivity*. Schools exist to do things, and what they *do* is productivity. A second outcome is what may be termed *organizational integration*, which is ". . . the meshing of the needs of the individuals and/or groups within the organization to organization goals and the linking of individuals and/or groups in the pursuit of organizational goals."[11] Third is *organization health*, a

[10] Glenn L. Immegart, "Systems Theory and Taxonomic Inquiry into Organizational Behavior in Education," in *Taxonomy of Organizational Behavior in Education*, Daniel E. Griffiths, editor. (Chicago: Rand McNally, in press).
[11] Glenn L. Immegart, "The Outcomes of Organizational Activity," unpublished paper prepared for The Ontario Institute for Studies in Education, University of Toronto, March 17, 1967, Mimeograph, pp. 6–7.

term used by social psychologists such as Miles to describe the ability of an organization to maintain itself in a dynamic state with purposive action and growth potential. The final category is *evaluation,* or feedback, in which an organization assesses the impact and value of its products, services, and other activities.

The most obvious category of outcomes for a school is the first one, productivity. The productivity of a school in strict economic terms is not completely measurable, but what the school *does* can be viewed in terms of its curricular programs. The *programs* of a program budget, for instance, constitute an important part of educational productivity.

Educational efficiency criteria

Thomas applied several systems analysis measures to schools as multipurpose productive units whose end products are classified as identifiable services. These services are both consumed and invested by the clients or learners. Education possesses social benefits and social costs that accrue to individuals other than the ones who are directly involved. Thomas asserted that ". . . the social benefits of education, whose value is almost impossible to express in quantitative terms, are a major portion of education's outputs." [12]

Inefficiency in schools is much less likely to include waste and corruption than it is to involve low performance levels, high dropout rates, poor usage of instructional materials, and poor vocational preparation for some students. These are the kinds of factors which contribute to the inefficiency of local school districts. The individual and social costs may be much greater than is generally estimated and provide at least a partial justification for the categorical aid which the Federal Government provides to combat specific school problems. Criteria for measuring efficiency are badly needed and the work of Thomas and others in urban school systems is a worthy beginning.

[12] J. Alan Thomas, "Efficiency Criteria in Urban School Systems," paper presented to the American Educational Research Association, New York City, February 18, 1967. Mimeograph, p. 4.

General systems theory in educational decision making

The philosophical roots of decision processes in education were analyzed by Gibson. The decision process was portrayed in a classification of five subsystems: *monitoring* (data collection); *diagnosis* (output evaluation); *selection; transformation;* and *intervention.* A person depends upon his own knowledge system and value system when he makes a choice. The former is influenced by empirical, scientific findings and the latter is made up of subjective preferences. Although little is known about how human value systems are related to decision making, they appear to be important, because ". . . decision processes have been seen as ways of bringing the conclusions of knowledge and value systems to bear upon the course of events, to shape them to desired outcomes."[13] In this sense, a school official may be a combination humanist-scientist, whose influence upon the shape of human affairs is a result of his own knowledge and value systems. Self-conscious rational action is the product of complex behavior that is most easily examined with the tools of general systems theory.

The school as an information system

A distinct category of systems procedures manifests itself in the analysis of information flow within an organization. Genetically, it is difficult to differentiate the origin of information theory from that of systems theory, although information theory can probably most directly be traced to the development of man-made, engineered communications systems. The electronic circuit is a common model of a cybernetic, or feedback system. It is a model of an open, fluid system with internal control capabilities self-generated by methods of signaling operational status and behavior. If we relate energy to human behavior outputs, we can include both physical action and symbolic communication as elements of information theory. In a narrow sense, information theory is defined

[13] R. Oliver Gibson, "A General Systems Approach to Decision Making," paper presented as part of the series *General Systems Theory and Education* at the Eleventh Annual General Meeting of the Society for General Systems Research, Berkeley, California, December 30, 1965, Mimeograph, p. 13.

as the science of human symbolic communication. In a broader sense, this science is interdisciplinary, and includes areas of philosophy, the work of A. Korzybski in general semantics, and contributions to the early development of theories of general information systems by N. Weiner, J. Miller, C. E. Shannon and C. W. Morris.

Viewing the school as an information system permits the systems analyst to focus upon the structural components and interfaces that comprise the communications network. The origin, storage, retrieval, recording, transmission, flow, reception, interpretation, and transformation of symbolic messages and other types of information are components of the complex process of communications in a school. There is much technical knowledge available within the communications sciences which can guide educators in the conduct of their institutional programs. Logic, mathematics, and other symbolic disciplines are contributing new structures for communicating and teaching that are perhaps most startling in their effectiveness when attached to the circuitry of the computer. Educators should also be aware of the research and development of semantics via semiotics and symbols. Knowledge of this nature is exercised daily in those media which seek to attract, persuade, exhort, and excite. Media of this type are of vital concern to politicians, advertisers, school administrators, and teachers, and to any other individual who attempts to lead and change the behavior of fellow human beings.[14]

Systems perspective for instructional processes and media

If an educational organization is viewed as a system, then certainly instruction is its most important subsystem. In fact, those whose primary concern is the teaching-learning process emphasize that one begins with instruction as "the system." Thus, the organiza-

[14] This section was prepared in collaboration with Professor Robert L. Granger, New York University. His contributions and critical comments were very helpful. A discussion of the application of information systems in schools is provided by E. F. Lindquist, "Implications and Potential of Information Systems in Public Schools," in *Computer Concepts and Educational Administration,* eds. Robert W. Marker, *et al.* (Iowa City: University of Iowa and University Council for Educational Administration, 1966), Chapter 3.

tion and its environment become suprasystems, and students and learning materials are regarded as subsystems.[15] Although many writers and researchers grapple with a systemic approach to the whole of education, students of the instructional process confine their attention to the power that systems concepts lend to the design and improvement of learning experiences. The progression of concept development in instructional systems tends to confirm this contention. Both learning theorists and instructional material specialists have noted the confluence of their interests describing instructional systems.[16] What has most influenced this mode of thought, however, and provided the necessary tools for testing the propositions is the advent of the computer. With its capacity to handle great complexity and conditional branching of programs, the instructional systems specialist had, at last, the implements for research and development of a multifaceted technology.[17] The growth of these technological efforts seems to be multiplying by a geometrical progression, constituting, in effect, a whole new field of educational engineering.

The "systems concepts" underlying these approaches to instructional technology vary widely. At the risk of generalization, a modest schema is offered in Figure 1 as representative of a rationale for the management of instructional processes. It shows that, beginning with some data base, for instance, literature sources, experiences, or thoughts, the instructor (control) selects some information to display to his students. This display function covers activities which range from referring to a page number to the use of oral presenta-

[15] For example, see David G. Ryans, "A Model of Instruction Based on Information System Concepts," in *Theories of Instruction,* J. B. Macdonald and R. R. Leeper, editors (Washington, D.C.: Asociation for Supervision and Curriculum Development, 1965), p. 86.

[16] See Donald P. Ely, editor, "The Changing Role of the Audio-Visual Process in Education: A Definition and a Glossary of Related Terms," *Audio-Visual Communication Review,* Supplement 6, January–February, 1963; Robert M. Gogne, editor, *Psychological Principles in System Development* (New York: Holt, Rinehart and Winston, 1962); Robert Glaser, editor, *Training Research and Education* (Pittsburgh: University of Pittsburgh Press, 1962).

[17] See Karl L. Zinn, *Computer Assistance for Instruction: A Review of Systems and Projects* (Ann Arbor, Mich.: Center for Research on Learning and Teaching, University of Michigan, 1967), Mimeograph; John Barson, editor, "A Systems Approach to Curricular and Instructional Planning," symposium, American Educational Research Association, February, 1965 (Lansing, Mich.: Audio-Visual Center), Mimeograph.

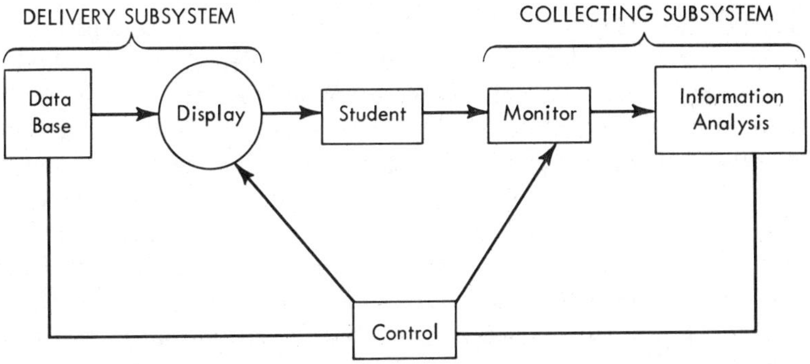

Figure 1. Instructional Technology System Schema.

tions or chalkboards. The student's responses to these displays are then monitored for accuracy, relevancy, promptness, and so on. Based on this monitoring, the instructor makes a control decision about the repetition, change, or sequence of consequent displays. The analysis of information patterns, in turn, yields implications for the overall instructional system of program design and its connection with the larger system.

The preceding notions express the conventional teaching functions in *systems* terminology. However, when the *display* function consists of a range of audio-visual devices plus cathode ray tubes, teletype hardcopy, and specially adapted computer-linked devices, then the system has new impact. Moreover, when the *control, monitoring,* and *analysis* functions are also computer based, then the potential of a man-machine system for the instructional process becomes considerable. In addition, the capacity of computer-based systems for handling complexity and magnitudes of displays, responses, and analyses permits a level of individualization that has been largely unattainable in education until now.[18]

School scheduling systems

A very practical application of systems analysis entails the use of computerized modular flexible scheduling to assign students to

[18] I am indebted to Paul A. Cullinan, professor of educational administration, New York University, for his aid in preparing the discussion on instructional media and process. Some of these ideas are derived in part from the joint research of Messrs. Paul A. Cullinan and Robert Ruderman of Educational Testing Services.

their classes each year. Pupil class schedules can be constructed from master schedules so that individual students receive a better "mix" of the prime variables of curricular offerings, teacher units, time, buildings, facilities, and student needs than was possible with standard schedules used in the past. Depending upon the output desired, the computer offers a wide array of educational plans for large group, small group, or individual study; team teaching; variable class time of less than or more than five class meetings per week; and for better pupil, staff, and plant utilization.

The computerized schedule probably has made its greatest contribution to date in allowing time to be considered as a variable rather than a constant, thus making less absurd some of the forced assumptions in the standard schedule. Along with the addition of time as a variable, the computer has vastly increased a school principal's ability to manipulate the variables with which he has always dealt. The very nature of computer programming encourages educational planners to view the educational process as a total interrelated system of variables that can be manipulated to predict, within fair limits, the desired output. The normal routine of trial and error is replaced by logical and progressive steps when computer science is applied.

The terminology surrounding computerized flexible scheduling sometimes tends to betray or obscure what it is in fact. Scheduling is and always will be a highly mechanistic procedure of bringing together the variables mentioned for more effective interaction. The schedule by itself is an inert schematic that says nothing of what occurs when the variables meet. This is to say, the schedule provides only potential opportunity. Although any schedule may be held to account for the degree of opportunity it provides, it may never be held to account for actual learning by students. This distinction is often lost by energetic schoolmen who, having expended great energy in developing an automated master schedule, are disappointed that changed organizational behavior and improved learning are not necessary concomitants.[19]

The greatest promise of the flexible-computerized-schedule system is its ability to treat each student as an individual in the in-

[19] Valuable assistance in preparing this section was provided by W. Deane Wiley, Professor of Education, Southern Illinois University.

structional process. As schoolmen perceive that they have the ability to schedule a single teacher with a single student for a given amount of time, or a group of students with a particular need with a highly competent teacher or team for a given amount of time, the use of the computer to systematize educational desire will become commonplace rather than a subject for headlines.[20]

UCEA task force on systems analysis

One of the first multi-institutional seminars devoted to the use of systems analysis in education took place in early 1966. Sponsored by the University Council for Educational Administration (UCEA), professors from twenty major universities met to study the relevancy of systems procedures for education. As a basis for discussing objectives and their measurement in a system framework, careful distinctions were made between a *concept* (mental image of a condition); *objective* (condition which is subject to measurement); *procedure* (process of action to achieve an objective); and *proposition* (verbal expression). An objective might be stated as: "teach each third grade child to read a passage in a text with 70 per cent comprehension." The proposition is that "each child should be taught to read." The task-force seminar was perhaps less significant in its immediate productive value than in its suggestion of next steps to be taken and indication of growing interest in the topic.[21]

Operations analysis in education

The United States Office of Education, through its National Center for Educational Statistics, embarked on an extensive program of operations analysis of American education. Although the

[20] A variety of computer based systems for school scheduling are in operation. Robert Holy of M.I.T. developed Generalized Academic Simulation Programs (GASP), Robert Oakford devised the Stanford School Scheduling System (SSSS) and Albert Holzman of Pittsburgh conducted research on a linear-programming approach and a heuristic approach to planning master schedules. Other programs are described by Judith Murphy, *School Scheduling by Computer* (New York: Educational Facilities Laboratories, 1964), Appendix A.

[21] Donald E. Davis and Vernon L. Hendrix, *Systems Analysis in Educational Administration* (Minneapolis: University of Minnesota and University Council for Educational Administration, 1966), p. 6.

number of significant problems that can be investigated by operations analysis is infinite, ". . . resources allocated to model building have the disconcerting characteristic of being resolutely finite." [22] Among the highest priority topics of exploration of USOE are the following:

1. Pupil flow model: analyzes the flows of pupils on the basis of grade levels, private-public schools, advancement rates, trade schools, higher education, region, race, and socioeconomic status;
2. Teacher flow model: traces flows of college graduates into teaching, migration rates, salaries, experience, age, and other characteristics;
3. Operational cost accounting: traces flows of funds;
4. Manpower and employment: will use 1970 census data;
5. Factors in educational attainment: analyze achievement factors;
6. Benefit-cost analysis: provides a basis for national policies regarding resource allocations for education.[23]

USOE held a major symposium on operations analysis in education in late 1967. The apparent purpose was to establish the usefulness of operations analysis and to build the kind of confidence and competence that would enable operations analysis to be a self-sustaining planning device. Approximately fifty papers and speeches were presented on a wide range of topics related to the all-encompassing term of operations analysis.[24] The widely attended conference may have been the signal for a major national thrust in the direction of quantitative analysis in educational planning. It laid the groundwork for increased mathematical model construction, but the final verdict on the efficacy of this approach in local schools has yet to be stated.

Other systems approaches in education

Brief mention of four additional applications of systems procedures in education follows:

1. *Pupil projections.* A simulation model for estimating public

[22] Alexander M. Mood and David S. Stoller, "USOE is Knee-Deep in Operations Analysis," *Nation's Schools,* LXXX, No. 4 (October, 1967), 74.

[23] *Ibid.,* pp. 74–77.

[24] The Symposium was entitled "Operations Analysis in Education," sponsored by the United States Department of Health, Education, and Welfare, Office of Education, National Center for Educational Statistics, Division of Operations Analysis, Washington, D.C., November 19–22, 1967. The papers were due to be published in 1968 by USOE.

school enrollments was developed recently, although it was not yet operational. Griffin and Schmitt of Boston College employed the "Monte Carlo Method" to make pupil-population projections on the basis of data for current enrollments, preschool age groups, birth rates, migration trends, dropout trends, and related factors. As a systems approach, this model may not always reduce uncertainty in predicting how many pupils will attend school in a given future year, but its procedures ". . . will result in a clarification of the cumulative effects of interaction by a large number of uncertain factors over an extended period of time.[25] Additionally, the model will mandate that all significant factors which affect pupil enrollments will be assessed by the analyst.

2. *School Plant Planning.* The University of Chicago announced its intention to replace the graduate administration course which pertains to buildings and school plant planning with a course in systems analysis.[26] Students are encouraged to view the design of educational systems as a variable that has systemwide implications. A curriculum is not viewed as something which must "fit" new buildings; rather, the planning of physical facilities is placed in the context of the design of a total educational system.

3. *Evaluation of Instruction.* Alkin used the systems approach to consider the problem of evaluating instruction and to identify the basic components of educational output. A skeleton of a general model was developed, and subsequent research may refine the outputs.[27]

4. *Defining Goals.* Open system theory was applied to educational goals and the functions they perform in educational organizations. Ohm constructed a goal-analysis model that included a classification scheme for the goal statement, constraints, policies, and strategies of a school. As a means of clarifying terms that are frequently

[25] Mary Griffin and John Schmitt, "A Monte Carlo Model for the Prediction of Public School Enrollments," a report presented to the 1966 Research Convocation of Educational Research Association of New York State and the New York State Education Department, Albany, N.Y., November 14, 1966, p. 12.

[26] The rationale for this approach is provided by J. Alan Thomas, "Probability Models and Computer Simulation and Preparation Programs for Educational Leaders," a paper presented to the Economics Conference sponsored by the University Council for Educational Administration, Columbus, Ohio, May, 1965, pp. 2–3.

[27] Marvin C. Alkin, *Towards an Evaluation Model: A Systems Approach,* CSEIP Working Paper No. 4 (Los Angeles: University of California, Center for the Study of Evaluation of Instructional Programs, August, 1967), 21 pp.

used interchangeably, Ohm distinguished between *goals* (used as the generic term); *objectives* (used to generate means and incorporated in measures of progress); *aims* (nonoperational general statements that require substatements of objectives); and *purposes* (statements that synthesize individual needs and organizational objectives).[28]

5. *Systems Planning Models in School Districts.* Finally, a number of urban school districts are developing information systems and simulation models that take full advantage of computer capabilities. Seattle Public Schools developed a total information system that supports sequential planning and benefit-cost considerations.[29] A typical flow chart is contained in Appendix I. The School District of Philadelphia was used as the basis for a simulation model. One objective of the simulation was to portray various conditions, such as staff salaries, space per student, and students per staff member, and then to estimate the financial requirements and operating statistics for each condition. Projections could then be made of the cost of operating the schools under various sets of policies.[30]

It is beyond the scope of this chapter to review *all* of the systems approaches in education.[31] The purpose for singling out more than a dozen projects for discussion was two-fold. First, it served to indicate the great diversity of projects that fall under the common heading of educational systems analysis; and second, it gave suggestive evidence of the extent to which implementation of rather abstract principles can actually take place in local school districts that seek to combine ingenuity with technical skills. For those who are interested in a particular application, and here the choice ranged from philosophical value systems in decision making to computerized operations analysis, references were cited which were

[28] Robert E. Ohm, "Organizational Goals: A Systems Approach," a paper presented at the Annual Meeting of the National Conference of Professors of Educational Administration, Indiana University, August 25, 1966, Mimeograph, p. 8.

[29] Forbes Bottomly, "How Seattle Gets Old Concepts Out of its System," *Nation's Schools,* LXXX, No. 4 (October, 1967), 60 ff.

[30] Roger L. Sisson, *Some Results of a Simulation of an Urban School District,* Report No. 042467 (Philadelphia: University of Pennsylvania, Wharton School of Finance and Commerce, March 30, 1967), 37 pp.

[31] For an interesting discussion of many of the dimensions of the systems approach in education, see *Phi Delta Kappan,* XLVIII, No. 5 (January, 1967). The entire issue is devoted to educational engineering, the systems approach, the role of big business in the expanding education market, and the future of educational technology.

thought to provide elaboration of the topic. Some recent contributions from General Learning Corporation, RAND Corporation, Systems Development Corporation, and other research groups and private consulting firms were omitted. Likewise, some extraordinary experimental designs for schools developed by specialists throughout the country were excluded due to space limitations.

The Human Use of Human Beings in School Systems

Man is more than a datum

A moral imperative and an absolute requisite for successful development in schools of any systems procedures such as program budgeting is convincing assurance that the desired end is human betterment. Students should be treated as something more than aggregative statistical data.

The salient feature of human groupings and organizational procedures is that they serve human beings. The extent of current disaffection, spiritual emptiness, disengagement, and dehumanization that seem to accompany technological advancements is illustrated by Goodman's *Growing Up Absurd*, Reisman's *The Lonely Crowd*, Galbraith's *The New Industrial State*, the poetry of Voznesensky, Sartre's novels and philosophical essays, university student riots, and contemporary religious and social critics who contend that man is being reduced to a datum, thereby losing his subjective, personalized human dimensions. In a large school, the student may be little more than a class ranking, a grade point average, or a college board score, and the teacher may feel the same loss of identity in his own lack of participation in those educational policies that directly affect his professional life.

Without exaggerating the potential dangers of systems procedures, it is understandable that some distrust of technical proficiency as the desired end of education is bound to exist with educators. Yet science, or more precisely, systems analysis, is a humanizing enterprise. As an expression of man's creative inquiry and interpretative response to given circumstances, it uses human terms to construct our knowledge and beliefs. Even though our social goals and educational ideals may not be achieved with finality, noetic experience implies behavior that achieves its objectives by a rational choice of means. Conversely, behavior that defeats its own purposes is nonrational.

If the Hegelian dialectic process of thesis-antithesis-synthesis may be used to describe human group conduct, each historical-belief pattern (*thesis*, such as organizational rationality) promotes the creation of an opposite point of view (*antithesis*, such as an individual's disaffection for his organization). From this model, we might anticipate a proliferation of nonrationalized behavior in complex school systems. However, individual growth need not be inconsistent with institutional objectives and programs, and a possible *synthesis* would combine educational programs that are rationally organized around two aims: (1) the central concern of sufficiently high individual development and self-realization of students; and (2) a meaningful reward system, or reimbursement pattern, for teachers and supporting personnel who comprise the formal system. If successful, this approach assures that systems procedures will be the servant of individuals, and not vice versa.

The notion of more humane treatment of individuals in organizations has been considered by such major contributors to the modern world of technics as Wiener, Michael, and Simon.[32] They hold that the goal of economic rationality is to support human judgment, not to dehumanize the environment. Simon spoke of the potential advantages of cybernation and technics to man:

> Perhaps the most exciting prospect of change resulting from our new technology of information processing is the likelihood that it will halt and reverse the progressive isolation of idea from idea and man from man. Mankind, in its professional as well as nonprofessional aspects, will again become the proper study of man.[33]

Process and Properties of Educational Systems Analysis

Although educational life contains elusive qualities, an attempt to grasp the nature of a school and its functions is made in Figures

[32] For example, see Norbert Wiener, *The Human Use of Human Beings* (Boston: Houghton Mifflin, 1950); Robert T. Golembiewski, "The Human Use of Human Beings: Organizing for Individual Development," in his book, *Men, Management and Morality* (New York: McGraw-Hill, 1965); and Donald N. Michael, "Some Long-Range Implications," in *Computer Concepts and Educational Administration,* Robert W. Marker, *et al.,* editors, Chapter 4.

[33] Herbert A. Simon, *The American Scholar,* XXXV, No. 2 (Spring, 1966), 264.

2 and 3. Simplified flow models of two important dimensions of the systems approach in education are illustrated. Figure 2 depicts the sequence of events in the process of systematic planning. Whether the level of analysis is that of an individual teacher planning for his classroom or of a superintendent planning for an entire school district, the procedures seem appropriate. The systems approach simply provides a total framework for formalizing many of the activities that schools are presently conducting in less formal terms.

Figure 3 is a schematic representation of the conversion of selected inputs into educational outputs. The properties of a school system are viewed from several vantages because one may define a school district in terms of an organizational structure, curricular programs, administrative functions, teaching-learning process, or in many other ways. It is noteworthy that the items typically found in present local school district budgets are viewed as inputs. By contrast, the program budget is designed to support outputs, or program activities. Some of the outputs in Figure 3 are descriptive, qualitative, and nonquantitative. As educators are able to define the product of behavioral outcomes more explicitly, the outputs may be stated in more precise terms. For the present, the ideal consists of the balanced functioning of all subsidiary components of the system.

Program Budgeting: An Application of Systems Analysis

Systems analysis is the general conceptual basis for program budgeting, and program budgeting is the detailed expression of the methodology of systems analysis. The programs of a school cannot be adequately designed and supported financially without an understanding of the total system that they support. In the discussion of the systems approach in this chapter and the one preceding it, a deliberate attempt was made to focus on more than just quantifiable elements of a system because decisions related to curricular programs of a school are not yet completely susceptible to that form of analysis. Operations research procedures are presently used in restricted areas but may be applied eventually to PPBS procedures.

PPBS required an analytical framework for educational planning,

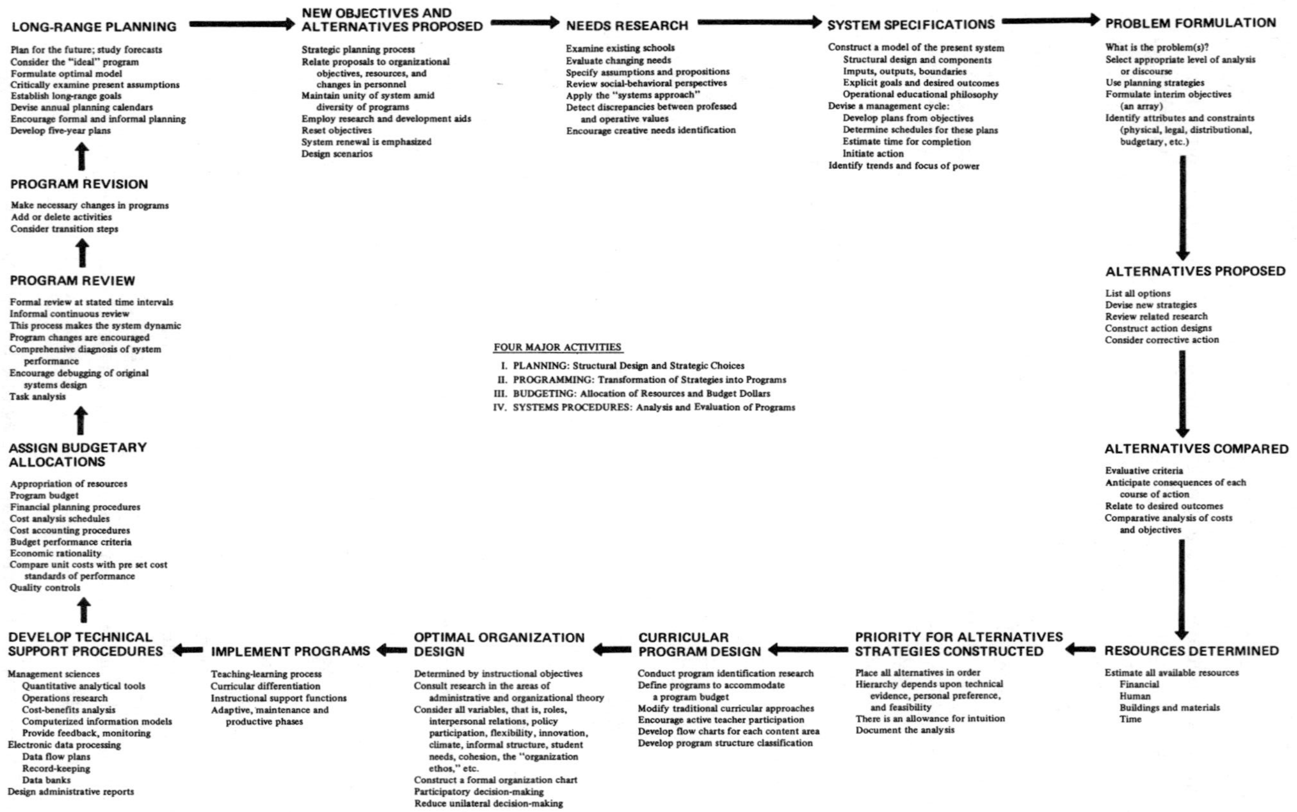

Figure 2. General Process of Educational Systems Analysis.

and this systems-oriented technique is applicable to institutions ranging from small, local school systems to large universities. Inclusion of systems analysis methods implies a careful consideration of alternative means-ends combinations. It also provides an integrative vehicle for blending the diverse values of participating educators into some shared, behavioral objectives and programs.

Conclusion

Advocating greater use of systems procedures in education does not necessarily reflect a belief that our present instructional endeavor is grossly inefficient. Instead, as our society undergoes rapid, disconcerting change and man's knowledge of himself is in the midst of a qualitative breakthrough, a proponent of systems analysis may be seeking to diagnose and revitalize current approaches while developing better articulation of future goals. The systems analyst need not abandon present procedures, providing he does not rely upon current instructional practice as the sole referent for charting the terrain of future action.

At the national level, recent legislation designed to reduce teacher shortages and improve training implies the use of systems analysis. The Education Professions Development Act, for example, provides for the appraisal of existing and future education personnel needs and supports the compilation of data for annual reports that (1) identify current and long-range trends in education and (2) indicate plans for allocating funds in relation to other federal programs.

At the local level, educators should benefit from increased planning procedures; Selden described the issue from the teacher's point of view:

> The implications for teachers and teacher organizations of the systems analysis approach to education must be confronted. Schools, teachers, and public education are under attack in a new, strange, and more formidable way. For a half-century, the foes of education were low-tax budget cutters and right-wing anti-liberty groups. Now, all at once, it seems, the attack is coming from the friends of the schools: social reformers, educationists, and parent and community groups.[34]

[34] David Selden, "The Future of Teachers According to the USOE," *American Teacher,* LII, No. 5 (January, 1968), 11–13. (Selden is Assistant to the President, American Federation of Teachers.)

Figure 3. General Properties of an Educational System.

Systems analysis in education is an extension of man's ability to reason. As a rational framework for planning, it imposes no particular dogma, educational philosophy, or curriculum. It offers a blueprint for planning, but there is no assurance that the pedagogue-architect's specifications will be followed in each system.

The Jeffersonian allowance for impulsive, nonrational proposals was that "Error of opinion may be tolerated if reason is left free to combat it." One systematic means of combating nonresponsible, irrational proposals in education is with a planning-programming-budgeting system. Proposals in education should contain operational objectives that are consistent with democratic ideals of public education. Otherwise, they subvert the school system from its mission of goal attainment prescribed by public policy. Systems planning is significant because it involves future action for all units of a school district. The issue which arouses controversy pertains to whether organizational objectives should *generate* a systems analysis or should be the *outcome* of a systems analysis. Using the program budget framework, a systems plan identifies a series of time-phased activities to be undertaken by each participating component of a school district. The next chapter describes PPBS in detail.

Suggestion for Discussion

State what you regard to be the most noteworthy application of systems analysis procedures to school districts with which you are familiar. You might up-date this chapter by reviewing more recent projects that applied the systems approach to a school context.

Selected References

Goodlad, John I., John F. O'Toole, and Louise L. Tyler, *Computers and Information Systems in Education.* New York: Harcourt, Brace & World, 1966, 152 pp.

Loughary, John W., editor, *Man-Machine Systems in Education.* New York: Harper and Row, Publishers, 1966.

Review of Educational Research. XXXVII, No. 4 (October, 1967), Chapters 2 and 6.

Ryans, David G., *An Information Systems Approach to Education,* TM-1945. Santa Monica, Calif.: Systems Development Corporation, 1963, 25 pp.

Smith, K. U., and M. F. Smith, *Cybernetic Principles of Learning and Educational Design*. New York: Holt, Rinehart & Winston, Inc., 1966.

Suppes, Patrick, "The Uses of Computers in Education." *Scientific American*. CCXV, No. 3 (September, 1966), 207–220.

United States Department of Health, Education, and Welfare, Office of Education. *A Bibliographic Guide to Operations Analysis of Education*. Technical Note No. 43. Washington, D.C.: National Center for Educational Statistics, Division of Operations Analysis (September 15, 1967), 20 pp.

Management is, in the end, the most creative of all arts—for its medium is human talent itself.

Robert S. McNamara

Chapter Four

PLANNING-PROGRAMMING-BUDGETING SYSTEMS

What Program Budgeting Is Not

Prior to describing the characteristics of PPBS, let us consider several inaccurate assumptions that can be made by persons in their first expressions of interest in this topic. To begin, the word *program* does not refer to computer programming; it does relate to the activities of an organization that are based upon desired outcomes. Second, program budgeting is not merely a new label for old notions such as performance budgeting or functional finance, where the functions were usually expressed in line-item, object classifications. Third, this conceptual approach to budgeting is not simply another cost restraint device that sacrifices goal accomplishment for minimum cost considerations. Fourth, it does not imply that the entire output of an organization can be quantified and measured. Fifth, the program budget is neither a substitute for good management nor a remedy for organizations who do not have sufficient resources to achieve their objectives.

Finally, a note of caution is in order for the educator who is searching for ways of "stretching" school dollars. Nothing inherent in the program-budget process enables it to avoid at least one pitfall of most school budgets: "worse than the last, but not as bad as the next." Although this feeling may typify certain economy-minded taxpayer groups, the trend of rising instructional and other school costs will probably continue, regardless of the budgetary process being used. The discipline of economics was born and exists now because of the presence of scarcity in the world, and the economic rationality of PPBS serves educators by providing a design for planning and allocating scarce resources among competing means. PPBS might not reduce the total costs of a school district.

What Program Budgeting Is

Program budgeting relates the output-oriented programs, or activities, of an organization to specific resources that are then stated in terms of budget dollars. Both programs and resources are projected for at least several years into the future. Emphasis is upon outputs, cost-effectiveness methods, rational planning techniques, long-range objectives and analytical tools for decision making. Probably the most important single task that must be accomplished in moving to this kind of planning and budgeting is the development of a program structure. Schools are presently more likely to be organized, for budget purposes at least, along a traditional line-item basis of objects, that is, debt service, instructional costs, board of education costs, administration costs, and others. It is difficult, if not impossible, to find a school system which can show that its total budget is organized completely on the basis of curricular programs and objectives. A program budget contains categorizations by programs, grade-level functions, outputs, or activities. It is one element of systems analysis, inasmuch as the program framework becomes a system within which program analysis is conducted and decisions are made. Some tend to use the term to encompass all systems-oriented procedures, not just the budget. The reason for much of this confusion in terminology is that as a program budget is prepared, the procedures of the systems approach should be followed, and it is not easy to delineate the discrete stages of budget preparation. The essential characteristic of PPBS is the projection of total resource and dollar needs for a suitable number of years and in relation to key decision variables of the organization's administration.

The sequence of topics that follow begins with budgetary reforms at the federal level and concludes with elements needed to design an educational program budget. Related subjects include the Department of Defense programs, RAND Corporation research, advantages gained from PPBS, and political-economic factors in budgeting.

Budgetary reforms in the federal government

Educational budgeting practices have been influenced a great deal by the budget systems being used in the federal and state levels of government. In reviewing the stages of budget reform in this country, one might be surprised to discover that the establishment of a national budget did not take place until the passage of the Budget and Accounting Act of 1921. The first year of the United States budget was 1922. The first budget had an object, line-item makeup, and the budget officers were concerned more with economic efficiency than with policy. Because of the federal influence, budgetary practices in local school systems before 1920 were relatively undeveloped and nonstandardized. The similarity between federal budgetary orientations and local school budgeting was portrayed in Table 1.

Schick contended that budgetary reform in the United States evolved through three distinct stages: central control, scientific management, and PPBS.[1] Each of these approaches had different emphases, with the program budget being a product of converging elements of its predecessors. The central control stage (1920–1935) was characterized by executive budgets that developed a system of expenditure control and limited the discretion and abuses of administrators. In the mid-1930's management-oriented budgets that focused upon efficient performance by workers were formulated. Organizational activities were prescribed and the budget was used, not as a control device for governing administrators, but as a management tool to assess work efficiency. The concept of performance budgeting was introduced to evaluate work-cost data and was an important contribution of the scientific management era. The third and final stage is exemplified by the planning orientation of the PPBS design. Program budgeting proposals began appearing in the early 1950's and received implementation in the early 1960's. The conceptual basis of this economic model can be traced to capital theory, the influence of John M. Keynes, macroeconomics, principles

[1] Allen Schick, "The Road to PPB: The Stages of Budget Reform," *Public Administration Review,* XXVI, No. 4 (December, 1966), 243–58.

of marginal analysis, a desire to combine policy with budgeting, and the growing contributions of the systems sciences to administration.

The planning aspects of program budgeting have their roots in Keynesian economics, although the basic notion behind program budgeting can be traced back at least to the 1920's, and the writings of A. E. Buck. This approach was strongly recommended first at the federal level by the Hoover Commission on Government Reorganization in 1949. It stated that the entire federal budget should be refashioned by the adoption of procedures that focus upon performance, functions, activities, projects, and programs. The Hoover Commission introduced a new term, "performance budgeting," which was a forerunner to current program budgeting practices.[2] The most extensive research and development of the program budget has taken place at the federal level, and so an examination of early attempts at program development in the Department of Defense is undertaken below.

Program budget for the Department of Defense

The pre-1961 planning and budgeting procedures of the Department of Defense (DOD) did not integrate military objectives and planning with either resource requirements or an incredibly detailed line-item budget. In an effort to achieve integrated action in defense planning, Robert S. McNamara, Secretary for seven years during the Kennedy-Johnson administrations, initiated program planning techniques that resulted in PPBS. If one believes that it is difficult to apply systems analysis procedures to an educational enterprise, imagine the almost insurmountable task of trying to specify the programs and objectives of an organization as complex as the Department of Defense.

With the aid of researchers and systems analysts, DOD was able to identify and assign its activities within nine major programs. The programs were defined on the basis of the primary missions to be performed, and each program contained the program elements necessary for goal achievement. In Table 3, the program-budget structure for the Department of Defense is outlined.

[2] The distinction between performance and program budgeting was made by Schick, *op. cit.*, p. 250.

TABLE 3

MAJOR PROGRAMS IN THE DEPARTMENT OF DEFENSE [3]

PROGRAM	DESCRIPTION
1. Strategic Retaliatory Forces	"The forces that are designed to carry out the long-range strategic mission and to carry the main burden of battle in general. They include the long-range bombers, the air-to-ground and decoy missiles, and the refueling tankers; the land-based and submarine-based strategic missiles; and the systems for their command and control."
2. Continental Air and Missile Defense Forces	"Those weapon systems, warning and communications networks and ancillary equipment required to detect, identify, track, and destroy unfriendly forces approaching the North American continent."
3. General Purpose Forces	"The forces relied upon to perform the entire range of combat operations short of general nuclear war. These include most of the Army's combat and combat support units, virtually all Navy units, all Marine Corps units, and the tactical units of the Air Force."
4. Airlift and Sealift Forces	"Those airlift and sealift forces required to move troops and cargo promptly to wherever they might be needed. Included in the airlift forces are both the MATS transports and the Air Force Tactical Air Command troop carrier aircraft. The sealift forces include the troop ships, cargo ships, and tankers operated by MSTS and the 'Forward Floating Bases.' "
5. Reserve and National Guard Forces	"Equipment, training, and administration of the Reserve and National Guard personnel of the several services."
6. Research and Development	"All research and development effort not directly identified with elements of other programs (i.e., where there has been no decision to produce for inventory)."
7. General Support	"Support activities of the several services and the agencies that serve the entire Department of Defense. It constitutes an 'all-other' or residual category of activities or programs and includes all costs not capable of being directly or meaningfully allocated to the other major programs."
8. Military Assistance	"Equipment, training, and related services provided for armed forces of allied and friendly nations."
9. Civil Defense	"Federal assistance for fallout shelters, warning and radiological monitoring systems, training and education for emergency preparedness, etc."

[3] Elaboration of this outline is contained in the testimony of Mr. McNamara before the Committee on Armed Services, January 27, 1964, *Hearings on Military Posture and H.R. 9637*, House of Representatives, 88th Congress, 2nd Session (Washington, D.C.. United States Government Printing Office, 1964).

Each of the nine DOD programs was differentiated to a large extent, first in terms of subclassifications and program elements and then in terms of specific resources that were subsequently related to budget dollars on an extended time horizon. As an illustration, consider Program I, Strategic Retaliatory Forces. It is made up of four basic program elements, and each program element has numerous components. The four program elements for Program I are provided in Table 4 along with two exemplary components for each.

TABLE 4

PROGRAM ELEMENTS AND COMPONENTS FOR PROGRAM I OF DOD, "STRATEGIC RETALIATORY FORCES"

PROGRAM ELEMENTS	ILLUSTRATIVE COMPONENTS
1. Aircraft forces	RB-47
	B-52
2. Missile forces, land based	Atlas
	Titan
3. Missile forces, sea based	Polaris System
	Regulus System
4. Command control,	SAC Control System
communications, and support	Base Operating Support

A major advantage of this program format is that all of the manpower, materials, and facilities are *not* grouped together in lump-sum categories, such as the total size of the Air Force. Rather, each military component is broken down and identified with the specific program and objectives that it is designed to support. Air Force personnel, for example, are included in each of the first five programs outlined in Table 3, but their designation is dependent upon the explicitly defined objectives of the particular program. In this manner, the Secretary of Defense has a better programmatic understanding of the operations, both current and long range, and of the allocation of resources within the Department. This approach systematizes the flow of internal evaluation and analysis. Earlier, the military branches had budgeted rather independently and with little effort to coordinate with each other's programs, but with PPBS, planning became centered on missions. Strategic elements from the Army, Navy, and Air Force were assembled into a comprehensive five-year plan which was referred to as a "mission program package." The new format did not contain decision making capabilities or substitute a computer for human judgment. On the contrary, the analytical techniques of PPBS placed an even greater premium on judgment based upon experience. It was affirmed that ". . . the better the factual basis for reflective judgment the better the judgment is likely to be." [4]

The Department of Defense initiated program budgeting in 1961, and the program structure model devised for the Pentagon may be appropriate for educational organizations. However, even the Pentagon's "major program-program element" model is not fully satisfactory for all sectors of the Department of Defense.[5] Some critics attacked the system for placing too much weight on cost and not enough on benefits, particularly in purchasing weapon systems, and of overanalyzing (and eliminating) promising solutions to security problems. A large share of past criticism has been generalized, vague, and aimed at personalities rather than techniques. The overall project of program budgeting and cost effectiveness analysis appeared to be successful, thus prompting the President to install PPBS throughout the government.

Research contributions of RAND Corporation

Among the first and most important sources of research on program budgeting was RAND Corporation, whose name stands for "research and development." It is an independent, nonprofit organization established to focus on governmental problems without being involved in partisan politics. As early as 1954, Novick published a RAND monograph in which he defined a program as the end objective of an agency that is developed or budgeted in terms of all of the elements necessary to its execution.[6] RAND was instrumental in refining PPBS and in aiding its adoption by the federal government. Numerous papers and memoranda have been prepared

[4] *Time,* April 26, 1964, p. 36.

[5] Charles J. Hitch, "What Are the Programs in Planning, Programming, Budgeting?" Speech delivered to the symposium on "Operations Analysis of Education," U.S. Department of Health, Education, and Welfare, Office of Education, Division of Operations Analysis, Washington, D.C., November 21, 1967.

[6] David Novick, *Which Program Do We Mean in "Program Budgeting"?* P-350 (Santa Monica, Calif.: RAND Corporation, May 12, 1954), p. 17.

by RAND on the allied topics of PPBS, program budgeting, systems analysis, cost effectiveness and others.

To illustrate how program budgets can be constructed, Hirsch identified twenty major federal government programs, many of which have state and local government counterparts, and described how they can be further classified into subprograms. Education, for example, contained seven subprograms: primary education, secondary education, higher education, adult education, library services, research, and international education.[7] These programs are appropriate for the United States Office of Education, as described in Chapter Ten (Table 23), but they do not adequately portray the curricular programs and activities of local school districts. Therefore, local schools should be able to formulate program budgets in creative, innovative ways, rather than looking to the federal government for a model that can be imposed arbitrarily on all local districts.

Fisher, a member of the RAND staff, considered some of the problems encountered in developing a program budgeting system. He suggested that if an organization desires to develop a program structure, at least two months of intensive work should be spent in designing an initial structure. It should then be put into operation with an awareness that modifications in the original structure will be desirable.

> One could spend many months and even years trying to develop the "perfect" program structure before implementation, but since a perfect structure does not exist anyway, it is best to try to come up with something reasonable soon, get it into operation, and then let it evolve over time.[8]

A significant RAND-sponsored publication that is referred to several times in this text is the 1965 book, *Program Budgeting,* edited by Novick. Program budgeting is not the exclusive domain of RAND, and other organizations have contributed to its development. Some of these are drawn upon in the next chapter, where I have reviewed several projects that pertain to program budgeting implementation in contexts other than the Department of Defense.

[7] Werner Z. Hirsch, *Toward Federal Program Budgeting,* P-3306 (Santa Monica, Calif: RAND Corporation, February, 1966), p. 11.

[8] Gene H. Fisher, *The World of Program Budgeting,* P-3361 (Santa Monica, Calif.: RAND Corporation, May, 1966), p. 27.

The PPBS Concept

PPBS is the comprehensive planning process that includes a program budget as its major component. This process received its greatest impetus when the Presidential directive of August 25, 1965, called for the introduction of this system throughout the federal government for the fiscal 1968 budget. The technical success of the PPBS concept experienced by DOD from 1961 to 1965 provided the background for this widespread adoption. DOD pioneered in producing a number of planning concepts which may be appropriate for education. These include systems analysis, strategic planning, needs research, "think tanks" decision centers, logic-sequence network diagrams, and the PPBS framework.

The success of DOD gave sufficient support for the President to instruct twenty-one nondefense departments to institute similar planning techniques by May, 1966. Included in this group were the Office of Education and the entire Department of Health, Education, and Welfare. The President defined a budget as a financial expression of a program plan, and he outlined several of the shortcomings of traditional budgeting practices that created the need for PPBS. These shortcomings may be summarized as follows: (1) under the existing format, objectives of agency functions and activities have too often not been explicated with clarity and concreteness; (2) alternatives have not been sufficiently provided for consideration by decision makers; (3) program review for decision making has been frequently concentrated within too brief a time period; (4) accomplishments have not always been specified adequately; (5) the future-year costs of present decisions have not always been considered; and perhaps most important, (6) formalized planning techniques and systems analysis have had an insufficient effect on budget decisions.[9]

The integrated PPBS actually provides relatively few innovations for the individual elements of planning, programming and budgeting; its value results from its systematic coordination of all of these.

[9] For a detailed discussion see Executive Office of the President, *Planning-Programming-Budgeting*, Bulletin Number 68-2 (Washington, D.C.: Bureau of the Budget, July 18, 1967), 12 pp.; and a 30-page Supplement to Bulletin Number 66-3 that was issued by the Bureau of the Budget on February 21, 1966.

A conceptual framework for the total budget making process is provided. PPBS attempts to structure a cohesive decision making procedure in such a way that resources are allocated efficiently to achieve specified objectives. Thus, the budget is an expression of the operating plans of an organization.

PPBS has at least six major distinctive characteristics: analytic modes, planning, programming, budgeting, structural cohesion, and administrative lines of action.

1. *Analytic features.* Systems analysis is used to examine alternative courses of action in terms of utility and cost. When possible, a quantitative analysis of comparative benefits is made. Otherwise, less rigorous analysis prevails. The options are made explicit in order to clarify relevant choices and their probable consequences. The analytical activity is used to generate new objectives and alternatives and to help specify the most appropriate courses of action. It is, therefore, intended to provide policy appraisal rather than mere budget justification.

2. *Planning.* The activity of means-ends considerations comprises the iterative process of making program policy decisions that culminate in a particular budget and multiyear projections. These stages cannot always be delineated neatly, because planning is also an analytic tool. In order to assess the future expenditure implications of current decisions, profiles of future conditions are linked to budgetary data and program objectives. Planning is the production of the range of meaningful potentials for selection of courses of action through a systematic consideration of alternatives.[10]

3. *Programming.* In this phase, the planned goals are related to specified alternative programs. Inputs are related to outputs by lines of action that may include immediate, intermediate and long-range objectives. Programming entails a review of existing objectives in relation to alternative means and encourages revision of procedures as needed. It is a multiyear process that may utilize a computerized information system to present current data to decision makers in the most accessible, comprehensible way. Programming is also the determination and assignment of the manpower, materials and facilities required to support a program structure.

[10] David Novick, editor, *Program Budgeting* (Cambridge: Harvard University Press, 1965), p. 91.

4. *Budgeting.* Instead of showing budget dollars by an object-of-expenditure classification, PPBS is designed to relate programs to resources that are then transformed into budget dollars for present and future years. As the nucleus of PPBS, the program budget expresses the dollars in relation to the outputs, or programs. At the federal level, this process translates broad program decisions into more refined decisions in a budget context, and the appropriate program and financial data for Presidential and Congressional action are presented. A program budget should delineate the legal basis that prescribes the budgetary process, composition, calendar, and responsibility for its formulation and administration. It permits the activities of several departments to be assembled as specific output packages, or programs, of various convenient levels of aggregation.

5. *Structural features.* An essential characteristic of PPBS is its output orientation. Each governmental agency is required to determine a series of output categories that cover the total work of the agency. This assemblage of output-oriented activities serves as the basic framework for the planning, programming, and budgeting processes. Following the pattern of systems analysis, there are several levels at which programs may be analyzed. At the most generalized level, there are *program categories* (or areas), which are groupings of agency activities that have generally similar objectives. An example would be the improvement of higher education, a broad objective and program category that is shared by more than one governmental agency.[11] *Program subcategories* are subdivisions within each program category that combine agency activities on the basis of narrower objectives. In the example cited above, improvement of graduate economics training might be one program subcategory under the improvement of higher education program category. *Programs* are the activities, missions, operations or outputs of a specific agency or organization. An example of a program for the United States Office of Education is adult education. Within this program fall all activities, or *subprograms,* such as vocational and technical training, veteran's education, and others that are a part of the adult education program. Finally, the most differentiated

[11] To illustrate the overlapping of objectives by governmental agencies, education expenditures of various kinds are incurred by approximately fifty agencies of the federal government.

parts of the program structure are the *program elements,* which comprise the specific components that contribute to the agency's objectives. There are variations of the program structure described above, but these levels of program differentiation will be used to construct the illustrative local school district structures shown in later chapters.

6. *Administrative features.* As an executive tool, PPBS is designed to facilitate the kind of information and data analysis that provides administrators with a complete basis for rational choice. It prescribes an organizational structure of programs but allows for much variance in the application of such bureaucratic elements as centralization, hierarchy, expertise, authority, span of control, and role definitions of particular organizations. Some might propose a highly decentralized operation in which each of the programs becomes a relatively autonomous power center, with an administrator who is responsible for the allocation of resources and review of performance within his program. Others may choose to initiate PPBS in the highly centralized fashion of a vertical rather than horizontal type of organization. As presently conceived at the federal level, PPBS contains a centralizing bias. It provides the means to administer budgetary decisions, but it should not be equated with efforts to reduce spending. It is neutral on the issue of cost reduction. From an administrator's viewpoint, PPBS offers at least four important advantages over traditional practices: (1) information on total system costs is output, or program, oriented; (2) analysis of possible alternative programs and of alternative means of meeting program objectives is more extensive; (3) the planning process is continuous and includes multiyear plans so that future year implications of present decisions are explicitly identified; and (4) policy is an ordered process in a well defined organization which directs major lines of action toward perceptible program goals. To a large extent, the federal planners modified the original norm of comprehensiveness, inasmuch as political considerations of policy implications reduced the scope of program design in some areas.

A potential administrative virtue of this systems approach is that it does not take human values for granted. Discrepancies in values that are unspecified may go undetected in traditional budget practices, and yet these values may have systemwide repercussions. Regardless of the level of discourse, the PPBS planner is charged with the responsibility of detecting differences among professed, conceived, or desired values on the one hand, and the operative, observed, or measured values on the other. Disparities between professed and measured values should be fed back into the system.

PPBS is a multipurpose system. It was designed at the federal level to enable the Executive Branch to analyze the uses of national inputs and to achieve identifiable needs of this country. Two of its products are a comprehensive multiyear program and financial plan that is systematically updated, and analyses, including ". . . Program Memoranda, prepared annually and used in the Budget Preview, Special Studies in depth from time to time, and other information which will contribute to the annual budget process."[12] Program memoranda should be prepared annually in each of the program categories of the agency. These summarize the program and financial plan approved by the agency administrator for that category and present a succinct evaluation and justification. In addition to appraising future needs and assessing the adequacy of the previously approved plan to meet those needs, the memorandum should propose revisions or modifications in existing programs.

In the budget message for fiscal 1968, the President contended that PPBS was helping to provide better methods of accomplishing program objectives and was contributing to greater overall efficiency. He cited five particular programs to which organized analysis and programming had been applied in the past year: disease control, child health, urban planning, agricultural research, and tax administration. After the second full year of operation, the President praised the PPB system in his fiscal 1969 budget message and described its usage in three specific areas: vocational rehabilitation programs, veterans' pensions, and employment programs in depressed areas. To what extent was PPBS fulfilling its expectations? The President indicated that ". . . the full effects of this effort will not be felt until next year and later, as the necessary data are gathered and analyses now in progress are completed."[13]

[12] United States Bureau of the Budget, *Planning-Programming-Budgeting*, Bulletin No. 66-3 (Washington, D.C.: United States Government Printing Office), p. 3.

[13] *The Budget of the United States Government—Fiscal Year 1968* (Washington, D.C.: United States Government Printing Office, 1967), p. 36.

Toward a single federal budget

Until the recent budgets, federal budgets were built almost entirely on an agency-by-agency basis, and to complicate matters further, three different "budgets" (the administrative budget, the consolidated cash budget and the national income accounts budget) were used to detail the Administration's plans and to provide data on the economic impact of government activities. With the advent of PPBS, the strategic Bureau of the Budget attempted to concentrate more on broad program areas, ". . . spotlighting programs aimed at the same objectives and trimming out programs that duplicate or run at crosspurposes with one another. The chief purpose of the reorganization is to cope with the growing interrelationship of independently run federal activities."[14] A number of persons believed that a unified summary budget statement should replace the three different federal budgets that were confusing and deficient in several ways. As a result, the President appointed a Commission on Budget Concepts whose objective was to recommend an approach to budgetary presentation which would assist both public and congressional understanding of government finance. The fiscal 1969 federal budget put into effect most of the major recommendations contained in the Commission's report, including the design of a *single unified budget document* to replace the three formats previously used. The 1969 unified budget accounting system reported all federal government outlays, whether from general funds or the trust funds; it carried a special section showing the relationship between the new and old concepts; and it reflected a greater concern for the portrayal of programmatic objectives, priorities, results, and resources.

An Office of Executive Management (OEM) was also created and program divisions were designated by the Bureau of the Budget in an exploratory attempt to integrate separate agencies. OEM was formed to analyze government structure, provide assistance to agencies in developing management information systems, coordinate operations with state and local programs and to assist in fiscal affairs related to PPBS. Six program divisions are shown in Table 5.

One way of illustrating the sequence of a federal program struc-

[14] *Business Week*, September 23, 1967, p. 129.

TABLE 5

PROGRAM DIVISIONS FOR THE UNITED STATES GOVERNMENT

SIX MAJOR PROGRAM AREAS	AN ILLUSTRATIVE AGENCY FOR EACH PROGRAM AREA
National Security Programs	Department of Defense Military Operations
National Resources Programs	Department of Agriculture
International Programs	Central Intelligence Agency
Human Resources Programs	Department of Health, Education, and Welfare
Science and Economic Programs	Department of Commerce
General Government Management	Civil Service Commission

ture is to start with a general objective, for example, "elimination of poverty." This can be broken down into a number of more specific objectives, such as "income maintenance" and "community improvements." These give rise, in turn, to narrower subobjectives, for example, educational "programs for disadvantaged youths" and "adult manpower development." From this level of subobjectives, the rationale is provided for such programs as "Head Start," "ESEA Title I," and "Student Scholarships." [15] Ultimately, the specific elements and means for accomplishing the end objective of elimination of poverty are found at the lowest level, or program element level, of a program structure. Current expenditures as well as the future projected costs can be determined both for the general objective and for each program element.

It is apparent that objectives and programs pertaining to "elimination of poverty," or any other general federal objective, will cut across organizational lines, thus creating additional problems for budget planners. In spite of the obstacles confronting OEM, some observers believe that the Bureau of the Budget may be better used by presidents as a prime tool for enforcing policy and exerting pressure against the inertia of entrenched federal programs. If PPBS succeeds at the federal level, the Bureau of the Budget can become an even more effective arm of the President. Budgetary reform is a continual process, and with the fiscal 1969 federal

[15] This type of program structure was prepared by Michael E. Levy, Manager of the Conference Board's Fiscal and Monetary Department, in his analysis of PPBS in the United States budget for fiscal 1968. See *The Federal Budget: Its Impact on the Economy*, fiscal 1968 edition (New York: National Industrial Conference Board, Inc., 1967), pp. 25–29.

budget, we moved closer to the day of a single federal budget document prepared almost entirely on a program basis.

Characteristics and advantages of PPBS: thirty theses

The thirty theses that follow are aimed at describing, in outline form, the process of a program budget (PB) as it should operate. Because the process lends itself to nearly any type of organization, these theses have inferred implications for education.

1. *Output Emphasis.* Perhaps the major characteristic of PB is that it describes accomplishment rather than things purchased. It is structured on the basis of outputs, missions, functions, activities, services, or programs, rather than on traditional input items. A program is related to operational objectives, and consists of activities to be performed, subprograms, and program elements such as human resources, materials, space, and facilities.

2. *Strategic Planning.* The planning orientation ensures that the budget is to be viewed as the financial expression of a well-defined program structure. It may serve also as an estimate of the requirements for a proposed plan of action.

3. *Input-Output Coordination.* PB provides meaningful information on the relation of inputs to outputs or programs of the organization. This represents a rational means-ends calculus which accommodates changes in interests and the priority of objectives.

4. *Explicit Objectives.* In order to avoid ambiguity of purpose, the objectives for the total system and for each program are specified in operational terms. Unless this is done, it is difficult to specify the needed programs adequately. Even though educators have remarkably poor unanimity regarding objectives and productive ways to attain them, desired directions should be articulated cogently.

5. *Evaluation.* Comparison of desired outcomes, as expressed in programmatic objectives may be made with actual accomplishments. Performance indicators are utilized, such as indices that measure changes in pupil cognitive development.

6. *Long-Range Fiscal Planning.* The annual budget is integrated with multiyear projections on a continuing basis. Typically, a pro-

gram budget document portrays estimates of needs and costs over a time horizon of at least five years.

7. *Planning Cycles.* Annual planning calendars, cycles, and flowcharts are constructed which unify procedural strategies with the budgeting process.

8. *Systems Sciences.* Systems analysis procedures are used extensively. Contributions from general systems theory, cybernetics, operations research, administrative theory, management science, and other systems sciences can be incorporated into the PPBS process in order to make it more responsive to complex human needs.

9. *Quantitative Analysis.* In order to analyze comparative benefits, quantitative measures are applied if they are available. These include such techniques as: input-output analysis, benefit-cost analysis, cost-effectiveness evaluation, operations analysis, management information system, linear programming, simulation, queuing, gaming, and others. Qualitative measures are also included, and they should play a major role in educational planning.

10. *Multiplicity of Options.* PB provides a framework for the consideration of all relevant alternatives for a particular course of action. These are then placed in order on the basis of desirability, feasibility, least cost, available resources, and other criteria.

11. *Programming.* Lines of action are drawn to coordinate the planned objectives, programs and activities, and costs along a protracted time dimension.

12. *Program Review and Revision.* In addition to program formulation and analysis, procedures for periodic review and modifications of programs are specified. This process is dynamic, viable, and promotes the adoption of innovations. Intraprogram studies are encouraged.

13. *Subprograms and Program Elements.* Each of the major programs contains delineated subprograms that minimize overlapping. Supporting program elements for each are specified.

14. *Expenditures by Program Category.* Conventional line-item objects are classified according to the end-product, program, or service they support. Thus, all expenditures are classified by program category.

15. *Optimal Resource Allocation.* PB is intended to allocate scarce resources in the most efficient manner possible. Solutions to

specific subproblems result in suboptimizations. In some cases, however, factors other than optimization may influence decisions.

16. *Future Needs.* More explicit assumptions can be made about future demand and production functions of the organization. Risk is reduced and assumptions are specified. Total cost implications of long-term undertakings are expressed.

17. *Economic Rationality.* There are at least two schools of budgetary theory, one subscribing to economic rationality and the other to political rationality. PB is essentially an economic concept designed to serve in the political arena.[16] It represents an encroachment of economics upon politics, and is an embodiment of classical political economy.

18. *Flexibility.* PB should not impose arbitrary constraints. Programs can be defined in any way suitable to a particular organization. This approach is feasible both for internal programming and control and for development of future policies and programs.

19. *Openendedness.* Expenditure items are not treated as givens. The amount available for the total system is determined, and then highest utility alternatives are selected for the specified budget programs. The major objective is not expenditure control in the fiduciary sense.

20. *Policy Determination.* Budgeting becomes an integral part of the general administrative process with PPBS. The financial administrator shares in policy formulation, and provision should be made for a continuing dialogue among the policy maker, systems analyst, budget officer, and the organization members affected by such policy.

21. *Models.* The construction of management information systems and behavioral-theoretical models is encouraged in order to process data, examine the system's operations, and to specify alternative options. If a computer is used, a model of the organization can be constructed for purposes of simulation and improved program design.

22. *Network Diagrams.* Complex development projects are created and budgeted for by programming of systematic task-sequence network diagrams. The costing of such packages may be done by PERT/Cost procedures, for example.

[16] Werner Z. Hirsch, "Toward Federal Program Budgeting," *Public Administration Review,* XXVI, No. 4 (December, 1966), 269.

23. *Decision Centers.* Within some organizations using PPBS, decision centers and cost centers are developed so that administrators can have at their fingertips historical and projected information from all phases of activity. These are retrievable from a computer data bank.[17] Simulators of the budget can be developed.

24. *Cost Neutrality.* PB is neutral on the issue of cost reduction. A cult of efficiency, measured by less spending, per se, is not the criterion of success for PPBS.

25. *Structural Variance.* Organizational structural variability is maintained, because the operations may be either centralized or decentralized. If the latter, participatory planning is encouraged so that policy making is shared by all members of the organization. If the former, lowest departmental level budget estimates form the building blocks for the next level where they are aggregated, reviewed, and transmitted upward to the highest level.

26. *Accountability and Performance Measurement.* PB can be used for control and internal management purposes to review personnel and facilities data, output data and resource data. It seeks to assess performance and affix accountability. Cost accounting procedures are generally a part of the PB format, although it may be necessary to redesign an existing accounting system so that it will provide information to meet line-item, legal accounting requirements and also provide data on program costs.

27. *Concise Budget Document.* The actual PB document should be concise, but complete, and should be understandable even to a lay reader. Local school budgets frequently use terminology and nonprogrammatic categories that are too technical and unclear for their citizenry. With PPBS, the programs should be clearly stated so that the public can grasp their contents easily.

28. *Time Factors.* A characteristic of PPBS is that achievement of a smoothly running system using this concept cannot be expected in less than a year or so. The size, resources, and complexity of operations of the organization will influence the amount of time needed to develop the new format. Generalists rush in where specialists fear to tread, and educational generalists should consider

[17] Donald J. Smalter and Rudy L. Ruggles, Jr., "Six Business Lessons from the Pentagon," *Harvard Business Review*, XLIV, No. 2 (March/April, 1966), 74–75.

the time requirements. PPBS specialists are well aware of time factors.

29. *Preservation of the Past.* The program budget encompasses the best features of previous budgeting formats: the executive budget; line-item, object budgets; and performance budgeting. It need *not* replace conventional budgeting procedures. For the time being, line-item *and* program budgets probably should be maintained concurrently as a means of describing an organization's expenditures on both an input and output basis.

30. *Proven Success.* PB has worked reasonably well in the Department of Defense, other federal agencies, municipal and state governments, and industry, and offers much promise for educational planning. If adopted, it can help to inform the public about future program plans and past accomplishments of the schools.

A hasty addendum to the list of thirty characteristics of PPBS should point out that program budgeting is not a panacea. It does not abolish the vulgarity of concern over dollars, nor does it ensure that this ideal-type blueprint will be maintained successfully in actual practice. The *original sin* in the world of finance is not inadequate budgeting, but comprises the many intervening variables that existed long before the program budget, that is, human errors, poor judgment, dishonesty, malfeasance, resistance to accountability, administrative short-sightedness, visions of orthodoxy, political factors, and the like.

Political Economy and the Budget Process

There is some question as to whether the budget process in government generally, and education in particular, has its deepest roots in economics or political science. One might sidestep the issue by claiming that the process of budgeting is a contemporary result of the original union of the two disciplines as political economy. Certainly, the ethos of program budgeting is economic rationality. However, in order for PPBS to continue to make inroads, it must show its worth in the political arena without becoming embroiled in political entanglements. Amidst the political realities of government, program preferences that ultimately are reflected in both the budget document and budget process occasionally may be unrelated to costs and benefits, where the objective is least-cost methods of achieving efficiency in resource allocation. There may be accidental facts; or the sources of revenue for a particular program may be easier to utilize than another; or the beneficiaries of a proposed program may be more politically powerful than those of a competing program; or jurisdictional disputes over programs that cut across organizational lines may offset economic rationality of program budgeting.

At the federal level, theoretical models can be designed and equations formulated that explain major facets of the budget process. A set of simple decision rules can explain or represent the behavior of participants in the federal budgetary process in their efforts to make decisions about complex situations. In one study, "The empirical results support the hypothesis that, up to a random error of reasonable magnitude, the budgetary process of the U.S. is equivalent to a set of temporally stable linear decision rules." [18]

In a school setting, local administrators are well aware that the budget process is both economic and political. The preparation and execution of the technical aspects of budgeting are mostly economic, whereas the gathering of public support is largely political. The budget process in most school districts, and especially in large city school systems, is highly complicated because so many interested and articulate parties are involved and the stakes are high. Chief school administrators seek to mobilize power on behalf of the schools. It is within this environment that the PPBS process will have to gain acceptance if it is to coexist with conventional line-item budgeting. In the political context, one may distinguish between several kinds of politics:

Partisan politics: Which political party will gain?
Policy politics: Which policy will be adopted?
System politics: How will decision structures be organized?

Wildavsky contends that program budgeting is not particularly involved with partisan politics, is manifestly concerned with policy politics, and is an integral part of system politics.[19] It is at the sys-

[18] O. A. Davis, M. A. H. Dempster, and Aaron Wildavsky, "A Theory of the Budgetary Process," *The American Political Science Review,* LX, No. 3 (September, 1966), 537.

[19] Aaron Wildavsky, "The Political Economy of Efficiency," *The Public Interest,* No. 8 (Summer, 1967), 41.

tem-politics level that local school officials will need to become better informed. PPBS may serve as a vehicle for integrating research contributions from the economics of education and the politics of education in a manner that will benefit school practitioners. The future of public education will not be determined solely by public need. It will be determined by those who can transform public need into public policy, and PPBS may serve as the vehicle of transformation.

Components of an educational program budget design

An educational budget should describe programmatic objectives in addition to objects of expenditure or things purchased. As a planning and management device, the program budget process is more comprehensive than the existing fragmented process of constructing incremental administrative budgets. Some of the conceptual aspects are described next as a general guide to educational planners who wish to design a program budget for their organization. There is fairly wide variation in approaches to this budgeting process, and each planner is truly an architect of a unique program design. A major objective of this format is to move budgeting from simply a justification-control-constraint function to an analytical framework for total organization planning. Alternative program structures are provided in Chapter Seven.

1. *Systems Analysis.* The first step in the design of a program budget consists of a rigorous analysis of the organization, culminating in the formulation of objectives expressed in operational terms. For a school system this means that the educational philosophy may be used as a basis for more specific curricular objectives. Truisms and clichés such as "meet the needs" and "teach the whole child" are inadequate as operational objectives. A more fruitful approach is to state objectives for appropriate curricular programs in terms of behavioral, achievement, or attitudinal outcomes. This is dependent upon the extent to which the results of the teaching-learning process can be specified by measurable variables or performance indicators. One purpose of systems analysis is to present an analytical comparison of alternatives. The quantification of output and benefits is, in effect, the quantification of the organization's objectives, and it serves as a test of the validation of the stated

objective. Systems procedures may indicate the deficiency of the objectives stated by a school district.

2. *Program Structure.* The flexible quality of program budgeting permits each educational institution to specify its programs in whatever manner it deems appropriate. The only constraint here is the extent to which certain programs are mandated by state departments of education or supported by federal aid or foundations. The program structure comprises the outputs, programs, program elements, human and material resources, and strategic missions or activities of the organization. Programming is the specific allocation of resources for the support of the various instructional programs. States may prescribe how a budget is to be developed, but no state expressly forbids program budgeting.

3. *Multiyear Planning.* A principal product of this process is a multiyear program document and financial plan for the organization. Program, or department, chairmen and others involved in school planning are required to project their needs into the future for a stated period of time, perhaps five years. Budget classification should facilitate the comparison of program outcomes over a span of time. In education, this is done in capital budgets much more than in operating budgets because there are formal, required procedures for estimating pupil enrollments and forecasting the number of buildings to be needed at a future time. What is needed is a decisional matrix and data flow plan ensuring that annual budgeting is not merely incremental, but is integrated with long-range planning on a continuing basis.

4. *Cost-Effectiveness Analysis.* In order to determine a pay-off function, the costs of a particular course of action should be compared with anticipated benefits and then weighed against alternative courses of action. This analytic approach is similar to cost-utility, benefit-cost, or even input-output analysis, and it is designed to aid in the evaluation of competing alternatives. Until educational benefits no longer defy complete quantitative measurement, it is desirable to articulate many of the benefits in nonquantitative terms. Attempts to quantify all program objectives of a school would probably suffocate the basic concept of PPBS.

5. *Budgeting.* Appropriations to the classifications of the program structure are made by the financial administrator, although the degree of centralization in this process may vary from school to school. Dollar amounts are assigned to program elements. It is not

necessary, and probably not even desirable, to abolish the traditional line-item type of budget. Rather, this traditional input budget may accompany the newer program budget so as to show a more complete breakdown of an organization's expenditures on the basis of both inputs and outputs. To illustrate, a particular teacher's salary might appear in the input budget as a part of line-item "instructional costs," and in the program budget, as a part of the specific curricular program or grade level program of which the teacher is a prime component. This should not double the work load of the budget officer because data processing could easily enable a given budgetary appropriation to be assigned to both the input and output budgets.

6. *Evaluation.* Program review is a year-round process of evaluating and revising program objectives, performance, and costs. It makes the planning-programming-budgeting system a dynamic procedure. The organizational structure should mandate periodic updating by means of planning calendars so that recommendations can be made within the annual budget cycle. Evaluative criteria should be developed to aid decision makers at all levels within the system.

Each of the six procedural steps should be employed if an educational institution wishes to phase-in the total process of program budgeting successfully. The analytical and structural components are necessary if the process is to be an improvement over traditional budgeting procedures. The ideal system is a multiyear program budget that is fully costed out in performance terms.[20] If successful, the program budget introduces a system for the evaluation of school output and school costs over time and provides a comprehensive framework for rational planning.

Conclusion

The educational budget is conceived as a financial expression of a comprehensive instructional-curricular program plan. The initial work in implementing the PPBS process should pertain to the de-

[20] Jesse Burkhead, "The Theory and Application of Program Budgeting to Education," *Trends in Financing Public Education,* Eighth National Conference on School Finance (Washington, D.C.: National Education Association Committee on Educational Finance, 1965), p. 185.

sign of a program structure that reflects the operational objectives of a school system. After a suitable program structure is developed, the allocation of resources and assignment of budgetary dollars can be accomplished. The conceptual framework for program budgeting is systems analysis, which is not limited in education to quantitative analysis. In the next chapter, I shall review selected examples of educational and noneducational organizations that recently developed program budget procedures with varying degrees of sophistication and success.

Suggestion for Discussion

Describe how some of the distinguishing characteristics of PPBS are precisely the reverse of those of traditional budgeting practice.

Selected References

Budgeting for National Objectives. New York: Committee for Economic Development, 1966, 65 pp.

Bureau of the Budget, Executive Office of the President. *Planning-Programming-Budgeting.* Bulletin Number 68-2. Washington, D.C.: United States Government Printing Office (July 18, 1967). This replaced Bulletin Number 66-3 (October 12, 1965).

Fisher, Gene H., *The World of Program Budgeting,* P-3361. Santa Monica, Calif.: RAND Corporation, May, 1966, 30 pp.

Hatry, Harry P., and John F. Cotton, *Program Planning for State, County and City.* Washington, D.C.: George Washington University, 1967, 72 pp.

Hirsch, Werner Z., *Toward Federal Program Budgeting,* P-3306. Santa Monica, Calif.: RAND Corporation (February, 1966), 27 pp.

Novick, David, editor, *Program Budgeting: Program Analysis and the Federal Government.* Cambridge, Mass.: Harvard University Press, 1965, Chapters 1, 2, and 4.

Public Administration Review. XXVI, No. 4, December, 1966, 243–310.

U.S. Department of Health, Education, and Welfare. *PPB: Guidance for Program and Financial Plan.* Washington, D.C.: the Department (April 6, 1967), 200 pp.

As interesting as watching what happens to government when confronted with program planning is observing what happens to program planning when confronted with government.

Elizabeth B. Drew

Chapter Five

RECENT PROJECTS IN PPBS DEVELOPMENT

Following the Executive Order which required the heads of all federal agencies to adopt PPBS for fiscal 1968, the planners in industry, municipal and state governments, and other nondefense organizations sought to discover what could be learned from the federal experience. There was an intensive interest in the sophisticated conceptual procedures developed for our nation's top priority organization (as reflected in the share of GNP expended for defense), the Department of Defense. Illustrating the applicability of these techniques to diverse types of organizations, subsequent sections describe in synopsis form noteworthy projects in government, industry, and education that were designed to result in a comprehensive program budget structure for each. The common aims were: (1) to chart the direction of future events less in response to impulse than to rational strategy and (2) to display the conversion of resource inputs into programs. The list is representative although, regretfully, many projects that may prove to be quite significant have been omitted. The range of projects encompasses a chemical company, government units other than schools, and ten urban public school systems selected from eight states. Inasmuch as the major initial concern at the conceptual stage should be for the design of a suitable program classification system, less attention is given to portraying the highly technical aspects of PPBS supportive elements.

Noneducational Projects

5-5-5 Project

One of the more notable attempts to develop program budget procedures is the State and Local Finances Project, which is part of a program of research and education on advanced fiscal planning supported by a grant from the Ford Foundation to the George Washington University. Under the direction of economist Selma Mushkin, the "5-5-5 Project" was undertaken to demonstrate the conceptual and operational feasibility of planning-programming-budgeting systems procedures for state and municipal governments in five states (California, Michigan, New York, Vermont, and Wisconsin), five counties (Dade, Florida; Davidson, Tennessee; Los Angeles, California; Nassau, New York; and Wayne, Michigan), and five cities (Dayton, Denver, Detroit, New Haven, and San Diego). The extent to which PPBS procedures have been developed varies greatly among these fifteen governmental units, but descriptive information, guidelines, and technical mannuals are generally available upon request from each unit.

The State and Local Finances Project provided a series of explanatory monographs on planning-programming-budgeting entitled *PPB Notes.* These dealt with issues such as alternative administrative frameworks for PPBS, program structures, staffing needs, and the role of cost analysis in a PPB system. One monograph provides an illustrative general program structure for a city government. It encompasses eight program areas, each of which has a statement of objectives, and includes subcategories and representative specific program elements.[1] This design was presented to a United States Senate subcommittee that was studying intergovernmental relations between and among the federal, state and local levels. It is shown in Table 6.

As was the case with the nine programs of the Department of Defense shown in the preceding chapter, these are general categories which must be differentiated in greater detail. Within each general program area, there are a number of specific programs. For

[1] State and Local Finances Project, *PPB Note* 3 (Washington, D.C.: George Washington University, January, 1967), pp. 10–19.

TABLE 6

ILLUSTRATIVE PPBS PROGRAM STRUCTURE FOR THE GENERAL PROGRAMS OF A MUNICIPAL OR STATE GOVERNMENT [2]

I.	Personal safety (Protection from personal harm and property loss)
II.	Health (Physical and mental well-being)
III.	Intellectual Development and Personal Enrichment (Education, libraries, museums, etc.)
IV.	Satisfactory Home and Community Environment (Creation of a livable and pleasant environment)
V.	Economic Satisfaction (Satisfactory individual work opportunities, welfare assistance)
VI.	Leisure-time Opportunities (Indoor-outdoor recreational and cultural opportunities)
VII.	Transportation-Communication-Location (Highways, urban transit, parking, air transport, etc.)
VIII.	General Administration and Support (Activities not assignable to the seven other major program areas)

example, in General Program Area I, *Personal Safety,* there are eight categories, or programs:

1. law enforcement;
2. traffic safety;
3. fire prevention and control;
4. safety from animals;
5. protection from and control of disasters;
6. prevention of food, drug, and occupational hazards and accidents;
7. unassignable research and planning, personal safety; and
8. unassignable support, personal safety.[3]

Furthermore, within each of these programs, there are subprograms which are supported by program elements. Within Program 1, Law Enforcement, as an illustration, there are five subprograms:

[2] United States Congress, Senate, Committee on Government Relations, Subcommittee on Intergovernmental Relations, *Criteria for Evaluation in Planning State and Local Programs,* 90th Congress, 1st Session (July 21, 1967), pp. 37–42.

[3] *Ibid.,* p. 38.

1. crime prevention;
2. crime investigation;
3. judging and assigning of punishment;
4. punishment and safekeeping of criminals; and
5. rehabilitation of criminals.[4]

The logic of this procedure is clear. The first step is to formulate approximately ten or twelve general program areas which include all of the activities of the organization, whether it be a government, corporation, or school system. The next procedure is to identify more specific programs within each program area. In the case of a school, these could be curricular in nature. Finally, each of the program elements, including the traditional budgetary line-items of personnel, materials and supplies, transportation, buildings, administrative costs, debt service, and others should be assigned to a designated program category. For those items which cannot reasonably be assigned to the other major program areas, there might be an "all-other," residual, or general support program. Examples of this are Program VII, General Support, in the Department of Defense program structure (Table 3) and Program VIII, General Administration and Support, in the State Local Finances Project (Table 6).

New York State

Since 1964, the State of New York has been developing a PPBS format that systematically relates the expenditure of State funds to the accomplishment of carefully conceived goals. This is being achieved through the combined efforts of the staffs of the Office of Planning Coordination and the Division of the Budget, working with the many line agencies. The most difficult task was to develop a complete program structure that included all activities of each agency, such as state operations, capital facilities, local assistance programs, and federally assisted programs.

In order to establish program planning on a recurring basis, an annual cycle was established to provide for the evaluation and coordination of program plans in line with statewide goals and to help coordinate annual budget requests with a detailed projection of long-range needs. There are six major phases of the annual planning cycle:

[4] *Ibid.*

1. *Organization Phase.* The PPBS cycle for the coming year is organized immediately following the submission of the Executive Budget to the Legislature. Revised central forecasts of economic trends, population growth, and public needs prepared during the past year are submitted to each agency to aid in planning and programming.

2. *Agency Report Preparation.* Each state agency begins the preparation of its program planning reports before the start of the new fiscal year.

3. *Executive Office Conferences with Each Agency.* Conferences are scheduled by the Division of the Budget with the agencies to discuss the major policy issues and administrative aspects of the agency reports that were submitted in Phase 2. This provides the Governor with a general analysis and evaluation of major trends of State programs.

4. *Program Coordination and Summarization.* The program plans are combined and analyzed for planning and budgetary implications. Meetings are held with the agencies to clarify policy issues and problem areas prior to the submission of their budget request.

5. *Integration of Program Plans and Budget Requests.* The agency budget requests, which are presented nearly four months after the program plan reports, are examined in relation to those program plans. During formal budget hearings, agencies present budget requests in the context of their program goals. This is the essence of the program budget structure.

6. *Budget Development.* The proposed Executive Budget of the Governor is developed in accordance with the priorities and resource requirements of the coordinated program plans.[5]

Dates for these six phases of the planning cycle can be stipulated well in advance so that each person involved in the planning process has prior knowledge of target dates and information required. Internal planning cycles for each agency are also established.

The most important single component of the New York State sys-

[5] The Office of Planning Coordination and the Division of the Budget prepared jointly a monograph describing in some detail the purpose, scope, procedures, program plans, and administrative plans for the program budget: *Guidelines for Integrated Planning-Programming-Budgeting* (Albany, N.Y.: Executive Department, State of New York, 1967), 63 pp. The annual planning cycle is presented on pp. 8–10.

tem is the *program plan,* which is submitted by each agency to the Division of the Budget. In this plan, the agency provides a complete design for each program, including clear statements of objectives, achievement schedules, and possible constraints. In a school setting, these would probably be prepared by curricular program heads in cooperation with teachers. The information requested on program plans by New York State is of three general types.

1. List the goals, and the constraints on them, for the major program area, including:
   a. the long-range goal of each major program area;
   b. general goals beyond a five-year period;
   c. specific goals over the next five years for each program in the major program area;
   d. the priority position, or ranking, of each specific goal; and
   e. the constraints which limit each goal.
2. Describe the design for major program areas, including:
   a. a specific design for each program which enables programs to meet the goals set forth above;
   b. major policy issues or administrative problems which may arise;
   c. anticipated major new capital facilities or changes in use, capacity, or function of existing capital facilities, extending beyond the next five years;
   d. requirements for new legislation; and
   e. the anticipated impact of each program in achieving the agency role in fulfilling the needs of major program areas.
3. Indicate the estimated achievements for each program for each of the next five years, including:
   a. a brief description of the program;
   b. the priority rank of this program relative to all other programs in the major program area;
   c. the status of each program (current, modified, or proposed); and
   d. the projected performance of each program to reach a stated goal, and the accompanying work load measurements that contribute to the achievement of this performance level.[6]

The New York State procedure requires cooperation among planners, budget analysts, administrators, policy makers, and sup-

[6] *Ibid.,* pp. 29–31.

port personnel at every level of government. The overall objective of PPBS in the State is to provide a framework within which alternative goals, programs, and resources can be organized and summarized for presentation to appointed and elected officials to provide them with a more objective basis for making policy decisions. Program budgeting applies to the State Education Department only in terms of its own operations. The Department has not applied it to the public schools and probably will not do so at least until the early 1970's.[7] In the meantime, the State's school district reorganization effort is directed toward a reduction in the total number of local districts from 859 in 1967–68 to 500 in the near future. Also, attempts are being made to regionalize the State for data processing functions and to implement this approach by 1973. As these goals for district reorganization and data processing are achieved, it is likely that the State Education Department will explore program budgeting as it relates to the local schools. Until the format is changed, local educational expenditures will continue to be reported on a conventional line-item, input, object basis. Emergent planning technologies should be applied to an area which is badly in need of improved procedural strategies.

California

Using the same general principles as PPBS, the State of California embarked upon a mission to establish a Programming and Budgeting System (PABS). In 1966 the State contended that the concepts underlying PABS were not new, although the total integrative package was:

> PABS formalizes what has gone on and is taking place in the framework of the management decision process in governmental jurisdictions. . . . PABS is a complete system; it encompasses *all* those

[7] A portion of the information was drawn from correspondence received from Maurice G. Osborne, Assistant Commissioner for Educational Finance and Management Services, New York State Education Department, August 9, 1967. Further evidence of future implementation of PPBS in local school districts throughout the State was indicated in a letter from Gordon M. Ambach, Special Assistant to the Commissioner of Education for Long Range Planning, November 29, 1967. Mr. Ambach was formerly Program Planning Officer for the United States Commissioner of Education and was trained in program budgeting; his State role may reflect the type of new, specialized position which PPBS will lead to in the near future.

> techniques associated with program and systems analysis. It is not simply an effort to improve budget narratives. It is not simply an attempt to improve performance standards. It is a system of program analysis which formalizes and records alternatives over a multi-year time span and the analysis upon which the program decisions were made.[8]

In relating PABS to its many departments and agencies, the State admitted it had difficulties answering the question, "What is a program?" It was suggested that, lacking a complete program structure, the answer depended on the position (organization level) held by the individual asking the question. To answer this question and to train department personnel in the intricacies of PABS, the State stressed ten principles:

1. Define problem (need);
2. Meaningfully describe objectives;
3. Quantify outputs (benefits);
4. Quantify inputs (costs);
5. Provide multiyear considerations;
6. Conduct analysis of alternatives;
7. Crossover;
8. Record assumptions and uncertainties;
9. Record relationships; and
10. Conduct evaluation.[9]

Because its lineage is traced to PPBS, California's PABS uses similar key documents such as program statements, multiyear program budgets, and program memoranda. The State emphasizes the consideration of all relevant cost considerations for programs, both immediate and future. It provides documents for listing additional costs, sunk costs (funds already spent), fixed costs, and variable costs.

California is phasing-in the concept of PABS gradually rather than prematurely installing it as an immediately workable total package. Local schools might heed this advice:

> It is going to take time to develop the analysis capabilities at the various levels of state programs. Even in PABS' most advanced de-

[8] *Programming and Budgeting System* (Sacramento, Calif.: Department of Finance, State of California, 1967), p. 1.

[9] *Ibid.*, pp. 26–34.

> velopments, we may not have the capabilities of advanced systems analysis, particularly those techniques of systems analysis dealing with intricate cost-effectiveness analysis. For three or four or perhaps five years, a good deal of the material will be prepared on a rather elemental basis. Just spending the necessary time in thinking through program need and objectives with fundamental considerations of quantification will be very productive to program managers, administrators and other decision makers.[10]

Pennsylvania

The Commonwealth of Pennsylvania, as an example of a state *not* participating in the "5-5-5 Project," considered the feasibility of PPBS independently. Using a private consulting firm, the Commonwealth ordered a four-month, first-phase assessment of Pennsylvania's current management and decision making processes and capabilities. From this preliminary study will come a detailed plan for PPBS. The goal of Pennsylvania is to develop a package of integrated management procedures that ". . . identifies broad objectives, establishes program structures, improves decision making capabilities, relates planning to budgeting, and provides a basis for the rational allocation of resources considering various alternative courses of action." [11]

Nassau County, N.Y.

One of the county units of government that participated in the State and Local Finances Project is Nassau County, Long Island, part of the metropolitan area of New York City. With forty departments and nearly 13,000 employees, the County established program budgeting procedures as part of a comprehensive management information system (MIS). The project was developed in four phases, with completion expected to be achieved by 1970. Phase One is the systems-design and pilot project that furnished the functional classification system and program structure. Phase Two is the implementation of Phase One by all forty agencies of the County. Management reports, work reports, work standards and basic instructions are included in this stage. Phase Three provides for the employment of MIS management analysis personnel

[10] *Ibid.*, p. 2.
[11] *The Pittsburgh Press*, August 29, 1967, p. 34.

and for the fully designed and implemented fiscal systems. Resources are allocated according to the program budget format. Phase Four, with no specified time limit, includes the development of mathematical models to be used in making financial projections and the furtherance of analytical management science techniques.[12] This final phase places great importance upon the computer, for the ultimate goal in using MIS is to secure information concerning every aspect of an operation, analyze it, and develop reports in any form desired. The computer is simply the processing device that makes complex systems feasible and manageable.

Nassau County seeks to develop a simplified input-output system for which multiple purpose management reports can be easily produced. These reports can be classified under one of four categories: (1) program development and control; (2) performance analysis and control; (3) financial planning and control; and (4) resource utilization and control. The most important step was the development of a comprehensive classification system in which every work activity of the various County agencies was spelled out, beginning with the general functions and concluding with highly differentiated tasks. All operations of the County were categorized in terms of the following:

1. *Functions:* the ultimate area of responsibility within which each department's operations are conducted. Examples include public safety, public health and public works.

2. *Objectives:* the basic missions of each department. Based upon the concept of mission, these objectives state the purpose of each department's work. Examples include prevention of crime under the function of public safety and disease control under the function of public health.

3. *Programs:* the fundamental groups of related activities around which the department is organized and upon which its policies are based. Examples of programs include police laboratory work under the objective of prevention of crime and venereal disease control under the objective of disease control.

4. *Activities:* the smallest group of related tasks that result in one measurable unit of work. Examples include fingerprint analysis

[12] Eugene H. Nickerson, *Management Information System* (Nassau County, New York: Office of the County Executive, June 17, 1966), pp. 5–6. A revised edition was published in March, 1968.

under the program of police laboratory work and nursing visits under the program of venereal disease.

5. *Tasks:* the specific jobs assigned individuals which in total comprise the activities. Examples include reading an X-ray, spraying chemicals, or filing fingerprints.[13]

Ideally, all activities and tasks are grouped in terms of their missions, as is the case with the Department of Defense. This is quite a difficult task for local governments and school systems that are required to provide continuous service, much of which is difficult to measure objectively.

New York City

Pursuing a strategy sharply different from that of the other government units described above, the City of New York initiated PPBS. The City's ". . . overall approach has, deliberately, been opportunistic, rather than systematic and comprehensive. We have concentrated our efforts on analysis, rather than on program structure and accounts, and we have focused on sectors of high apparent yield." [14] A partial justification for this approach is that the massive effort to classify City expenditures by program category and to articulate and quantify all program objectives would stifle the basic concept of rational planning.

The City suggested that a number of factors contributed to its limited capacity to engage in conceptual budgeting: (1) a highly developed budget making apparatus was lacking; (2) inadequate information systems; (3) lack of personnel and inexperience in program planning; (4) centralization of budget control; (5) line-item basis for budget construction and administration; (6) predominance of established practice in key municipal programs (for instance, police, fire, sanitation, education); and (7) lack of funds for innovation and experimentation.

The frankness of city officials is a refreshing contrast to organizations who describe their ascent toward Nirvana with PPBS. "Our strategy was based upon a recognition of realities, the strengths and weaknesses, the constraints and limitations inherent in the existing

[13] *Ibid.*, pp. 8–9.

[14] Statement by Frederick O'R. Hayes, Director of the Budget, City of New York, "PPBS in New York," September 19, 1967. Mimeograph, p. 1.

pattern of municipal government."[15] A number of first steps were taken in 1967–1968 toward the PPBS format, including:

1. recruitment efforts to employ program analysts;
2. establishment of a Policy Planning Council;
3. analysis of the capital and operating budgets by objective;
4. review of projects by community area within the City;
5. efforts to establish proximate goals for new projects;
6. establishment of a Division of Program Planning;
7. PPBS *probes* in key areas;
8. usage of cost-effectiveness procedures;
9. project information and scheduling systems; and
10. proposals for a "think tank"[16] to analyze city problems.

In addition, the City hired RAND Corporation to conduct a $600,000, six-month study of the police, fire, housing, and health agencies in 1968. This new commitment by RAND to urban problems accounted for more than 5 per cent of the Corporation's annual budget.

Applications of PPBS procedures to a private corporation

Corporate executives are interested in new planning strategies, and as might be expected, have applied the PPBS concept to business environments in creative ways. An exemplary project is that of International Minerals and Chemical Corporation (IMC), whose program structure and planning procedures were well designed. IMC developed a product-classification scheme and planning framework that included strategic planning and sales development by missions, a centralized "decision center," a scheduled annual planning cycle, quantitative techniques and systems analysis, needs research and other formalized studies, and logic-sequence network diagrams for controlling complex projects. Two systems specialists

[15] *Ibid.*

[16] The proposed research institute is similar to, but independent of, RAND Corporation. Such a "think tank" would possess some of the same advantages as RAND, in that it would give the City the chance to employ scientists, sociologists, educators, and others who are unwilling to work in a bureaucracy for Civil Service salaries. See the *New York Times,* November 10, 1967, p. 65. The Federal Government proposed the establishment of a similar type of program analysis center to deal with urban problems.

described how this chemical company applied the following six lessons from the experience of the Department of Defense:

1. Resources were allocated through the use of the concept of strategic missions;
2. Annual budgeting was integrated with long-range planning on a continuing basis;
3. Systems simulation and other operations research techniques were applied to complex strategy questions;
4. Planning and program analysis were based on a logical, systematic sequence of analytical steps;
5. Task-sequence network diagrams were used in the programming and administration of complex development projects; and
6. Decision making centers were designed for analyzing and reviewing corporate plans.[17]

The corporation did more than merely understand PPBS; it provided this concept a position from which to operate by establishing a Corporate Planning and Development Division headed by a vice president. Some school districts have followed suit by employing management consultants. The role of these specialists may be defined in different ways, but in IMC, top management stated that it wanted ". . . its past methods of decision making challenged, its proposals soundly evaluated by a distinterested team of specialists, its strategic moves made in the light of penetrating environment *intelligence,* and its alternative courses of action systematically identified and weighed." [18]

The federal government

The experience of the Federal Government with PPBS is used to answer two questions: Why was PPBS an improvement over existing practices? What does the PPBS enable each agency to do? Many publications describing the Government's encounter with PPBS are available, including Bulletin Number 68-2 issued by the Executive Office, and these are of value to educators.

[17] Donald J. Smalter and Rudy L. Ruggles, Jr., "Six Business Lessons from the Pentagon," *Harvard Business Review,* XLIV, No. 2 (March/April, 1966), 67.

[18] *Ibid.,* p. 75.

Why was PPBS better than existing practices?

1. Program review was concentrated within too short a period;
2. Objectives of agency programs and activities were not specified with enough clarity and concreteness;
3. Accomplishments were not always specified concretely;
4. Alternatives were insufficiently presented for administrative consideration;
5. Future year costs of present decisions were not provided; and
6. Formalized planning and systems analysis had too little effect on budget decisions.[19]

What can PPBS enable each agency to accomplish?

1. Each agency can make available to top management more concrete and specific data relevant to broad decisions;
2. It can spell out more explicitly the objectives of Government programs;
3. It can analyze systematically and offer for agency head and Presidential review and decision possible alternative objectives and alternate programs to meet these objectives;
4. Each agency can evaluate completely and compare the costs and benefits of various programs;
5. It can provide total rather than partial cost estimates of programs;
6. It can present on a multiyear basis the prospective costs and accomplishments of programs; and
7. Each agency will be able to review and revise objectives and conduct program analysis on a continuing, year-round basis, instead of on a crisis schedule to meet budget deadlines.[20]

The applicability of conceptual planning is demonstrated by the increasing number of government and industry units that are employing PPBS procedures. The choice of the several units described above was arbitrarily made, partially on the basis of the availability of information. Similar qualifications apply to the educational projects described next.

Educational projects

A number of local urban and suburban school districts claim to

[19] Executive Office of the President, Bulletin 66-3, *Planning-Programming-Budgeting* (Washington, D.C.: Bureau of the Budget, October 12, 1965), p. 1.
[20] *Ibid.*, p. 3.

be operating under at least a modified program budget structure. Close observation of their procedures often reveals that they have simply continued their traditional planning and budgeting approaches but under the disguised name of the program budget. Name-changing and minor modifications are insufficient. Districts which purport to be using a program budget format fall into one of several categories.

Some school systems change the name of the line-item functions, or objects of expenditure, contained in the state mandated school budget codes to "programs." Little else is done in the way of fully implementing the PPBS concept.

Second, some districts provide a great number of unit cost analyses to show, for example, the annual per pupil cost of the eighth-grade algebra program. Unit cost analysis is an important type of information, but its usage does not imply that the district has revamped its curricular program structure as required with the program budget.

A great number of districts, particularly hard-pressed city systems, have looked to the program budget as a way of reducing costs. These administrators apparently do not realize that PPBS is neutral on the issue of cost reduction, although it does promote rational efficiency in the allocation of resources.

Perhaps the most common misuse of PPBS by school districts is to assume that the concept applies only to the operations of the school business administrator. Most districts which claim that they are moving toward a PPBS design do not involve curriculum-instructional specialists until a later phase, if they involve them at all. If this new approach is to be successful, it is imperative that instructional specialists be involved from the very beginning in the design and classification of the program structure. Continual dialogue and cooperation between instructional specialists and financial administrators are essential.

Finally, some districts that say they are using PPBS procedures are, in fact, doing so. Progress has been impeded by the newness of the topic, the lack of familiarity of most school administrators with recently developed management science concepts for planning, the resistance to innovation that has always plagued education, and lack of venture capital to engage in research and development projects of any kind. Ten school districts attempting to implement PPBS procedures in various degrees are mentioned below.

Baltimore City Public Schools

A somewhat traditional approach was taken to define twelve general programs of the school district.[21] Ninety-seven activities are reported as components of the basic programs. All costs associated with a given program or activity are posted to that program or activity. An official of the Baltimore Schools indicated that an ideal program budget was difficult to put into practice, and his comments support the compromise model developed by his district. He stated:

> If program, activities, and subactivities were required, this alone would be a herculean task . . . only an absolute minimum of programs and activities should be costed out. . . . For over a century, educators have worked on costing out educational programs. . . . Some persons think that school districts, particularly the large systems, should seek to attain the ideal—in other words program costs for subject matter by grade level, with costs assigned to each school in the system. The literature abounds with such proposals *particularly by college professors* [italics mine]. Too much unnecessary data will hamper those persons who are in decision-making roles just as much as too little data.[22]

Chicago Public Schools

Chicago made progress in reclassifying accounts within broad functional areas so that emphasis was placed on programs rather than on the traditional objects of expenditure. As was the case with Baltimore, this is not a complete PPBS structure, but it represents a substantial revision of the budget and accounting procedures. Research is under way to identify ways to relate expenditures to expected outcomes in more specific terms than simply the quantitative measure of the number of pupils served, which is the present procedure.

Little published evidence is yet available on the Chicago project, but one advantage which the District gained from program budget-

[21] The twelve programs are almost identical to the categories of expenditures, by objects, contained in United States Office of Education *Handbook II* (for example: instruction, debt service, transportation).

[22] Orlando F. Furno, "Program Budgeting and School Quality," *Association for Educational Data Systems Monitor*, V, No. 9 (April, 1967), 14.

ing is described by the former budget officer. In one year's tentative budget for the Chicago Schools, twelve programs from the previous year were omitted because of inadequate funds.

> When it became apparent to the public that there were insufficient funds to continue these programs with the current tax rate, an urgent plea from the public for restoration of these programs prompted the Board of Education to raise the necessary taxes to provide them. In this instance, program budgeting worked to the advantage of improvement in the educational program by identifying precisely what the funds were to be used for in terms that no one could misunderstand.[23]

Similar benefits may be gained by other local districts.

Dade County, Florida, Public Schools

Among the first school districts to launch a comprehensive project in program budgeting was that of the Dade County Board of Public Instruction, which includes the area of Greater Miami. At the time of this writing, the school district had prepared a proposal for federal assistance (Title IV) for a $600,000, three-year project and was awaiting formal notification concerning the status of the funding. If accepted, this comprehensive project could have national impact upon schools that seek to adopt program budgeting and are looking for guidelines for action. Inasmuch as any work that was underway in the Dade County Public Schools on program budgeting prior to 1968 was exploratory and related to the subsequent preparation of the federal proposal, the discussion that follows is less detailed than it might be otherwise. After the funding of the proposals, several years will probably be needed to prepare guidelines and make them available to interested persons from other schools. One of the unique aspects of this project is that the proposal for federal assistance is jointly sponsored by the district and the Association of School Business Officials (ASBO), the latter organization serving as the dissemination agent for this venture.[24]

[23] Donald W. Hill, former Assistant to the Superintendent of Chicago Schools, "Progress Report on Program Budgeting in Chicago," *Trends in Financing Public Education* (Washington, D.C.: National Education Association, Committee on Educational Finance, 1965), p. 190.

[24] Letter from E. L. Whigham, deputy superintendent, Dade County Public Schools, Miami, Florida, October 25, 1967. Additional information was provided in several letters from former superintendent Joe Hall. Whigham replaced Hall as superintendent in January, 1968.

The district developed a comprehensive program called a "Strategy of Teaching," which pertained to the overall improvement of its instructional program. One part of this project involved the design and implementation of a management system capable of providing support to the teacher in specified ways. Teacher support was organized into three major efforts:

1. *Instructional Services.* This category includes research, developing and pilot testing experimental, instructional programs, evaluation of results, and massive in-service training for personnel to acquaint them with the "Strategy of Teaching."
2. *Administrative Services.* Included are services related to personnel, procurement, finance, planning, data processing, management reports, and others.
3. *Operational Services.* This category contains physical services needed by teachers, such as building and capital outlay programs, maintenance, operations and custodial services, transportation and others.

Each of these service areas was described in greater detail by the district.[25] For example, one objective for administrative services was the development of a five-year operating plan with a program budget in which all costs of the schools would be identified in three distinct ways: by object class, by responsibility, and by program. In addition, PERT networks were prepared and a data bank designed as a means of providing school officials with reports by which they could better evaluate the qualitative and cost performance of various programs. A management training course was developed to introduce personnel of all administrative levels, from assistant principal upward, to the new format. Efforts were directed toward the development of a series of procedural manuals in the areas of overall system design, cost systems, program identification, accounting procedures, program budgeting, evaluation, electronic data processing, and others. Included in the actual program budget research proposal was a one-page table that could serve as a model of conciseness in summarizing projects. The areas of research, or functions, were listed across the top of the table, and beneath each area was a summary of (1) objectives, (2) procedures, and (3) the

[25] *A Strategy of Teaching,* paper prepared to describe the First Research Proposal (Miami, Fla.: Dade County Board of Public Instruction, October 10, 1966), 7 pp.

products of research that the "Strategy for Teaching" project was intended to yield. See Appendix K.

The Dade County project appears to be quite promising, but early results will probably not be available until at least 1970.

Los Angeles City Schools

The district developed a plan that would permit it to move into program budgeting and accounting on a "phasing-in" basis. In 1968, the Los Angeles Schools were in the preliminary stages of program budgeting and were awaiting more definitive guidelines from the state level. The ten programs shown in the budget summary were based upon grade level and support services. The State of California Board of Education appointed a State Advisory Commission on School District Budgeting and Accounting for the purpose of advising it concerning the development of PPBS in the public schools. The enabling legislation setting up such a commission was adopted during the 1967 session of the Legislature. Potential future developments in Los Angeles may be significant, inasmuch as school officials examined other PPBS projects rather carefully prior to designing their own format.[26]

Memphis City Schools

The Memphis School District has a hybrid planning system that combines elements of functional budgeting and performance budgeting. The financial coding structure is designed around functions, and the budget presentation is not made completely in accordance with a PPBS format. The building of a curricular structure in Memphis is based upon teacher involvement in the determination of priorities. Financial support of curriculum is related to personnel, materials, equipment, supplies, and the availability of funds to project curriculum change. The district's Department of Instruction, in building an annual budget and working with the supervisory staffs, projects curriculum change as a part of a new budget. This varies from year to year and also reflects itself in specific subject matter areas that have been given top priorities.

[26] I am grateful for the information and assistance provided by Frederick G. Fox, Assistant Superintendent of Budget Division, Los Angeles City School Districts.

Responsibilities for instruction and for administration are delineated. The former has three major duties: to teach, to evaluate what is being taught, and to provide plans as to how to do a better job of teaching. The latter is expected to plan, execute, review, and evaluate operations of the system. The planning cycle encourages cooperation between instructional and financial specialists. The development and adoption of the annual budget, the execution and administration of the budget in which expenditures are controlled by the budget, long range planning, ". . . and the evaluation and appraisal of experience in preparation for the next year's development of a new budget are all a part of the total responsibility." [27]

Memphis makes some use of cost-effectiveness techniques, which involve arraying ends and means so that school planners possess a keener awareness of the options available and better bases for measuring results against both expectations and objectives. Systems analysis is used to predict the outcomes and changes resulting from individual program actions. It is also used to help define quality education more precisely and to improve the curriculum. Priorities are determined along with a specified level of funding for each program. The district points out that its program budget is *never* adequate to meet all educational needs, but is necessarily a compromise with the realities of politics and tax rates. However, in its experimentation, it has tried to provide a creative atmosphere and organization, where new ideas are actively sought and there is freedom to be wrong many times for each significant success.

The district is developing a management information system and allied techniques that will exploit the capabilities of its computer system. A student development data bank is being implemented that will relieve teachers of clerical tasks, keep them informed about the needs of individual students, and provide an important tool for educational planning and budgeting. The Superintendent believes that program budgeting has been of great value.[28]

[27] E. C. Stimbert, "Progress Report on Programmed Budgeting in Memphis," *Trends in Financing Public Education, op. cit.*, p. 195.

[28] Much of the information resulted from correspondence and descriptive materials provided by E. C. Stimbert, Memphis superintendent of schools, and John F. Merrill, supervisor of systems and computer programming. These were provided in July, 1967, as the district was in the process of revamping its system design.

New York City Public Schools

In early 1967, the City of New York Board of Education announced first phase plans for the development of a comprehensive PPBS, promising that ". . . this will be the first such installation in a large-city school district."[29] The Board's announcement followed closely the Mayor's request of a similar format for municipal agencies, which was spelled out in particular detail in the proposal for the organization of the city's Human Resources Administration. The City Schools, with an expense budget approaching $1.5 billion and serving more than one million pupils, hoped that the new budgeting system would provide better accountability and guide the Board in policy decisions.

The first step was a feasibility study by a nonprofit research organization to determine the merits of program budgeting and to develop a plan for installing the system. From the district's standpoint, one objective was to obtain a breakdown of every function of the school system into component cost factors, so that policy makers could determine whether the amount allotted to each function, or general program, was yielding its stated objective in the most efficient way. A second objective was to improve long-range planning. After a full examination of alternative ways of achieving a given objective, the district can spell out in specific detail the objectives it wants to accomplish over a five-year period and relate these to available resources. Long-range planning in New York and many other districts is irreversibly contingent upon such factors as collective negotiations, urban rioting, changes in revenue allocations, mobility patterns, political considerations such as fiscal dependence, and others that contribute to the perils of making long-range projections.

The Superintendent's 1966–1967 budget proposal called for the establishment of a budget analysis unit to determine whether each of the many programs of the system was attaining its goals efficiently. His premise was that the district had limited resources with

[29] Bernard E. Donovan, Superintendent of Schools, *Staff Bulletin,* The Public Schools of New York City, V, No. 5 (December 12, 1966), p. 1. A general description of the approach to be taken was provided in *PPB: An Introduction,* prepared by the Board of Education's PPBS Staff and Stanford Research Institute, OPPB Bulletin No. 1, June, 1967, 14 pp.

which to achieve instructional excellence. In a separate area of concern, the Deputy Superintendent for Business Affairs expressed concern over how to use the program budget as an instrument of decentralization of budget controls. This is an unresolved issue, and the challenge was posed thus:

> A billion dollar budget becomes a rather monstrous thing and there are many tendencies to centralize its administration for efficiency reasons. However, I feel that we must find ways to decentralize budget administration if democracy is to survive and I believe this is one of the important problems of our time.[30]

Shortly after Hill's statement was made, the New York City School District was the subject of a major study headed by McGeorge Bundy, president of the Ford Foundation. The following observation was included in the study report:

> Budget formulation now is incremental, fragmented and unprogrammatic. Approximately sixty headquarters, divisions or bureaus submit budget requests for the areas under their jurisdiction; the requests are based on past expenditures plus increased student enrollment or for specific programs in particular schools. The budget is thus so fragmented that school headquarters has not been able to provide information on the actual expenditures for any individual school. . . . There exists now a system with little accountability to the public—either to the Mayor or to local communities—on the way it allocates resources to meet the educational needs of the city.[31]

Some changes are underway, including PPBS, and several of the forms being used by the District are contained in Appendix D. The purpose of PPBS in the District is described by the official in charge of the program:

> It is the intent of PPBS to relate costs to objectives of the New York City School System. In that way, we can more realistically determine if we get maximum value for our dollar. Output measures, or what industry would call productive units, would be examined and financial resources reallocated, if desired results are not maintained.
>
> In addition, we are trying to bring costs down to the school level so that in the process of decentralizing New York City schools we

30 Letter from Frederick W. Hill, Deputy Superintendent of Schools, Board of Education of the City of New York, March 1, 1967.

31 Mayor's Advisory Panel on Decentralization of the New York City Schools, *Reconnection for Learning* (November 9, 1967), p. 53.

shall know, and the communities will know, what the total costs are for each school. It will be possible, therefore, to reallocate resources even on the individual school level in an attempt to facilitate optimal achievement of the children.[32]

If good, workable solutions can be developed with PPBS in the administration of so large an enterprise as the New York City School System, a pattern may be set that will have utility for other complex organizations. The jury is still out in the case of New York.

Philadelphia Public Schools

A Program Budgetary System initiated in 1966 presented the expenditures of the School District of Philadelphia in thirteen functional areas, according to the general purpose served. The only activities not classified by purpose were those covered under a special allowance for contingencies and federal programs. The district's budget document used the terms program and function interchangeably, and listed expenditures by the following functions: (1) early childhood education, (2) elementary education, (3) junior high school education, (4) senior and technical high school education, (5) special education, (6) community education and services, (7) health services, (8) transportation and attendance, (9) plant operations and maintenance, (10) administration, planning and staff development, (11) fringe benefits, (12) debt service, and (13) contingencies for impending wage increase.[33]

Sacramento City Unified School District

The Public Schools of Sacramento operate within a program-budget framework. This school district, with about 55,000 pupils and total expenditures of $37 million for 1967–1968, prepares its budget in terms of three program areas: administrative services, instructional programs and services, and supporting services. The largest of the three program areas is instructional programs and services, and it is further subdivided, largely on a grade level basis, into twelve programs: (1) instructional administration; (2) cur-

[32] Letter from Murray Hart, Assistant Superintendent for Office of PPB, Board of Education of the City of New York, January 10, 1968.

[33] *Proposed Operating Budget of the School District of Philadelphia,* Fiscal Year beginning July 1, 1967, pp. 9–11.

riculum development; (3) special services; (4) special programs; (5) elementary schools; (6) junior high schools; (7) senior high schools; (8) schools for adults; (9) continuation high schools; (10) summer school programs; (11) staff training and summer demonstration school; and (12) special projects.

The district uses a computer to prepare the school budget in the three different ways that are described below: (1) presentation format, (2) working format, and (3) state budget code format. The working budget is used by the involved departments, services, and schools. It is the most detailed of the three budgets, showing all applicable direct charges in the programs. The Director of Budget Services, Henry J. Moeller, described the budget in these terms:

> The budget for Sacramento City Unified School District is a combination, or hybrid, of a budget by programs and a program budget. By use of account codes in the computer, it is run in three formats: (1) by State required classifications, which is an object budget; (2) by programs, which is the working budget; and (3) in publication format for presentation to the Board of Education and to the public. Some programs, notably federal ones, include appropriations for indirect costs. Most programs include only appropriations for direct costs.[34]

Some of the program budget documents for the Sacramento Schools are included in the appendixes. These include budget classification codes (Appendix G) the "popularized budget" (B), and samples of computer-run program budget statements (E and F). Appendix C contains a program budget summary of expenditures.

A number of other California school districts are developing somewhat similar program structures and procedures.

Seattle Public Schools

Although the district produced only the conventional style of annual budget for 1968, it was starting to develop program budgeting. The initial emphasis was upon the interpretative phase to show the public and staff what they are receiving for dollars spent by the

[34] Letter from Henry J. Moeller, Director of Budget Services, Sacramento City Unified School District, November 13, 1967. For more details, see the *1967–68 Adopted Budget and Financial Information* (Sacramento, Calif.: Sacramento City Unified School District, October 16, 1967), 147 pp.

district. It was hoped that program budgeting would encourage school personnel to consider all related costs when proposing a change or experimental project. The Budget Director described the objectives as follows:

> Program budget implementation in Seattle will be a gradual process. Ultimately the approach will enable the administration and school board to recognize resource requirements for different programs on a long-range basis as well as on a short-term basis. The program budget information should enable the administration to assign priorities more comfortably to proposed or existing programs within the context of current policies and long-range educational goals.[35]

Westchester County (N.Y.): an intermediate school district

Table 7 shows how one school district reports its expenditures in two ways: first in a conventional, line-item format, and second in a program budget format. The total expenditures for the two budgets are equal, but the categories for classification differ. In this illustration, the institution is not a local school district, but an intermediate school district (Board of Cooperative Educational Services, First Supervisory District) overlaying thirteen component local school districts. It provides supplementary educational services to these local districts beyond the basic program of instruction they furnish. The controlling board is separate from the local boards. Twelve programs are reported in the program budget.

Outlook for the Future

Some of the most prominent specialists in educational finance have expressed interest in, and support for, the concept of program budgeting as applied to local schools. These include Professors Benson of California, Burkhead of Syracuse, James of Stanford, and Thomas of Chicago. Thomas examined the administrative advantages,[36] and James provided a forecast that large city school

[35] Letter from Ken Sato, Budget Director, Seattle Public Schools, December 7, 1967.

[36] J. Alan Thomas, "Educational Decision-Making and the School Budget," *Administrator's Notebook,* XII, No. 4 (December, 1963), 1–4.

TABLE 7

COMPARATIVE BREAKDOWN FOR AN EDUCATIONAL INSTITUTION OF BUDGET EXPENDITURES BY LINE-ITEM FUNCTIONS AND BY PROGRAMS [a]

CONVENTIONAL BUDGET			PROGRAM BUDGET		
Functions	Appropriations	Relative share	Programs	Appropriations	Relative share
1. Administration	$ 301,379	8.6%	1. Administration	$ 301,379	8.6%
2. Teaching	2,000,545	57.2	2. Shared teacher services	235,488	6.7
3. Transportation	112,253	3.2	3. Special education	1,651,486	47.7
4. Operation and Maintenance	585,391	16.8	4. Psychiatric services	44,450	1.4
5. Undistributed	490,631	14.1	5. Testing and counseling	119,515	3.5
6. Transfer to Other Funds	1,500	0.1	6. Evening career counseling	5,130	0.2
			7. College conference	6,501	0.2
			8. Technical vocational education	574,195	15.9
			9. Educational services and research	119,419	3.3
			10. Data processing	258,688	7.4
			11. Cerebral palsy, outside contract	55,000	1.6
			12. Transportation	120,448	3.5
Total	$3,491,699	100.0%	Total	$3,491,699	100.0%

[a] Calculated from: Board of Cooperative Educational Services, First Supervisory District, Budget Estimates for Shared Services—1967-68 (Yorktown Heights, N.Y.: Westchester County, First District, March, 1967). The program format was designed by Dr. Gray N. Taylor, Director of Administrative Services for this BOCES district.

districts, in particular, would adopt program budget procedures during the decade of the 1970's.[37] Burkhead criticized the lack of reforms in budgetary analysis and classification by school administrators and described a needed program budget as a ". . . system for the evaluation of school output and school costs over time."[38] Benson helped to stimulate interest in this conceptual approach by preparing several reports on fiscal policy for the State Senate of California. He recommended that ". . . the State Department of Education investigate the feasibility of establishing a uniform system of school accounts under which the concept of program budgeting can be applied."[39] His committee's justification was concisely stated, "Presently, school districts are enjoined by the State to employ a combination function-object scheme of classification which in our view is not a very useful tool in determining which alternative allocations of school resources have the strongest effects in raising pupil achievement."[40]

As of 1968, it was probably accurate to state that there was insufficient evidence to predict the extent to which program budgeting and systems analysis would be installed successfully in school systems. Each of the projects described above was somewhat exploratory and is not yet a finished product. However, the lag in implementation is not confined to education. Chase Manhattan Bank noted the following at the beginning of 1968:

> In no sector of government is PPBS fully implemented. Converting line budgets into a multiyear framework focused on goals can run into hurdles. Few competent cost-benefit analyses have been completed, and even fewer are integrated into the program budgeting process.
>
> The fact that problems are cropping up should not be a surprise. Shortages of manpower and funds put limits on progress. Changing from one system to another inevitably causes bottlenecks. And

[37] H. Thomas James, *et al., Determinants of Educational Expenditures in Large Cities of the United States,* United States Office of Education Cooperative Research Project No. 2389 (Stanford, Calif.: School of Education, Stanford University, 1966), p. 89.

[38] Jesse Burkhead, "The Theory and Application of Program Budgeting to Education," *Trends in Financing Public Education,* p. 188.

[39] Charles S. Benson, *et al., State and Local Fiscal Relationships in Public Education in California* (Sacramento, Calif.: Report of the Senate Fact Finding Committee on Revenue and Taxation, Senate of California, March, 1965), p. 15.

[40] *Ibid.,* p. 63.

there is a more fundamental problem: Moving from theory to fact opens up a host of pragmatic questions.[41]

Let us hope that within the decade of the 1970's educational planning will shift more rapidly from blind, doctrinal faith toward conceptual strategies emerging from administrative theory and management science. PPBS provides a framework for coping with disconcerting changes and awesome responsibilities that will face the schools with increasing intensity each year. If there is a systems apocalypse in education, advance guard school districts may find refreshingly different *life styles* among their students, teachers, and administrators. Until then, existing planning formats should not be viewed as permanent and irrevocable. Weaknesses in present local school budgeting practices are examined in the next chapter.

41 "The Planning-Programming-Budgeting System," *Business in Brief* (New York: Chase Manhattan Bank, December, 1967), pp. 3–4.

Suggestion for Discussion

Examine in some detail one organization that uses PPBS procedures and critically review its program structure, manuals, budget documents, analytical methods, and other available materials.

Selected References

Fitzsimmons, Warren B., *A Model for a Public School Program Budget.* Unpublished doctoral dissertation. Greeley, Colo.: Colorado State College, 1966.

Hartley, Harry J., "Economic Rationality in Urban School Planning: The Program Budget," *Urban Education,* III, No. 1 (1967), 39–51.

Hatry, Harry P., and John F. Cotton, *Program Planning for State-County-City.* Washington, D.C.: State-Local Finances Project of The George Washington University, January, 1967.

Nickerson, Eugene H., *Management Information System.* Nassau County, N.Y.: Office of the County Executive, March, 1968.

Sherwood, Robert P., *Cost Implications of Specific State Legislative Requirements: An Application of Program Budgeting to Selected California Unified School Districts.* Unpublished doctoral dissertation. Berkeley, Calif.: University of California, 1965.

Budget formulation (in New York City Public Schools) is incremental, fragmented, and unprogrammatic. . . . There exists now a system with little accountability to the public.

McGeorge Bundy

Chapter Six

THE NEED FOR BUDGETARY REFORM IN LOCAL SCHOOLS

by Sol Levin *

The local school budget, as presently used, has developed as a consequence of the general governmental reform movement over the past half-century. Traditionally, therefore, it has been viewed as a device for providing strong fiscal accountability and managerial-control accountability to the public for their funds and control between and within the governmental agencies responsible for the expenditure of the appropriations.

More recently an apparent need for budgetary reform has been evolving, but with a new emphasis. In competing for public funds, educators are now being challenged to justify their budgetary requests in terms of student achievement, rather than with the costs of objects and services. The school budget, as currently composed and presented, does not provide satisfactory answers to the questions being asked. However, educators must be able to provide such answers.

Early Development of the School Budget

Historically, the formalization and standardization of the school budget lagged behind that of either private or other governmental

* Dr. Levin is the Assistant Superintendent for Business Affairs, Ramapo Central School District No. 2, Spring Valley, New York.

agencies. It was not until after World War I that a trend in the development of a school budgeting system was noted. By the 1930's, considerable progress had been made in growth of acceptance as well as in reform of practices.[1] Today it is exceptional for even the smallest school system not to be using a formally adopted budget consisting of estimated expenses supported by a plan for financing its total operation. Characteristic of the budgetary structure is a system of classified subdivisions that is now almost universally employed in this country.

The budgetary process of governmental agencies, including school districts, has been evolving through the following relative stages of development: (1) the object budget; (2) the function-object budget (the present type used by most public school systems); and (3) the planning-programming-budgeting system (or program budget).

The *object-oriented budget* is the simplest form, consisting of a listing of objects of expense, such as salaries, supplies, equipment, contracted services, and so forth, without regard to their function. Many school districts that operated under the most rudimentary management throughout the first quarter of this century found an object-oriented budget to be an adequate fiscal device. The primary emphasis was upon fiscal accountability.

The *function-object budget,* which appeared prior to 1920, has developed with some modification into the type of budget structure utilized almost universally today by the local public schools. This type of budget identifies costs under several broadly defined function and object categories and then delineates these by their component subdivisions, both function and object, as subexpenses. It tends to be used more as a tool for management, in contrast to the strict control emphasis of the earlier object budgets.

The broad categories of the function-object budget are identified by the following titles, which date back to as early as 1912:[2] (1) administration, (2) instruction, (3) plant operation, (4) plant maintenance, (5) auxiliary agencies, (6) fixed charges, (7) capital outlay and (8) debt service. Items 1 through 5 are function activities,

[1] C. A. DeYoung, *Budgetary Practices in Public School Administration* (Evanston, Ill.: Northwestern University Studies, 1932), p. 152.

[2] John W. Twente, *Budgetary Procedure for Local School Systems* (Montpelier, Vt.: Capital Press, 1922).

whereas 6, 7 and 8 are objects of expense that cut across all functions.

The expenditures under this budget format are tabulated in summary form in Table 8 to provide a two-dimensional configuration. It has the obvious operational advantage of totaling objects of expense, as well as those of the major categories.

An Analysis of Traditional Budgetary Classifications

Administration

The function "administration" is a misnomer because it encompasses the systemwide functions of the superintendent's office as well as those of the board of education, the latter being legislative, not administrative. In some school systems, this category is referred to as "general control" and is subdivided into the board of education and the superintendent's office. Furthermore, this category, by being separate from the instruction classification, infers that the superintendent or members of his immediate staff do not administer the instructional program. Ironically, it is generally assumed in the profession that instructional leadership is a major role of superintendency. In larger school systems, one or more assistant superintendents who are specifically designated as being responsible for the instructional program are included under "administration," not "instruction."

The isolation of "administration" as a single classification resulted from an attempt to facilitate a scrutiny of the salaries and other related overhead costs of the top brass. Administrators have traditionally been viewed by the public, and frequently by the staff, with suspicion and distrust, and at best, as a necessary evil. However, this classification, as currently interpreted, does not represent the total administrative cost. Actually, the major administration expenses, those of the building principals and their staffs, are included under "instruction." The administrative expenses of other programs, such as transportation, plant and school lunch, are usually included under their respective functional headings. The apparent inconsistency has arisen from a dilemma in attempting to identify administration costs and, at the same time, to retain an identification of the costs for instruction and the other functional activities in the budget. The focus on systemwide, or central administration, as a budgetary item has resulted in a variety of sometimes artificial organizational structuring employed in the interest of dispersing and thus minimizing the costs appearing under this vulnerable category.

Instruction

The major functional budgetary classification, "instruction" usually accounts for 50 to 60 per cent of the dollar amount of the budget, of which from 80 to 90 per cent is represented by teachers' salaries.[3] The subdivisions under this category follow several patterns, one of the most common being:

1. Principals, directors, supervisors and clerical staff.
2. Teaching staff, regular program, by grades:
   a. kindergarten through sixth.
   b. seventh through ninth.
   c. tenth through twelfth.
3. Specialized services (guidance, psychological, etc.).
4. Special instructional programs (handicapped students, adult education, etc.).

Under this organization, the salaries, supplies, equipment, and other expenses may be given for each heading; or, the salaries may be itemized for each, while the supplies, equipment and other expenses may each be a composite for instruction as a whole.

Other minor variations exist between states and individual systems as follows: (a) textbooks may be extracted as a separate item; (b) school nurses, dental hygienists, and librarians may be under "instruction" or under "auxiliary agencies"; and (c) library books may be part of instructional supplies or capitalized under "capital outlay."

In general, this category loosely outlines the parameter of instructional costs. However, there are expenses included under the other major categories discussed elsewhere, which logically should be charged to instruction. These could add another 15 to 20 per cent to the total amount of this classification.

[3] Paul R. Mort, *et al., Public School Finance* (New York: McGraw-Hill Book Company, 1960), p. 408.

TABLE 8

TRADITIONAL SCHOOL BUDGET IN SUMMARY FORM SHOWING MAJOR CATEGORIES OF FUNCTIONS AND OBJECTS OF EXPENSE

	OBJECTS OF EXPENSE				
MAJOR CATEGORY	SALARIES	EQUIPMENT	SUPPLIES	OTHER	TOTALS
ADMINISTRATION					
Board of Education	18,028	375	4,550	20,890	43,843
Superintendent's Office	59,878	550	2,000	1,500	63,929
Business Administration	184,806	6,492	6,265	22,791	220,354
Curriculum and Instruction	85,733	342	2,400	30,900	119,375
Sub Total					447,501
INSTRUCTION					
Supervision, District	180,512	29,122	9,106	22,100	240,849
School Principals	681,197	14,541	6,215	27,860	729,813
Teaching, Regular Program	7,099,019	59,277	524,939	140,064	7,823,299
Special Programs	73,187	——	2,800	795	76,782
Adult Education	18,030	——	400	2,300	20,730
Sub Total					8,891,473
PLANT OPERATION					
Custodial Services	677,518	15,382	124,626	23,800	841,326
Fuel	——	——	121,000	——	121,000
Utilities	——	——	——	176,200	176,200
Other	——	——	——	58,347	58,347
Sub Total					1,196,873
PLANT MAINTENANCE					
Buildings	106,091	18,041	35,220	18,362	177,714
Mechanical Equipment	70,500	12,752	14,380	11,800	109,432
Grounds	22,000	8,575	21,250	2,700	54,525
Sub Total					341,671

TABLE 8—continued

TRADITIONAL SCHOOL BUDGET IN SUMMARY FORM
SHOWING MAJOR CATEGORIES OF FUNCTIONS AND OBJECTS OF EXPENSE

	OBJECTS OF EXPENSE				
MAJOR CATEGORY	SALARIES	EQUIPMENT	SUPPLIES	OTHER	TOTALS
AUXILIARY AGENCIES					
Attendance	8,700	——	325	1,650	10,675
Health Services	186,262	——	5,900	31,174	223,336
Library Service	57,362	1,700	13,682	8,600	81,344
Pupil Transportation	52,370	23,860	3,263	693,903	773,396
Lunch Program	284,000	9,000	45,000	15,000	353,000
Community Services	4,800	——	——	11,000	15,800
Sub Total					1,457,551
FIXED CHARGES					
Employee Retirement	——	——	——	1,218,285	1,218,285
Social Security	——	——	——	338,911	338,911
Other Employee Benefits	——	——	——	84,711	84,711
Insurance	——	——	——	85,200	85,200
Sub Total					1,727,107
CAPITAL OUTLAY					
Building Improvements	——	46,200	——	——	46,200
Grounds Improvements	——	16,500	——	——	16,500
Furniture and Equipment	——	68,285	——	——	68,285
Sub Total					130,985
DEBT SERVICE					
Principal Retirement	——	——	——	810,000	810,000
Interest Charges	——	——	——	1,036,513	1,036,513
Sub Total					1,846,513
				TOTAL BUDGET	$16,039,674

Despite the scope of the instructional category, which dwarfs all of the others, its total dimension cannot be too meaningful, other than for serving as an indicator of the relative amount to be spent for teaching as compared with that for the peripheral but essential services otherwise categorized. The breadth of this function makes its subclassifications of particular significance. Some of these components are actually more costly than certain of the major budgetary categories. However, these subclassifications are heavily object-structured, so that costs for subfunctions or programs of instruction become obscured. Instead there appear: (a) salary listings for principals, teachers and clerks; and (b) the costs of supplies, textbooks, and conferences.

Plant operation

The categories "operation of plant" and "maintenance of plant" are usually developed as separate activities or functions for budget purposes. The former encompasses mainly the expenses for cleaning the buildings and grounds, the operation of the heating plant and related mechanical equipment, and fuel and utilities. "Maintenance of plant" includes primarily the expenses for repairing the buildings and grounds. The reason for the separation of these categories is not clear. Actually, the function of the building custodian varies. In most instances, he performs some maintenance work, depending on personal skills, while cleaning and operating the plant. Surely, cleaning of the building and the correct operation of the mechanical equipment are preventative maintenance functions.

A less serious concern, but of interest, is the question of the traditional placement of building insurance and rental of property under the category of "Fixed Charges," rather than with the more appropriate plant operations costs.

Plant maintenance

In addition to the expenses for repairing the building structure and the site, as described above, this category also includes the costs for repairing and replacing all moveable furnishings and equipment, regardless of the function of the items. It is not difficult to argue against the logic of charging the costs for the replacement or repair, for example, of instructional equipment, cafeteria kitchen equipment, and administrative vehicles other than to their respective functions.

Auxiliary agencies

"Auxiliary agencies" is a residual, catch-all category that developed over the years as school districts assumed areas of responsibility justified as school-related but not accepted as part of the regular program. Included here have been such services as libraries, transportation, school lunch programs, attendance, health services (doctors, nurses and dental hygienists), community-sponsored programs, interscholastic sports, recreation, out-of-school youth programs. The term "agencies" originated from the practice in many districts of contracting for these services from other public and private agencies. In certain systems the term "coordinate activities" was associated with several of these functions. In more recent years, the intrinsic educational value of such programs as library, interscholastic sports, and health service, has been recognized, and they have been incorporated under the "instruction" category.

Fixed charges

The item "fixed charges" mainly consists of employee benefits such as retirement, Social Security, hospitalization, and insurance for the school district. This accounting expediency epitomizes the entire budgetary process of which it is a part. The components of this category cut across all the major activities of the school district and are true expenditures chargeable to all of these activities. By isolating the benefit costs from the salaries of the administrators, teachers, maintenance men, and other employees, the results achieved are as follows:

1. Because all of the significant expenditures are not included under each of the listed major functional categories, the total costs of the functions are obscured.
2. Looking under either function or object, the uninitiated cannot determine true personnel costs by examining the salary listings in the budget.
3. It expedites financial accounting and reporting to interested state and national agencies.

Capital outlay

The category "capital outlay" similarly cuts across the activities of the school, representing costs for the purchase of a projector, a truck, the renovation of a maintenance building, or the addition to a library. The extraction of these items from the other costs of the activities is justified on the accounting theory which provides that the costs for additional equipment and building improvements should not be a charge against a current fiscal budget. This theory is supported in many states and municipalities by statutory requirements. In the process of practical budget construction, this category, along with the contradistinctive "plant maintenance" category, has caused frustration in determining which items may be classified additional or replacement, renovation or repair. This is further complicated by the type of financing (short and long-term obligation) possible with capitalization. The inherent indefinitiveness of the "capital outlay" components provides budget makers with ample opportunity for fiscal maneuvering between this and the "plant maintenance" categories. Again, as with "fixed charges," accounting and fiscal considerations have been major influencing factors in the budgetary structure.

Debt service

The annual payment for long-term financing for major new school construction and renovation is in essence an object of expenditure. Its components are the annual financing (interest) cost in addition to the amortized (principal) cost. The separation of these costs from the various functions for which they provide facilities, while generally a statutory or regulatory requirement, causes everyone to lose sight of any relative cost-space relationships that exist between the various school functions. Space and facilities utilization do not become cost considerations to school budget makers.

Where property accounting is employed, and this is rare in school districts,[4] its main concern is the establishment of insurable value. It is not concerned with space utilization for programs as a factor in pro-rata cost accounting.

[4] Stephen J. Knezovich and John G. Fowlkes, *Business Management of Local School Systems* (New York: Harper & Row, Publishers, 1960), p. 244.

Sources of funds

The sources-of-funds items, or the categories of receipts, in the object-budget as well as in the function-object budget are similar. The exception is that in the latter the refinements that evolved consisted of a more definitive categorizing of the sources of funds.

Summary of shortcomings of the traditional budget structure

In summation of this structural analysis of the traditional school budget document currently in general use, the following conclusions may be drawn:

1. The budget has been structured primarily as a device to facilitate fiscal accounting, and secondarily to identify some broad functional programs.
2. The organizational structure of the budget, with its traditional and legalized description and interpretation of categories has established the stereotyped models currently employed as the basis for all stages of the budgetary process in local schools.
3. There are inconsistencies in that the categories do not include all of the costs that would be assumed from their descriptive titles. Segments of inherent components of the function have been extracted and included under other categories, generally to meet a special fiscal or other expediency.
4. Although most of the major categories are described as broad programs, they are subdivided with primary concern for objects of expenditures, salaries, materials, and other, rather than for meaningful subprograms.
5. The emphasis on objects rather than on programs in the budgetary process encourages an automatic incremental approach to existing objects, rather than a consideration of the cost-output relationship of programs that are either in effect or proposed.

Some reforms have been made in the budget structure in recent years; most significant has been the influence of the cooperative projects on school accounting, spearheaded by the United States Office of Education.[5] Although the purpose of the work, completed

[5] Paul L. Reason and A. L. White, *Financial Accounting for Local and State School Systems,* United States Department of Health, Education, and Welfare (Washington, D.C.: Government Printing Office, 1957), p. 235; and Allan R. Lichtenberger, *et al., Principles of Public School Accounting,* United States Department of Health, Education, and Welfare, Office of Education (Washington, D.C.: Government Printing Office, 1967), p. 257.

in 1957 (and a subsequent handbook to be published soon), was to standardize and improve the financial accounting of schools, it has done as follows: (1) suggested modifications in the organization of certain categories of expenditures and receipts; (2) provided long-needed definitions for terminology; (3) encouraged accounting for certain instructional program areas, and (4) specified methods of analyzing and prorating costs among functions and objects. Many school systems have adopted several or all of the accounting concepts recommended in this manual, which have been reflected in turn, in their budgetary organization. It is interesting that, as in the past, budgetary organizational changes are being brought about primarily as a result of a need to improve and standardize accounting procedures. The result has been an improvement built onto an *existing* structure of concepts, whereas the basic structure, still remaining object, input-oriented, with many of the same inconsistencies, has needed a complete remodeling that cannot be achieved from a primary perspective of accounting practice.

The Traditional Budget Document

The terms "budget" and "budgetary process" are often used loosely and interchangeably. A clear distinction between them must be made in the interest of understanding the topic. The school budget is a legal document, adopted by a legislative authority and its structural format is generally prescribed by law or regulation in most states.[6] It itemizes with varying degree of detail the anticipated expenditures and receipts for a fiscal year; this, in essence, is a financial plan. It imposes a ceiling on expenditures, varying by locality in the flexibility allowed to the school authorities for the transfer of appropriation between the listed categories. It becomes the basis of audit and accountability for the stewardship of public monies, and it is backed by penalities under the law. It is, therefore, understandable why the school business administrator and his accounting staff may tend to view the budget in the same manner as the fundamentalist views his Bible. In this context, the budget is a fiscally controlling device supported by the law.

An important condition, which is not often understood, is that

[6] Mort, *op. cit.,* p. 359.

since a budget is an estimate or plan for a given fiscal period, *at the termination of the defined period, the budget technically no longer exists,* other than as an historical document. At the termination of the period, a composite financial record of the itemized *actual expenditures and receipts* replaces the budget. With this understanding, two things should become evident: (1) the budget or budget document serves mainly financial management purposes, and (2) the *actual financial records, not the budget,* become the source of statistical data for the school system for analysis and audit.

Therefore, it may be reasonably concluded that, once formalized and adopted, the only value of the budget to those who have planned and formulated it is in observing the accuracy of their projected costs and receipts. The *actual* (not budgetary) *costs* become the basis for appraisal of planned goals, or output, against expenditures. The budget is meaningful to the planners only to the extent that there is incorporated within it financial provision for the programs of interest to them; *and this takes place before the budget is adopted in the budgetary process.*

The Traditional Budgetary Process: A Critique

The budgetary process, defined in its broad sense by most authorities, is a continuous affair that includes planning, development of the document, presentation to the approving authority, formal adoption, implementation, fiscal administration, and appraisal.[7] But, because the budget document is confined to a fiscal year, the budgetary process under way during any fiscal year cannot apply to a single budget. Three budgets must be involved. First, the preliminary stages of planning and development relate to the budget of the succeeding year; second, the fiscal administration is devoted to the current budget; and third, appraisal of the previous year's budgetary experiences, both program and fiscal, serve as the basis for current planning.

The significant role of the format of the budget document in the budgetary process is frequently overlooked. By indicating how the data must be categorized, the budget structure gives direction to

[7] Henry H. Linn, *School Business Administration* (New York: The Ronald Press Company, 1956), p. 143.

all the participants in the process. The budget request forms for personnel, materials, and services that are distributed to all departments follow the pattern of the budget format. In all stages of the budgetary process, most of the discussion and writing are confined to reference to these categories, some of which are not clearly interpretive. There is no question that the traditional format of budgetary classifications has been an important factor in restricting the development of educational budget concepts and procedures to a more meaningful level.

The process of developing the annual school budget today has as its primary objective the generating of the input data that will need to be distilled into a fiscally and politically realistic document. Necessary to achieve this goal are numerous activities, each of which at certain stages of the process is operating independently of the others. This process occurs generally during the seven to eight months' interval prior to the date of the budget's adoption, and usually includes the following:

1. negotiation with the teachers and other staff members for salary adjustments and other personnel considerations;
2. determination of changes in numbers of staff based on projected student population and facilities;
3. compilation of departmental requests for additional and replacement materials, equipment, and services for existing programs;
4. crystallization of the highest priority program changes, and the estimating of staffing and material costs related to them;
5. computation of the costs for fixed charges (Social Security, retirement, other employee benefits, insurance, etc.) and debt service (outstanding indebtedness); and
6. computation and projection of the potential revenue limits from the various sources that will ultimately confine the budget fiscally; the state, the Federal Government, the municipality (dependent districts) and the public, where budgets and tax rates require a vote of the residents.

In the final analysis, after the results of the activities above are compiled and evaluated, decisions that determine what is to be included in the budget are based inevitably in the following sequence of priority. These range from the most to the least politically defensible items, as budget makers weigh the strategy for obtaining budgetary approval:

1. items mandated by law or regulation (fixed charges, debt service, pupil transportation: 15 to 30 per cent of the budget);
2. negotiated salaries of existing staff (50 to 60 per cent of the budget);
3. replacement of used materials for existing program;
4. addition of staff and materials for numerical increases in pupil population, but based on existing programs; and
5. changes in staffing and materials to implement significant program changes.

There is no question on the mandated items. Salaries are usually scheduled with automatic increments that are commitments of prior years' actions; further adjustments beyond this must follow the trends to compete for personnel. Frequently, as is the case with recent militant stands by teachers in negotiation proceedings, there is such an inordinate amount of time and energy devoted to salary determination that this completely dominates the budgetary process. Between mandated items and salaries, approximately 75 per cent of the monetary value of the budget has been accounted for, and very often these result in 90 per cent of the increase of the total budget over the previous one.

It is a significant fact that, except in isolated instances, it is current practice for proposals for salary change for both the teacher-professional and the nonteaching supportive personnel to be considered independently of the output and cost effects of existing programs or of proposed new ones. This occurs despite the fact that salaries are the major cost factor of the programs. It is understandable how this occurs with the present budget format, where salary and employee benefits are not closely identified with specific programs. Rather, salaries are identified with general position titles (teachers, clerks, and so forth) as objects of expense under the broad headings such as instruction or administration. Employee benefits become a conglomerate, nondefensible entity divorced from either position titles or programs.

The process of determination of material needs for the budget follows a similar separate track, or incremental pattern. These are compiled from school building requests, usually on a per pupil or per staff-member allowance basis. The prior use-experience in the various activities is the basis of the appropriation. The justification for modification relates to changes in numbers of students, spaces, curriculum, or across-the-board adjustments for rising costs. Regardless of the purpose, the mere fact that there is a slot in the budget designated for instructional and custodial supplies, a separate slot for new replacement equipment, not only establishes the channels for the mechanics, but also the thinking behind the budget process. In essence, the budgeted material amounts are usually the arithmetic product of the predetermined unit of allowance times the number of students, not the result of an actual listing of items needed for specific programs.

In some school districts, the costs for materials are accounted for by departments, grades, or buildings. This serves primarily as a useful experience guide in appropriating allowances from year to year and to control expenditures by these departments. It would be rare for these to be used for program evaluation purposes. But this procedure in itself is still not too meaningful, being divorced from the other more substantial costs of these programs, each being in its own track.

Inadequate Budget Planning

The earliest authorities on school finance, as well as the present ones, have purported to emphasize educational planning as the foundation of the school budget.[8] Texts have traditionally defined the school budget as a financial plan for the implementation of an educational plan. The financial plan of dollars committed for expenditures and the revenues required to finance them are relatively clearly stated. On the other hand, the educational plan has not been definitive or set forth in terms of specific programs, objectives, or true costs. This may be attributed in part to the fiscally oriented budget, which has encouraged the practice of explaining the educational plan completely apart from the financial plan or attempting to fit the former into the accommodating financial plan. The problem basically has been twofold. First, the component programs of the educational plan have never been defined so as to have general acceptance by all educators. In contrast, there has been nearly universal agreement on the definition and labeling of the fiscal categories now in use. Second, complete, true costs of the programs that

[8] C. A. DeYoung, *Budgeting in Public Schools,* revised ed. (Chicago: John S. Swift Company, Inc., 1950), pp. 509–544.

are itemized are rarely developed, or are not presented as such in the budget. This does not infer that those responsible for developing school budgets are not concerned with programs and costs; it exemplifies their deep involvement with object costs and total budget costs of the current school budgetary process, from planning through implementation and evaluation.

In the interest of public understanding and acceptance, it has become the usual practice for school boards to include in the budget their education plan, commonly referred to as "educational specifications." This consists of generalized statements of educational philosophy, policy, and program contents in explanation and justification of the budgetary costs.[9] The organization of the material and extent of detail vary with the sophistication of the school administration and the approving bodies. There are often included such items as a brief reference to the various courses of study offered in the school system; the achievement of local students; a description of existing and needed facilities; a projection of pupil enrollment; the aspirations for the year ahead for which the budget is submitted.

Adaptability lag

The planning process associated with the traditional budget follows the consistent pattern in setting a separate course for program planning and financial planning. Although universally acknowledged in the profession as a desirable, if not essential, practice, true long-range comprehensive planning, either financial or instructional, is a rarity in school administration. Burkhead[10] considers this the weakest point in the administration of schools today. The little planning that is done is short-range, incremental, and fragmentary, and is generally limited to a small segment of the budget being prepared, or of the one for the succeeding year. It is a logical assumption that this has been a factor in the inordinate *adaptability lag,* noted by Mort,[11] between innovation, experimentation and adoption of educational program changes, that has been character-

[9] Charles Bracken and A. S. Hurlburt, "A Checklist of Public School Budget Message Content," *American School Board Journal,* CLXVI (March, 1963), 15.

[10] Jesse Burkhead, *Public School Finance* (Syracuse, N.Y.: Syracuse University Press, 1964), p. 47.

[11] Mort, *op. cit.,* p. 37.

istic of the American public schools. Actually very few school districts are equipped or willing to support an on-going comprehensive planning program. Planning and research have not been generally accepted, as in industry, as essential investments for the local educational enterprise.

It is fair to assume, however, that all school districts are engaged to some degree in planning. For example, the building maintenance department is developing a five-year painting program; the modern language department is planning to implement a foreign language program in the elementary schools within two years; the need for establishing a class for handicapped children is under study; a lay committee is studying proposed salary schedules.

Financial expertise is lacking

Frequently, the planners completely ignore costs as a factor in the program they are developing. Or if costs are included, they are incomplete, and specifically for the first year of implementation, not projected for long-range financial implications. It is not unusual for a decision to have been made, with the role of the planners being one of implementation and justification of the program. Coordination and expertise are generally lacking in the planning procedures described above. It is a most unusual school district that has qualified persons on its staff who are continuously concerned with overall long-range budgetary planning.

Persons involved in planning, especially those volunteering their own time, expect to have their work implemented, when it is completed. The concept of feasibility planning, where alternative programs are studied with the possibility that all may be rejected, is a relatively new one to educational planners.

Long-range budget planning, has generally been interpreted to relate to the projection of annual budgets,[12] working with the traditional categories of expenditures and revenues. A common device is to extend the "curve" of prior expenditure experience, adjusted by anticipated changes in pupil growth and general cost trends. Revenue projection depends on "second-guessing," the state's future aid

[12] Leon Ovsiew and William B. Castetter, *Budgeting for Better Schools* (Englewood Cliffs, N.J.: Prentice-Hall, Inc., 1960).

program, and the pliability of the local real estate assessments to yield tax income.

This budget projection activity, commonly referred to as "financial planning," may generate for the board of education simulated budgets for as much as five years ahead. However, since fiscal planning is usually performed independently of the educational policy and program planning, the validity of the financial projection may be tenuous. The school financial planner works on the assumption of a continuation of existing programs, whereas the curriculum planners assume that there will be a change in program, but are not certain of costs or time of redesign.

The budgetary projection process described above does not in itself constitute planning. However, if its economics and statistics are sound, the results could serve as a useful tool to knowledgeable program planners by providing the inventory of overall costs for the current program enlarged quantitatively in a five-year projection. The resulting model could then be modified to accommodate projected alternative program changes or placed in juxtaposition with a completely new model if major program changes are contemplated. This process, of course, would be a technique in program budgeting, and is incompatible with traditional budgeting.

Innovation is stifled

Under traditional budgetary concepts of planning, the projection of budgets may produce the negative consequence of restricting innovative planning. Also, because of the projection of rising costs and taxes that may occur, taxpayer apprehensions and disapproval may result. In a recent paper, Fowlkes stated:

> The budget process seems intimately intertwined with educational innovation. The foundations of most school budgets seem to be inherently antagonistic to the support of innovation.[13]

The board and administration typically view the projection as something over which they can exercise little control because their

[13] J. G. Fowlkes, "Some Implications of Educational Innovation," *Long Range Planning in School Finance,* Sixth National Conference on School Finance (Washington, D.C.: National Education Association Committee on Educational Finance, 1963), p. 76.

perspective is object-oriented, in terms of salaries and materials with their inevitable increments. On the other hand, with the program budgeting concept, the inviolability of existing programs is more likely to be challenged. Furthermore, an on-going evaluation of output and costs of existing programs would be required, and alternative solutions along with comparative costs and anticipated outputs would be expected with new proposals. With this approach, budgetary planning can become one of positive action to achieve long-range goals.

Educational outcomes are not budget related

In traditional budgetary planning, the factor of output measurement of instructional programs has not been a serious consideration. It is logical to assume that without an appropriate concern for output in relation to objectives, the faddish trend in curriculum change that Corbally [14] labels "The-Thing-To-Do," or "Bandwagon" approach, may continue and proliferate without regard to costs or even reasonably substantiated education output. Faddism is nearly as dangerous as inertia, but imaginative innovations are needed. Program budgeting does not provide a ready solution to the problem of curriculum change. It does, however, offer a more defensible approach to the planning for change by focusing on output, costs and alternative solutions to a much greater extent than has heretofore been brought to bear by traditional school budgetary planning. Pertinent is the pioneer research of Mort, Woolatt, Cornell, Vincent, Newell and Furno.[15] All confirmed positive correlations between expenditure levels and quality of educational output on the basis of measurement criteria and instruments that they developed. More recently Thomas [16] found a positive relationship between the level of resource input and mean test scores in achievement tests. Possibly even more significant was his finding that the manner in which the money was spent was a more important factor than the level

[14] John E. Corbally, *School Finance* (Boston: Allyn and Bacon, 1962), p. 171.

[15] Paul R. Mort, *et al., The Growing Edge* (New York: Metropolitan School Study Council, 1946); and Lorne H. Woolatt, *The Cost-Quality Relationship on the Growing Edge* (New York: Bureau of Publications, Teachers College, Columbia University, 1949).

[16] J. Alan Thomas, "Efficiency in Education: An Empirical Study," *Administrators Notebook,* XI, No. 2 (October, 1962).

of expenditures. By placing new emphasis on the importance of output determination, program budgeting will undoubtedly encourage further research in this field of educational measurement.

The Program Budget Format

Program budgeting as conceived, is a truly continuing process, a snapshot of which at any given point should ideally portray the input and output for each program as it has existed, and is projected ahead for approximately a five-year span.[17] The division into fiscal years then becomes an arbitrarily imposed structure. It is unrealistic to assume that this long-ingrained universal concept of annual financing and accounting will be eradicated in the foreseeable future. This suggests that the annual program budget might have incorporated within its format the costs and revenues for the immediately projected year, as well as those for the two preceding and two succeeding years. Many school districts today follow the practice of including in the publicly distributed budget material one or two prior years' cost data; projections of costs for any long-range planning are rarely included. The requirement for publishing projected costs and revenues for more than the one year would undoubtedly initially create some consternation among school board members and administrators. However, the right of the public and approving bodies to have this information cannot be questioned. With program budgeting, there is the inherent requirement for the school district to generate this information on a more accurate and comprehensive basis heretofore not known to them. Furthermore, this could have the positive aspect of proving to the skeptics that the board of education is planning ahead and knows at least the direction of its programs and finances.

The official program budget document, whether publicly or otherwise adopted, would in essence consist of a listing of programs and subprograms, each with its costs and justification data to support input and output, and with historical and projected programs and costs as previously discussed. Objects of expense for personnel and material would not be "line items" in this budget, but may be in-

[17] David Novick, editor, *Program Budgeting* (Cambridge, Massachusetts: Harvard University Press, 1965), p. 21.

cluded with supporting data, where desired. This could pose an interesting problem in those districts where an outside approving authority has the privilege of passing on specific line items in the budget.[18] Whereas the "cutting" of an object line item, such as salaries, can be viewed in general terms, the decision on whether to cut one specific instructional program line or another would place a novel burden on the approving authority.

The traditional budget as presented to the public and approving agencies is somewhat of an enigma. The category headings are nondescript, fragmentary, and may appear misleading, with the result that it is difficult for the uninitiated to extrapolate true costs of programs and even some objects. The prescribed budget structure is obviously responsible for this confusion. It is not unusual for school boards to be blamed unjustly for complicity in concealing items that may be controversial.

In the interest of maintaining public confidence, school boards generally include explanations of certain of the contents under each budgetary category, indicating how costs have been affected by the number of added students and staff; the impact of salary schedule adjustments; or justification for additional costs of materials. However thoroughly these explanations are presented, at best they can be only generalized in terms of identifying meaningful costs of programs.[19]

On the other hand, the budget document that would be the result of the PPBS process should be more meaningful, defensible, and understandable to the public. It would help to demonstrate to the taxconscious community that school officials are interested in performance and productivity, as well as product, and in the most efficient use of available, scarce community resources.[20] Whether the budget stands or falls would then depend on justification of specific, planned programs, supported by evidence of output potential. It would be a revelation to the public to be shown how costs

[18] Twenty-three states require that proposed school budgets be approved by some state agency, eleven of which are noneducation agencies. See H. C. De Bruni, "Will Outside Control on School Budgets Increase?" *American School Board Journal,* CXLVII (August, 1963), 5–6.

[19] Harold E. Akerly, "For Better Public Relations Use a Performance Budget," *Nations Schools,* XLVII (February, 1951), 37–39.

[20] James Mauch, "A System Analysis Approach to Education," *Phi Delta Kappan,* XLIII (January, 1962), 158.

are distributed among defined school activities. The principal focus very likely would then be brought to bear on how the money is used, rather than on how much is spent. With this information, community lay participation in the budgetary process, which is now frequently prefunctory, could take on a new dimension of significance.

The accounting aspects of the program budgeting process would have the dual objectives of providing records for fiscal accountability as required by the laws of the various states and recording and controlling program costs against appropriations. On the assumption that the laws of the states are modified to accommodate program budgeting completely, the recording of program expenditures could also serve as the means of auditing for fiscal accountability.

Problems in Implementing Program Budgeting

The process of implementation of program budgeting would obviously require a great effort, as well as an expenditure of state and local funds. Progress would relate to state and local motivation; however, federal financial and leadership support of the project could constitute the most significant motivating influence. This would seem realistic with the federal government's growing commitment to education and to program budgeting as a concept.

The success of the project will depend on its acceptance. A serious impediment to an early achievement of this goal could be the sophistication of the image imparted to it—the image of a system that can be operational only with a staff of highly specialized systems experts backed by an expensive computer installation. Such misconceptions arise because today program budgeting is used primarily in large city school systems and in government agencies that have such facilities and trained personnel.

Carried to an extreme, program budgeting could become a relatively complex and costly process that would seem to be unrealistic for the vast majority of small school districts. However, the increase in cost can be balanced by the increase in efficient use of resources. James describes the advantages as follows:

> This [the implementation of program budgeting] would require substantial increases in accounting staff, developing a separate department of budget planning and systems analysis and appraisal.

> Such innovation would take us a long way in the direction of rational assessment of the effects of financial input into the system in terms of output services for which schools are operated.[21]

The question of how to reconcile the advantages to be gained in the general use of program budgeting with the realities of the capabilities and economics of the average school district is an important one. The resolution of the dilemma will be found either in the simplification of the process, while retaining the basic principles, and/or in the sharing of the costs and know-how by the cooperating units. The latter would seem to be potentially the more productive in long-range perspective, whereas the simplification approach may have to be the interim expediency.

The transition would conceivably include the following approaches: (1) programming the full implementation over an extended interval, such as five years; (2) restricting this form of budgeting to selected programs, possibly on an alternating basis;[22] and (3) experimenting with pilot projects in school systems of different sizes, types, structures, objectives, and programs.

Compounding the problem of programming the implementation on a limited basis over an interval of years would be the necessity to maintain a parallel, traditional budget while the latter is being phased out. This requirement would be a costly but essential ingredient and could be mitigated to an extent by the states' modification of their reporting and accounting requirements. In short, statutory budget codes will need to be streamlined.

The conversion to program budgeting will require the application of the principle of allocating the various responsibilities in accordance with the level of complexity and costs, to those with the appropriate resources of leadership, knowledge, funds, and hardware. The output from these would then be made available to those with lesser capabilities.

[21] H. Thomas James, "Modernizing State and Local Financing of Education," *A Financial Program for Today's Schools,* Seventh National Conference on School Finance (Washington, D.C.: NEA Committee on Educational Finance, 1964), p. 59.

[22] Allan R. Lichtenberger, "Program Planning, Budgeting and Accounting in School System Operation—A Position Paper" (Washington, D.C.: United States Office of Education, Mimeograph, September, 1967), p. 15.

State and Federal Support and Control

Aside from certain special programs funded over the years by the states and federal government, including school lunch and vocational education, the funding for the totality of the regular school program has been provided by general funding from state aid and local sources. The current experiment of funding by the federal government under ESEA and other acts, suggests interesting implications for future "aiding" patterns on the state as well as national levels. This may become particularly significant with program budgeting, where for the first time the expenditures for programs would be exposed to the scrutiny of state and national statisticians. Incentive funding for specific programs could therefore be expected to assume a more significant role in the implementation of state as well as federal education policy. An heretofore undefined "foundation" or "basic" program supported by the state could then be subject to the requirement of delineation of its specific components and their expenditure levels. Output data, such as from standardized achievement tests or behavioral measures, which would be part of the program budget, could also become a basis for funding. For example, a district may receive additional financial and/or professional aid, for reading programs, if its output in this area is below certain norms. The equalization principle of state support, in addition to, or in place of, being applicable to the traditional base of local wealth, could become contingent upon factors such as local achievement and effort, in terms of types of programs offered and the relative amounts spent locally for each of its programs.

As some view it, program budgeting may be condemned as a device for further reducing local controls of schools. First, the complexity of the process, conceptually and mechanically, suggests a need for assistance in know-how and money for implementation, that could only be available from a broader base than the typical school system can provide. This portends further consolidation of districts or increased dependence on state participation. Second, with the exposure of program definitions, costs, and outputs inherent in program budgeting, prospects would be enhanced for program funding to become a more significant basis of local support from the state and nation. Then where the eligibility for aid is made contingent upon the approval of the programs, based on predetermined criteria from above (such as required for ESEA programs), local prerogative could presumably be weakened.[23]

If a concomitant outcome of program budgeting might be an impingement on local prerogative, this factor needs to be weighed against the potential local gains in the output and efficiency of its educational enterprise, as well as in the possibilities for reduction of the local burden to finance it.

Conclusion

Let us review briefly the characteristics of traditional budgetary planning: it is minimal and fragmentary; its fiscal and program planning are conducted as separate activities; and, particularly in instructional areas, output consequences, if given consideration at all, are generalized.

In contrast, inherent in the program-budgeting concept is an emphasis on integrative, long-range planning that integrates cost accounting into the process. All programs must therefore be definitive before a price-tag is attached. In addition, and of equal significance, is a concern for a determination of the program's measurable output. The general acceptance and use of program budgeting by the local schools portend significant educational as well as fiscal management improvements.

Suggestion for Discussion

Review the categories contained in the function-object school budget code for a particular state and analyze the advantages and disadvantages of this format.

Selected References

DeYoung, C. A., *Budgeting in Public Schools*, revised ed. Chicago: John S. Swift Company, Incorporated, 1950.

[23] Harold Howe, II, United States Education Commissioner, in an appeal to the Senate Education Subcommittee, urged that his office not be reduced to a "mere paymaster," as is being threatened by pressure from states' rights advocates in Congress, who fear Federal control in the disbursements of Federal Aid. (From a report in the *New York Times*, September 24, 1967, p. 26).

Gauerke, Warren E., and Jack R. Childress, editors, *The Theory and Practice of School Finance.* Chicago: Rand McNally & Co., 1967. Chapter 8.

Linn, Henry H., *School Business Administration.* New York: The Ronald Press Company, 1956.

Mort, Paul R., *et al., Public School Finance.* New York: McGraw-Hill Book Company, 1960.

Ovsiew, Leon, and William B. Castetter, *Budgeting for Better Schools.* Englewood Cliffs, N.J.: Prentice-Hall, Inc., 1960.

Reason, Paul L., and A. L. White, *Financial Accounting for Local and State School Systems.* United States Department of Health, Education, and Welfare, Office of Education. Washington, D.C.: Government Printing Office, 1957.

To prepare an ideal educational budget is difficult, more difficult than the corresponding process in a private business firm. The objectives of school systems are multiple, and there is not absolute agreement among parents, educators and taxpayers on the importance or relative weighting of these different objectives.

Charles S. Benson

Chapter Seven

PROGRAM STRUCTURES AND ECONOMIC ISSUES IN LOCAL SCHOOLS

Program design and budget planning in local school districts have two fiscal dimensions, one pertaining to expenditures and the other to revenues. Inasmuch as the program budget essentially is designed to accommodate systematic planning on the basis of expenditures, the major portion of this chapter is devoted to the development of program categories. The very heart of the PPBS concept is the program structure, for it makes the outputs of a school district visible and identifies the resources required to yield these outputs. There is no single *best* program format for public schools. If local school districts are worth preserving as such, it would seem that schools which differ in size, location, clientele, staff, pupil needs, and fiscal resources would also differ in the goals they specify, the programs they offer, the priorities they assign to competing program elements, and in their achievement as measured by performance indicators. It would be unrealistic to consider PPBS in education without at least a brief examination of where the money will come from to support proposed programs. Revenue sources, of course, are related to any kind of budget, not only program budgets, and the final part of the chapter focuses upon some of the revenue issues of educational economics.

Designing Program Structures

Precisely how to create the most desirable structure for a program budget in local schools is not yet evident, but this problem can be resolved as more professional educators become interested in, and committed to, PPBS procedures. Several illustrative program structures are offered. Although they are arbitrarily put forth by one not specially trained in curriculum design, they suggest the type of format that is called for by PPBS. Many refinements are needed. Some administrative implications of program budgeting for local school officials are contained in this chapter, but they are described in greater detail in Chapter Eight. These two chapters may serve as a point of departure for local school planners who will be developing curricular program designs, management information systems, program budget documents, performance indicators, and other PPBS supportive elements that reflect the unique needs and capabilities of their schools.

The public is certainly justified in asking: What is obtained in educational services for the dollars spent? Until now, these services were measured for the most part by the dollars spent for salaries, materials, and buildings, and *not* in terms of program objectives, activities, and accomplishments. The possible categories that would lead to a program structure for an educational institution are illustrated in Table 9. The categories become narrower in scope at each lower level.

Preparing a statement of educational philosophy

A procedure that might be followed after a school district decides to accept program budgeting procedures is to prepare a formal statement of educational philosophy. From this statement, the systemwide goals may be derived, and ultimately transformed into the programs of the program-budget structure. The undertaking should result in something more than the poorly worded, rhetorical statement and cliché-ridden mythology that presently passes for an educational philosophy in many schools. The need is for clarity, precision, and quality in preparing the written philosophies, objectives, and program structures.

TABLE 9

ILLUSTRATIVE PROGRAM CLASSIFICATION SCHEMA FOR A SCHOOL DISTRICT WITH LEVELS OF CATEGORIES SHOWN IN DESCENDING SEQUENCE

GENERAL SYSTEM GOALS
(Written philosophy of education and formal board of education policies);

- INSTRUCTIONAL OBJECTIVES
  (Differentiated curricular objectives for a school district);
  - GENERAL PROGRAM AREAS
    (Groups of instructional program activities with similar objectives);
    - PROGRAMS
      (Specified curricular programs, outputs, activities or unassigned supportive services);
      - SUBPROGRAMS
        (Specialized offerings within grade levels or content areas);
        - PROGRAM ELEMENTS
          (Personnel, salaries, facilities, supplies, subsidies, debt service, and other line-item expenditures);
          - PROGRAM COMPONENTS
            (The nature of the program determines the definition of program components); and
            - TASKS
              (Activities performed within each program).

Most written school philosophies contain terms such as individual needs, self-realization, democratic values, meet the needs, whole child, sound learning, member of society, and maximum development or potential. This window dressing, lacking in operational specificity, consists largely of ". . . collections of educational jargon, psychological shibboleths, philosophical generalities, metaphysical tenets, and socio-political dogmas."[1]

One explanation for this lack of quality may be that school philosophies in many districts are prepared by board of education members, many of whom ". . . are completely incapable of writing, or understanding, a genuinely philosophical statement about educa-

[1] Donald C. Orlich and S. Samuel Shermis, "Educational Philosophy as Mythology: A Critical Analysis of School Philosophies," *Administrator's Notebook,* XIV, No. 4 (December, 1965), 3.

tion."[2] Orlich and Shermis, two professors trained in educational philosophy, analyzed numerous school board philosophies, including all written school philosophies of an entire state, and subsequently offered guidelines for school districts who seriously wish to prepare a useful statement of educational philosophy. Briefly, they proposed a means of spelling out the operational values of the school system; they advocated that all assumptions should be specified; and they described a hierarchy of values in which a district could list its priorities. These guidelines are consistent with the procedures prescribed by PPBS. The suggestion of an arrangement of priorities is particularly helpful. "Too many school philosophies reflect the cultural tendency to say that *all* values are important and further, that all are *equally* important. If all values are of equal importance, then no value can serve as a guide to conduct."[3] Persons who prepare the statement for a school should be aware of the history and scope of the subject, including ". . . theories of knowledge, metaphysics, human nature, ethics, aesthetics, and social philosophy. In practice, however, educational philosophies are typically written by a committee brought together for an evening to 'get the job done.'"[4]

A simplified flow chart, Figure 4, portrays the way in which educational philosophy is related to a proposed sequence for integrating the four operations of planning, programming, budgeting, and systems analysis.

Specifying the educational program objectives

After preparing the formal statement of educational philosophy, a school district can focus upon the systemwide objectives from which the instructional programs will be derived. The degree of generalization with which the objectives are to be expressed should be determined. Constructing an exhaustive list of very specific educational objectives would transform this document into a useless catalog; perhaps a taxonomy (classification schema) should be constructed. School planners are advised to consult some of the available sources on educational objectives. Two well-known publications are: *Taxonomy of Educational Objectives: Handbook I,*

[2] *Ibid.*
[3] *Ibid.*, p. 4.
[4] *Ibid.*, p. 3.

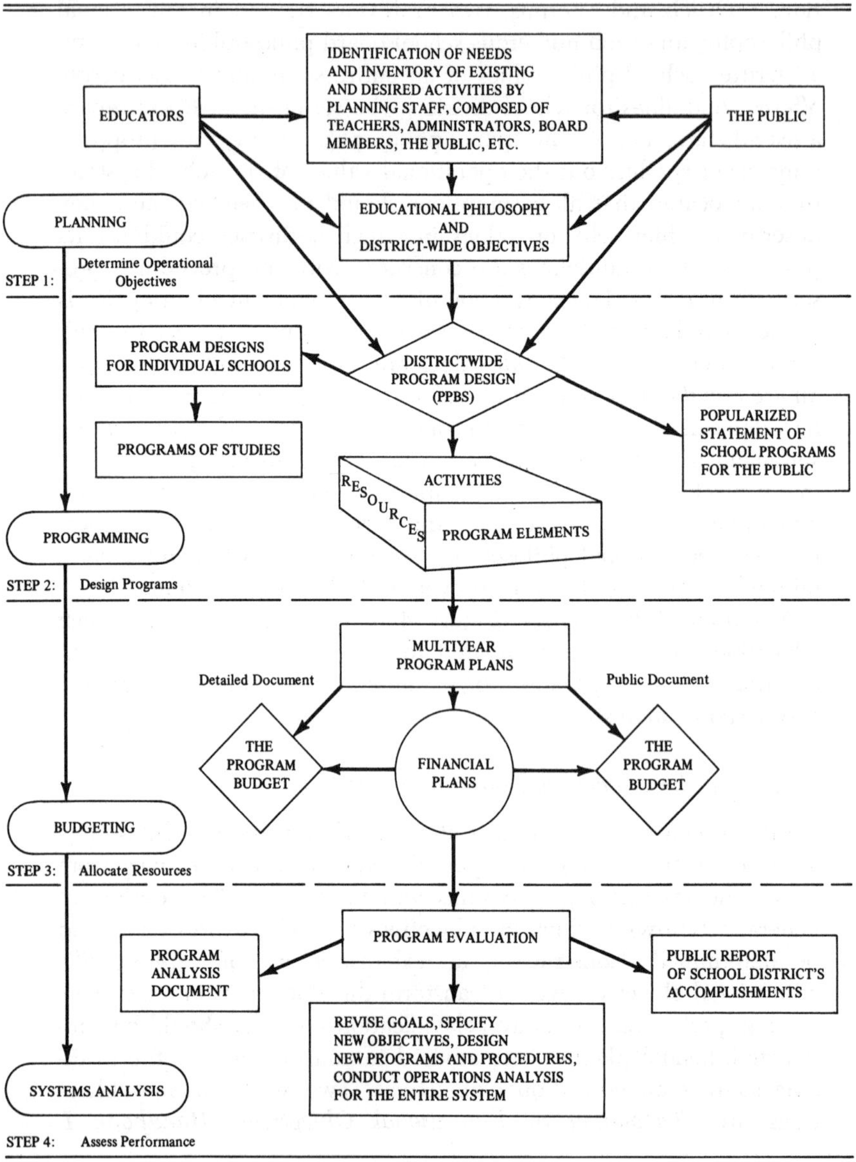

Figure 4. Flow Chart for PPBS Implementation by a Local School District.

Cognitive Domain; and *Handbook II, Affective Domain.*[5] These references provide a comprehensive analysis of levels of learning and the meaning, types, and formulations of educational objectives. Operational illustrations are provided. Professional associations also have published a number of worthwhile aids.[6]

There are various ways to examine educational objectives and there is a danger that an over-emphasis may be placed upon objectives that can be stated readily in behavioral terms and measured by simple recall or direct application skills. A taxonomy approach seems to be appropriate if it takes into account the structure of a discipline and complex cognitive skills as well as affective objectives and psycho-motor skills. A carefully prepared taxonomy could serve as a vehicle for assessing curriculum materials, analyzing learning and teaching behavior, and judging consistency with the professed instructional aims.

The United States Office of Education offers guidelines that may be helpful. The topic of instructional programs is dealt with in State Educational Records and Reports Series, Handbook VI, one of a group of manuals developed cooperatively to facilitate and improve the collection, maintenance, and reporting of educational information. One result of this cooperative project is likely to be improved standardization of terminology in instructional programs of both local and state school systems. This 690-page handbook contains three principal kinds of information: "(1) items of information about the organization, administration, content, resources, and processes of instruction; (2) items of information about the subject matter of the curriculum; and (3) information about related terminology and other considerations." [7] The handbook provides data

[5] Benjamin S. Bloom, editor, *Taxonomy of Educational Objectives, Book I: Cognitive Domain* (New York: McKay, 1956); and David R. Krathwohl, Benjamin S. Bloom, and Bertram B. Masia, *Taxonomy of Educational Objectives, Handbook II: Affective Domain* (New York, McKay, 1964).

[6] One example of a reference that deals with selection of curriculum content and setting of priorities is *Rational Planning in Curriculum and Instruction: Eight Essays* (Washington, D.C.: National Education Association, Center for the Study of Instruction, 1967), 203 pp.

[7] United States Department of Health, Education, and Welfare, *Standard Terminology for Instruction in Local and State School Systems: An Analysis of Instructional Content, Resources, and Process,* Handbook VI, preliminary edition, Office of Education (Washington, D.C.: United States Government Printing Office, May, 1967), p. 5.

on the basis of levels, or classes, of items in a manner suggestive of the way in which local school objectives may be differentiated by levels of generality. The five levels are as follows:

1. An entire school system
2. An individual school
3. A program of studies
4. A self-contained class, course, or cocurricular activity
5. A section, or instructional service activity.

The importance of defining objectives operationally cannot be overemphasized. Precise statements of desired outcomes are essential. There is a propensity among some educators to adopt only the jargon of innovations such as PPBS, while omitting the more rigorous requirement of specification. The danger is that this planning innovation will become as bastardized as some other innovations "adopted" by the local schools in which the adoption is in name only.

Illustrative program structures: five alternatives

Where does one look for ideal program structures? Several systems analysts have observed that "programs are not made in heaven"; rather, they are imposed on the natural world by man. If an educator wishes to use a program structure, probably he will have to develop one himself, with or without divine intervention. After some familiarity with PPBS, the next step is to get on with the business of structuring the activities of the organization within a workable number of programs, meaningfully defined.

> There are as many different ways of putting together a program structure as there are people who will attempt it. It is very difficult to formulate generally acceptable specific "rules" for constructing one. . . . The basic principle of an objective-oriented program structure is the grouping of activities that serve the same purpose. . . . The topmost level of a program structure should consist of the broad categories directed toward the fundamental objectives of the jurisdiction. . . . The lowest level in any structure would be comprised of the programs that have been implemented as the specific means for moving toward the end objectives.[8]

[8] State and Local Finances Project, *PPB Note 5* (Washington, D.C.: George Washington University, April, 1967), p. 6.

Five examples of program structures are offered in Tables 10 to 14. The first option, which retains some of the present function-object budget categories, emphasizes conventional grade levels as the basis for designing programs.[9] Option No. 2 is similar to the first, except for the provision for a middle-school program, a junior college program (K-14), and other contemporary types of school organization. An ideal, curricular-based program structure is shown as Option No. 3. The programs can be devised by instructional specialists, and the direct and indirect costs apportioned to subject areas. This is perhaps the most desirable, yet most difficult type to develop. Assigning program costs by subject matter and grade level involves a vast amount of effort and time. As a hybrid format, the fourth option combines grade level organization at the elementary level with subject matter organization at the secondary level. Generally, this combination reflects existing state certification procedures whereby educators are certified as elementary teachers through grade six and as English, mathematics, or social studies teachers at the secondary level. The fifth option uses services performed as the basis for a program structure.[10]

It is desirable to list under each program its related activities, elements, components and tasks. Then, a chart of expenditure objects and corresponding codes should be provided along with a program analysis document and a multiyear program and financial plan. It would be premature to develop these documents until an appropriate general program structure is developed and agreed upon. As an aid to designing programs and assigning the many instructional topics to broader general program areas, some of the guidelines offered by the United States Office of Education may be helpful. For example, Table 15 lists the *instructional areas* and *service areas* described by USOE in *Instructions for Preparing ESEA Title I, Project Applications.* Each of the more than forty curricular areas might be included at some level within a school district's program structure.

The five illustrative program structures indicate the diversity in

[9] This program structure is somewhat similar to the ones used by the Sacramento City Unified School District (California) in its 1967–68 general fund budget and the School District of Philadelphia in its 1967–68 proposed operating budget.

[10] The program design is similar to the one developed by a Westchester County, New York, intermediate district and described in Chapter Five.

TABLE 10

PROGRAM STRUCTURE (OPTIONAL #1) BASED UPON CONVENTIONAL GRADE-LEVEL ORGANIZATION

GENERAL PROGRAM AREAS	PROGRAMS	SUBPROGRAMS
Instructional Programs		
	Early childhood and elementary schools	
		Prekindergarten
		Kindergarten
		Primary level
		Intermediate level
	Junior high schools	
	Senior and technical high schools	
	Adult and continuing education	
	Curriculum development (might be apportioned elsewhere)	
	Summer schools	
	Instructional administration (might be apportioned elsewhere)	
	Special services, programs and projects	
Central Direction Programs		
	Board of education	
	Office of superintendent	
	Planning and research	
	Personnel services and staff development	
	Business services	
		Administration, financial
		Budget development
	Management information services	
	Plant planning services	
	Purchasing services	
	Special business services	
Supporting Programs		
	Transportation	
	Maintenance and operations	
	Food services	
	Community services	
	General capital improvements	

TABLE 11

PROGRAM STRUCTURE (OPTION #2) BASED UPON MIDDLE SCHOOL AND JUNIOR COLLEGE GRADE-LEVEL ORGANIZATION

GENERAL PROGRAM AREAS
Early childhood education
(Examples of costs for each program include teacher salaries, fixed charges, equipment, supplies, operating and maintenance costs; each program has a number of subprograms.)
Elementary education
Middle school education (grades 5–8)
Technical high school education
Comprehensive high school education
Special education
Continuing education
Junior college education
Community service
Health service
Transportation and attendance service
Debt service
Central direction and planning service
Unassigned support service

TABLE 12

PROGRAM STRUCTURE (OPTION #3) BASED UPON CURRICULAR SUBJECT-MATTER ORGANIZATION

GENERAL PROGRAM AREAS	DIRECT COSTS				INDIRECT COSTS				CURRENT AND PROJECTED TOTALS		
	Teacher Salaries and Related Benefits	Classroom Supplies, Books, Equipment	Support (ex., library)	Research Curriculum Development	Adminis-tration	Main-tenance	Operating Expense	Debt Serv.	Current Year Total	Next Year Total	Fifth Year Total
English Language Arts											
Foreign Languages											
Mathematics											
Science											
Social Studies											
Creative Arts											
Physical-Health Education											
Business, Vocational, Homemaking											
Kindergarten											
Special Education											
Community Relations											
Adult Education											
Pupil Personnel											
Pupil Welfare:											
Health Service											
Transportation											
Food Service											
Auxiliary Services											
Noninstructional											
TOTALS											

TABLE 13

PROGRAM STRUCTURE (OPTION #4) BASED UPON GRADE-LEVEL AND SUBJECT-MATTER ORGANIZATION

GENERAL PROGRAM AREAS
Early childhood education (pre-K and K)
Primary grades education (grades 1–3; includes reading, English, etc.)
Intermediate grades education (4–6)
Social sciences and humanities (7–12)
Mathematics and science (7–12)
Creative arts (7–12 or K–12)
Physical and health education (7–12 or K–12)
Business, vocational, homemaking education (7–12)
Pupil personnel services (K–12)
Special education (K–12)
Adult education and community services
Administration and general support services

TABLE 14

PROGRAM STRUCTURE (OPTION #5) BASED UPON SERVICES PERFORMED BY AN INTERMEDIATE SCHOOL DISTRICT FOR LOCAL SCHOOL DISTRICTS

GENERAL SERVICE PROGRAMS
Elementary grades special education
Secondary grades special education
Psychiatric services
Shared teacher services
Testing and counseling services
Technical and vocational education services
College conferences and career counseling services
Educational research services
Data processing services
Transportation services
Administration and planning services

approaches that may be taken. Although it will be difficult to abandon traditional thinking, creative planners may find it desirable to dismiss the departmental concept. Inasmuch as a program will cut across departmental lines, the notion of departmentalization may inhibit systems (or programmatic) thinking. A school district should reserve at least several months of intensive work for preparing the initial program structure.

The project to revise USOE Handbook II

It is probable that helpful financial guidelines for local officials who are interested in PPBS soon will be made available by the United States Office of Education. USOE is revising Handbook II, *Financial Accounting for Local and State School Systems,* which was first published in 1957.[11] This manual is credited with helping

TABLE 15

INSTRUCTIONAL AND SERVICE AREAS OF A LOCAL SCHOOL DISTRICT AS SHOWN IN DIRECTIONS FOR PREPARING ESEA-TITLE I PROJECT APPLICATIONS [a]

INSTRUCTIONAL AREAS	SERVICE AREAS
Art	Attendance Services
Business Ed./Office Occupations	Clothing
Cultural Enrichment	Curriculum Materials Center
English Language Arts	Food: Breakfast
English as a Second Language	Food: Lunch
Reading	Food: Other
Foreign Language	Guidance and Clothing
Home Economics	Health (Specify)
Industrial Arts	In-Service Staff Training
Kindergarten	Library Services
Mathematics	Pre-service Staff Training
Music	Psychiatric Services
Physical Ed./Recreation	Psychological Services
Prekindergarten	Related Services for Parents
Science	School Social Work
Social Studies/Social Science	Transportation
General Elem. and Sec. Ed.	Tutoring
Speech Therapy	Waiver of Fees for Books, etc.
Special Ed. for Handicapped	Other (Specify)
Vocational Ed.	
Work Study	
Other (Specify)	

[a] U.S. Department of Health, Education, and Welfare, *Instructions for Preparing ESEA Title I Project Applications* (Washington, D.C.: Office of Education, 1966), p. 14.

[11] The manual is part of a series of cooperatively developed handbooks devoted to standardized records, terminology, and planning. Handbook I, for state education use, is a reporting manual; Handbook II, described above, was being revised in 1968; Handbook III deals with property information; Handbook IV with staff records; Handbook V with pupil data; and Handbook VI, still being developed, with curriculum.

to standardize the language of school finance accounting and with achieving a degree of comparability for school finance data that previously had been elusive. In the proposed revised manual, emphasis will be upon program planning, budgeting, and accounting for school systems.

A USOE staff member pinpointed the weakness of financial practices suggested in the old Handbook II by noting that budgeting formats include broad receipt and expense categories which are poorly defined. "In reality, the process is not budgeting at all. It is a presentation of appropriation categories in which the emphasis is on *not overspending the array of estimates* rather than on relating the achievement of objectives to the dollars spent. For decision making purposes, the information they yield has most limited value." [12] The revised Handbook II will support program budgeting.

Developing program performance indicators

After a program structure has been devised, some means of evaluating performance should be agreed upon by school district planners. Standardized tests of academic achievement have long been used as indicators of system performance, although they may have created more problems than they resolved. A common approach has been to try to predict from a pupil's IQ scores what his achievement *should* be and then to compare his actual achievement test scores with the predicted scores. Critics have noted a number of fallacies in this procedure.

Several attempts to devise better performance indicators in education include the Quality Measurement Project (QMP) of New York State and recent projects undertaken by the Educational Testing Service (ETS) of Princeton, New Jersey. QMP was an attempt by the New York State Education Department to develop a series of differentiated achievement test norms that would provide data by which a local school administrator could compare the performance of his district's students with that of students in other systems of similar economic condition and IQ.[13]

[12] Allan R. Lichtenberger, "The Project to Revise Handbook II: Financial Accounting for Local and State School Systems," *The Challenge of Change in School Finance,* Proceedings of the Tenth National Conference on School Finance (Washington, D.C.: National Education Association, Committee on Educational Finance, 1967), p. 166.

[13] W. D. Firman, "The Quality Measurement Project," *Science Education,* L (April, 1966), 259–279.

Dyer, an ETS measurement specialist, noted that "A further step along the road toward believable educational performance indicators was taken by Educational Testing Service in the development of a plan for measuring the quality of education provided by the school systems in Pennsylvania." [14] This was a refinement and more comprehensive version of New York's QMP; it was mandated by the Pennsylvania legislature. The State Board of Education was given the charge to develop in two years' time ". . . an evaluation procedure designed to measure objectively the adequacy and efficiency of the education programs offered by the Commonwealth." [15] If successful, this evaluation procedure eventually could provide two kinds of results: (1) it could enable each district to appraise the effectiveness of the programs shown in a program budget in sufficient detail to indicate what should be done to strengthen them; and (2) it could provide state education departments with program performance standards to aid in allocative decisions to all districts across a state. Dyer explained that the idea behind the development of educational performance indicators is

> to achieve a method of measuring the performance of educational systems in a way that is easily interpretable by educators and educational policy makers and at the same time avoids as far as possible assumptions that cannot be empirically supported. . . . To depict how a system is performing, we require a matrix of performance indices (time dimensions; changes in cognitive development, attitudinal development, interpersonal behavior, etc.).[16]

In this illustration, the performance indicators as developed by ETS provide a series of estimates of how well a school district is doing in comparison with other districts working under presumably comparable advantages and handicaps. The matrix of indicators helps to show the general areas in which a district may be strong or weak.

Economic Aspects of Local School Revenues

The success of program budgeting in public schools will be inextricably related to the ways in which programs of financing education are resolved. Without sufficient funds to support programs,

[14] Henry S. Dyer, "The Pennsylvania Plan," *Science Education,* pp. 242–251.

[15] Pennsylvania General Assembly, Public Law 564 (Act 299, The School District Reorganization Act of 1963).

[16] Henry S. Dyer, *The Concept and Utility of Educational Performance Indicators,* paper presented at the 1967 Systems Science and Cybernetics Conference, Boston, Massachusetts, October 12, 1967, Mimeograph, pp. 6 and 9.

even the most creative planning framework will not result in improved learning. Several questions arise. What are the financial implications of economic-educational expansion? What are some of the contingency variables that could alter revenue distribution patterns? To what extent will fiscal constraints (such as ceilings on cost-sharing formulas) detract from the optimal educational program structures proposed by program budget planners? What is a desirable intergovernmental relationship in the sharing of resources? These questions are not easily answered, for the topic of future patterns of financing education has controversial facets that preclude consensus of judgment.

School revenue and GNP

National economic growth has direct implications for local public schools, because of the increasing proportion of gross national product (GNP) that is absorbed in supporting the schools. For the school year 1967–68, public school revenue from all sources (taxes, grants-in-aid, earnings, and tuition) was approximately 30 billion dollars and accounted for about 4 per cent of GNP. The National Education Association estimated that from 1956 to 1967, the revenue receipts of public schools increased 176.9 per cent at an annual rate of 9.7 per cent.[17] In this eleven-year period, school revenues increased at a rate which was 1.6 times as fast as the rate of increase of GNP. When one considers that national wealth, as measured by GNP, increased at an annual rate of approximately 6.5 per cent, the changing proportion of public school revenues is impressive and suggests the greater role that education may play in future economic growth. If one wishes to make a hazardous projection of aggregative educational revenues for a future year, he might attempt to use a trend line to relate GNP estimates to the proportion assumed to be allotted to public schools.

Some have estimated that the total revenues which support the annual public school budget will rise from the 30 billion dollars of 1968 to 82 billion dollars in 1975,[18] an amazing increase.

[17] Committee on Educational Finance, *Financial Status of the Public Schools, 1967* (Washington, D.C.: National Education Association, 1967), p. 47.

[18] This estimate was provided in an editorial in *Phi Delta Kappan,* XLIX, No. 3 (November, 1967), 113. By contrast, an earlier and more conservative estimate placed the 1980 total cost of public elementary and secondary schools at between 50 billion dollars and 60 billion dollars. See R. Oliver Gibson and Herold C. Hunt, *The School Personnel Administrator* (Boston: Houghton Mifflin, 1965), p. 290.

The method of estimating future school revenues may range all the way from divining rods to elaborate econometric models, such as the one developed by the Brookings Institution. The four hundred equations in this model depict numerous variables affecting the United States economy. As educational program-performance measures are developed, perhaps they can be included in such models as a guide to school officials.

Intergovernmental distribution patterns

The revenue for local school districts is, and probably will continue to be, largely dependent upon local sources of support. However, no massive infusion is likely to come from local or even state sources; the need for federal assistance is apparent and will probably result in shifts in the pattern of distribution of support by the three levels of government. The greatest revenue potential is the federal government.

Table 16 illustrates the percentage of school revenue contributed by the three sources from 1930 to 1967.

Substantial increases in school revenue will be necessary in order to support unconventional educational program structures. In the past ten years, all three levels of government have more than doubled their aid for public elementary and secondary schools. The flow of federal dollars to the nation's public schools was set into motion with the National Defense Education Act of 1958 and the Elementary and Secondary Education Act of 1965. Now that federal funds are a regular source of school subsidy, there is increased speculation that a larger share of total school revenue eventually will come from the federal government. There is additional concern among some persons, particularly state education officials, who perceive their power threatened by the new patron of education, the federal government.

In the past, federal funds have usually been given in the form of *categorical aid* rather than *general aid*. In other words, the aid was provided for specified categories such as foreign language, science, or vocational education programs. If the present annual rate of increase in school revenues is to be sustained, it seems inevitable that there will need to be widespread general aid, in addition to categorical aid, from Washington. This will enable local schools

TABLE 16

PROPORTION OF SCHOOL REVENUE FROM GOVERNMENT SOURCES, 1930 TO 1967 [a]

SCHOOL YEAR ENDING	PER CENT OF TOTAL SCHOOL REVENUE FROM		
	FEDERAL SOURCES	STATE SOURCES	LOCAL SOURCES
1930	0.4	16.9	82.7
1940	1.7	30.3	68.0
1950	2.9	39.8	57.3
1960	3.6	40.0	56.4
1967	8.0	39.9	52.1

[a] Data provided by National Education Association Committee on Education Finance.

to use federal aid to support teachers' salaries and other line-item objects in the operating budget. Education has become politically attractive and represents a large element in the Congressional pork barrel. Ideally, federal funds could enable, and perhaps challenge, local schools to be more imaginative in their planning and programming of instruction. They might serve as a type of *venture capital* with which local schools could experiment with proposals for new programs. An implicit assumption in supporting the trend toward a greater federal role in local school support is that the issues which arouse traditional fears of federal controls will not come alive. A general observation is that the federal government, ". . . contrary to the fears of some, is not using its new financial powers in support of education in the way of an all-powerful European Ministry of Education." [19]

Trends and outlook for local government finances

School finance is essentially a subdivision of public finance, which in turn is one of the many areas of specialization within the disci-

[19] Fred M. Hechinger, "Howe on Federal Purse Strings," *New York Times*, September 24, 1967, p. E-9. A concise analysis of questions revolving around federal aid to the schools and a discussion of future aspects of this problem are contained in Sidney W. Tiedt, *The Role of the Federal Government in Education* (New York: Oxford University Press, 1966), 243 pp.

pline of economics. In order to better understand the economic problems that confront local schools, a brief analysis of local government finance is in order. For the past twenty years, local government has been among the most dynamic and rapidly expanding sectors of the United States economy. Expenditures for local units increased at an average annual rate of nearly 9 per cent, in current dollars, and were influenced by such factors as: rapidly expanding local government services, population growth, and demographic changes, increases in per capita real disposable income, and inflationary effects upon cost and prices. A study by the National Industrial Conference Board suggested that the rapid and continual growth in local spending can be financed without a sizable further erosion of local autonomy only if the local financial structure undergoes comprehensive reforms through a concerted and cooperative local-state effort. These structural reforms ". . . will have to encompass: (a) extensive improvements in the administration of the local property tax; (b) a more efficient and more widespread utilization of local sales and income taxes, facilitated by a closer coordination of tax efforts at the state-local level; and (c) a broader and more rational application of service and user charges at the local level.[20]

Most states allow local districts to tax for school revenue, usually in the form of property taxes. However, the level of direct state support varies dramatically. Collins observed, for example, that the average state support in Nebraska is approximately 5 per cent, and this may be compared with Delaware, where the average is nearly 80 per cent from state tax sources. "The national average for state support of education (in 1967–68) is 40 per cent, excluding federal aid, which is primarily special aid." [21]

Local revenue from local sources is lagging more and more behind the increase in expenditures, and is resulting in greater state and federal aid to municipal governments. The federal grant programs to state and local governments are expected to exceed 30 billion dollars by 1975.[22] Increasingly, concern by critical observers

[20] Michael E. Levy, "Trends and Prospects in Local Government Finances," *The National Industrial Conference Board Record,* October, 1966, p. 20.

[21] George J. Collins, "How Public Schools Budget, 1967–68," *Nation's Schools,* LXXX, No. 6 (December, 1967), 38.

[22] First National City Bank, *Monthly Economic Letter* (New York: First National City Bank, January, 1967), p. 4.

is directed toward the possible erosion of local autonomy and complete subordination of weak local governments. Another possibility is that the municipalities will go directly to the federal government for grants and thus weaken the role of the states. Since the principal revenue sources for state and local governments, taxes on property and on sales and gross receipts, are not overly responsive to rising incomes and economic growth, these levels of government will probably be in a persistent fiscal bind.

The property tax

As the main revenue source of schools, the property tax is a relatively inflexible device, and its burden upon tax payers tends to be distributed in a regressive fashion. This means that lower-income residents of lower-valued properties tend to pay a higher percentage of their income on this tax than high-income groups. Richer families spend less proportionately for housing than poorer families. Inasmuch as regressive taxes are generally not popular with large numbers of voters, the schools are handicapped by their dependence upon an undesirable fiscal instrument. Critics of the tax have charged that it has a number of shortcomings, including: (1) regressivity and inequitability; (2) lack of correlation of the tax with benefits received by the taxpayer; (3) lack of theoretical justification;[23] (4) shortcomings in assessment practices and poor administration;[24] (5) deterrent to investment in housing; (6) sluggish response to changes in economic conditions; and (7) excessive exemptions.

Although the postwar growth of property tax revenues surprised many economists who considered this tax to be income-inelastic, or not very responsive to increases in income and overall economic growth, "there is reason to believe that the performance of the property tax during the next decade will not match that of the last two decades, unless the local property tax undergoes an extensive

23 "In short, the property tax has no theoretical justification and must be defended in terms of expediency or tradition." Charles S. Benson, *The Economics of Public Education* (Boston: Houghton Mifflin, 1961), p. 165.

24 One economist estimated that property can be efficiently assessed by local tax officials only in communities with over 40,000 to 50,000 people, a test that is met by fewer than 500 government units in the U.S. See Dick Netzer, *Economics of the Property Tax*, Studies of Government Finance (Washington, D.C.: The Brookings Institution, 1966), p. 176.

reform."[25] The National Industrial Conference Board recommended that the needed reform would have four major parts:

1. More uniform and equitable assessment within each community;
2. More uniform assessment ratios among the communities within each state;
3. Curtailment of property tax concessions and exemptions; and
4. State leadership to coordinate local efforts.[26]

A comprehensive analysis of the local property tax was made by Netzer, who observed that adverse criticism of this levy has been replaced by a "new complacency."[27] In fairness to the tax, it does possess some advantages. It can be defended, at least partially, on the basis of two principles of taxation: ability to pay and benefits received. It is rather closely linked to local autonomy and thus serves local preferences. However, its unique advantage is that it alone is amenable to small incremental changes in rate, which means that it reduces what has been called *tax tension.* In spite of the flaws of the property tax, it appears more desirable to strengthen it than it does to eradicate it. Promising reforms in some states are already discernible.

In addition, there is continuing interest in the economic implications of alternative means of financing education. Perhaps some kind of tax-credit approach will gain greater acceptance in the future. Under this plan, taxpayers use a fixed percentage of their state or local income tax payments as a credit to offset against their federal income tax liabilities. Some propose that parents of school children should be provided with specific education vouchers that would pay for the cost of schooling. This form of indirect subsidy would replace, or perhaps supplement, direct state and federal subsidies to the public schools. Other persons have argued for greater use of private resources in the financing of education, so as to reflect our "mixed" economic system that blends private initiative with public policy.

Economic factors and trends will have an important bearing upon future patterns of school finance. Two examples derived from

[25] Michael E. Levy, "Trends and Prospects in Local Government Finances," *The National Industrial Conference Board Record,* October, 1966, p. 24.

[26] *Ibid.*

[27] Dick Netzer, p. 3.

the urban context deserve mention. In many cities, the ratio of tax-exempt to taxable property is rising, as more and more property is taken over by charitable, religious, educational, and other tax-exempt owners. This places a greater burden on the small property owner. A second trend is also related to the erosion of the tax base and pertains to the distribution of total population and school-age population in urban areas. Between 1950 and 1960, the total population of New York City declined 1 per cent but the school-age population increased 20 per cent. Furthermore, in fourteen of our largest cities, the mean population decline in the same time period was 6 per cent and the mean school-age population increase was 20 per cent.[28]

Human capital

A school system exists to serve human clients. Self-evident though this may seem, it is only within the past few years that economists have become concerned with *human capital.*[29] Man is a special type of capital asset who invests in himself in many ways, perhaps the most important of which is in the form of education. The cost may be stated in dollars, time, effort, or leisure foregone, and the yield certainly cannot be expressed entirely in dollar terms. The return on educational investment is quite high, with some specialists stating that it is a principal cause of economic productivity and growth. Adam Smith was one of the first economists to detect a benefit-cost relation between education and wealth. Recent research by Becker, Denison, and Schultz establishes that education contributes to a *residual* factor which accelerates wealth as measured by gross national product. One implication is that it provides justification for additional government support for educational programs. Another is that it directs attention to human resources as program structures are designed. Until recently, the very thought of investment in human beings was rather offensive to some people. However, the

[28] H. Thomas James, *et al., Determinants of Educational Expenditures in Large Cities of the United States,* United States Department of Health, Education, and Welfare, Office of Education, Cooperative Research Project No. 2389 (Stanford, Calif.: School of Education, Stanford University, 1966), p. 8.

[29] This concept is described in two major sources: Theodore W. Schultz, *The Economic Value of Education* (New York: Columbia University Press, 1963), and Gary S. Becker, *Human Capital* (New York: Columbia University Press, 1964).

human capital approach places supreme emphasis upon maximizing human worth, without reducing the dignity of personal existence. Furthermore, it indicates that some economists are truly concerned with the basic moral values of society.[30]

The outlook

Almost every one of the fifty states has enacted a complex system of laws defining the financial relationship between the state and local school districts. The recently formed Education Commission of the States, whose objective is to stimulate state action for schools, designated as one of its key studies "Financing Elementary-Secondary Education at the State Level."[31] The results of this and many other research projects could be used as a basis for policy recommendations for federal-state-local school finance plans. A possible outcome could be even greater usage of systems procedures and program budgeting to plan intergovernmental educational activities. The increased demand for state and local services of all types continues unabated, and it is obvious that there is a lack of coordination in planning and fiscal matters among the various levels of government. An economic analysis of intergovernmental fiscal relations by Break pointed out some of the proposed reforms and fiscal prospects for the future.[32]

In a rather provocative paper, Benson suggested that present-

[30] Some suggest that contemporary economic theory is a type of verbal tic tac toe that is not really concerned with the kinds of individual human values expressed in the human capital concept. Contemporary economists, including those who devised PPBS, are increasingly called upon to help formulate public policy that touches each person in the nation. A symposium that did not deal specifically with human capital, but that challenged Kenneth Boulding, Milton Friedman, and Paul Samuelson to discuss moral questions raised by leading philosophers is of interest and relevant to any discussion of the relation of economics to education; see Sidney Hook, editor, *Human Values and Economic Policy* (New York: New York University Press, 1967), 268 pp.

[31] Allan R. Lichtenberger, "The Project to Revise Handbook II: Financial Accounting for Local and State School Systems," *The Challenge of Change in School Finance,* Proceedings of the Tenth National Conference on School Finance (Washington, D.C.: National Education Association, Committee on Educational Finance, 1967), pp. 20–23.

[32] A treatment of systems analysis and program evaluation of metropolitan fiscal problems is provided by George F. Break, *Intergovernmental Fiscal Relations in the United States,* Studies of Government Finance (Washington, D.C.: The Brookings Institution, 1967), pp. 192–203.

day school districts are *standardized service systems,* but in the future they are likely to become *differentiated output accountability systems.* He offered several ideas for future means of financing education such as: (1) state determination of minimum costs of maintaining basic programs via performance audits; (2) mandatory state-wide uniform property tax rates; (3) establishment of "Educational Improvement Funds" by states; (4) greater usage of local income taxes to support local activities; and (5) the linking of flow-of-funds to state-approved definitions of program priorities.[33]

Any realistic projections of future revenue and expenditure levels represent an uneasy compromise between public needs for services such as education and the political and economic constraints within which governments must operate.

Summary

Five program structures were presented for illustrative purposes. Because more detail for a local school district would be needed, subcategories and budget coding systems were not presented. However, these programs should provoke some disagreements and constructive dialogues among professional educators as they describe their areas of specialization within the program budget systemic framework. It would be contrary to the intent of systems procedures to view any program structure as a finished product. Continuous refinements contribute to system renewal[34] and to educational betterment.

The program budget provides an array of estimates of expenditures for both "have" and "have not" districts, and is intended to promote a more efficient allocation of scarce school revenues. It emphasizes not only what is to be spent, but more important, what

[33] Charles S. Benson, "Possible Break-throughs in the Financing of Public Education," paper presented at the symposium entitled *Operations Analysis in Education,* sponsored by the United States Office of Education, National Center for Educational Statistics, Division of Operations Analysis, Washington, D.C., November 19–22, 1967.

[34] A self-renewing social system is defined as one that possesses the capacity to recognize, protect, and encourage creative and innovative individuals (those who possess the traits of openness, independence, and flexibility). See John W. Gardner, *Self-Renewal: The Individual and the Innovative Society* (New York: Harper and Brothers, 1964).

is to be achieved. Several issues in the economics of education were discussed in terms of their influence upon patterns of raising revenue to support school programs of tomorrow. The upward spiral of per capita educational costs is likely to continue. One reason is that educational services are almost completely personal services, and the costs of personal services tend to rise even more rapidly than the costs of goods and other services. PPBS may produce a convergence of intergovernmental long-range expenditure and revenue planning for local schools.

Suggestion for Discussion

Design a local school district program structure that incorporates the existing curriculum and transforms the conventional school budget categories for your state; discuss operational problems (such as evaluating performance); and analyze economic dimensions of local educational programs.

Selected References

California Association of Public School Business Officials, *Program Budgeting in Public School Districts.* Los Angeles: Southern Section CAPSBO, School Budget Research Committee, April 4, 1967, 30 pp.

National Education Association, Committee on Educational Finance, *Financial Status of the Public Schools,* published annually.

State and Local Finances Project, *P–P–B Notes.* Washington, D.C.: George Washington University, issued periodically.

United States Congress, Senate Subcommittee on Intergovernmental Relations, *Criteria for Evaluation in Planning State and Local Programs.* 90th Congress, 1st Session. Washington, D.C.: United States Government Printing Office, July 21, 1967. 42 pp.

Wright, Gordon, *A Selected Annotated Bibliography on Educational Systems,* Working Paper No. 1, Division of Organizational Sciences. Cleveland: Case Institute of Technology, April 1, 1966, 225 entries.

In my judgment, well-informed legislators, governors and administrators will no longer be content to know, in mere dollar terms, what constitutes the abstract "needs" of the schools. The politician of today is unimpressed with continuing requests for more input without some concurrent idea of the schools' output.

Jesse M. Unruh

Chapter Eight

ADMINISTRATIVE ISSUES AND IMPLICATIONS OF PPBS

The encroachment of economics upon the field of educational administration brings with it some predictable implications, including greater concern for economic rationality and efficiency criteria. A number of other issues and implications are less apparent and are dealt with in the following paragraphs. Attention is given to administration-related issues pertaining to areas such as general administrative organization, board of education and community, management of information, reports and accounting, instructional administration, financial administration, informing the staff and community, and in a speculative vein, the impact of program budgeting upon collective negotiations between teachers and boards of education.

The nature of the implications will be dependent partially upon the extent to which program budgeting is adopted by local school districts and state departments of education, and supported from the federal level with Congressional appropriations for public schools. At any rate, it seems certain that practicing administrators and students of school administration will benefit from studying economic approaches to systems planning. For the most part, discussions of PPBS have been at the conceptual-theoretical level, whereas this chapter focuses more upon the technical-operational level; it is intended for school administrators generally rather than only school business officers.

Administrative Organization

Innovations such as PPBS do not just happen, nor do they slowly evolve in local school districts. They require deliberate effort and planned implementation. While the general executive leadership will be supplied by the chief school officer, with the cooperation of other administrative personnel and the legislative support of the board of education, the ultimate responsibility for PPBS development is likely to fall upon one man, whose title will vary from district to district. In all but the smallest and poorest districts, this will probably require the creation of a new position or positions. Unless the school district has available personnel who are skilled in the techniques required, responsibility for overall system design, program management, and budgeting will be given to a consultant or preferably, to a member who is new to the organization. The first administrative implications therefore revolve about the relationship of the program budget specialist to the existing organization.

Organization structure

Figure 5 depicts a possible organizational structure for the central office of school districts ranging in size from small to moderately large. It shows how the PPBS format integrates the operations of curriculum planning and financial administration, without abolishing present school structures. It also indicates that the position of Administrative Assistant, Planning Coordinator, is essentially a staff role. Unlike most other staff members, whose jobs are advisory within one general area, this person should be able to articulate both curriculum and fiscal needs. His specialization and loyalty reside with neither, but to the system as a whole. What is required is the proper mix of technical competency in budget development and information analysis with curricular training and program design. His concern for the system as a whole, however, should not restrict him to activities only with the chief school officer. His influence on the responsible specialists throughout the system will largely determine the success or failure of the undertaking. Personnel with this type of training are not easy to obtain, but as districts are able to identify

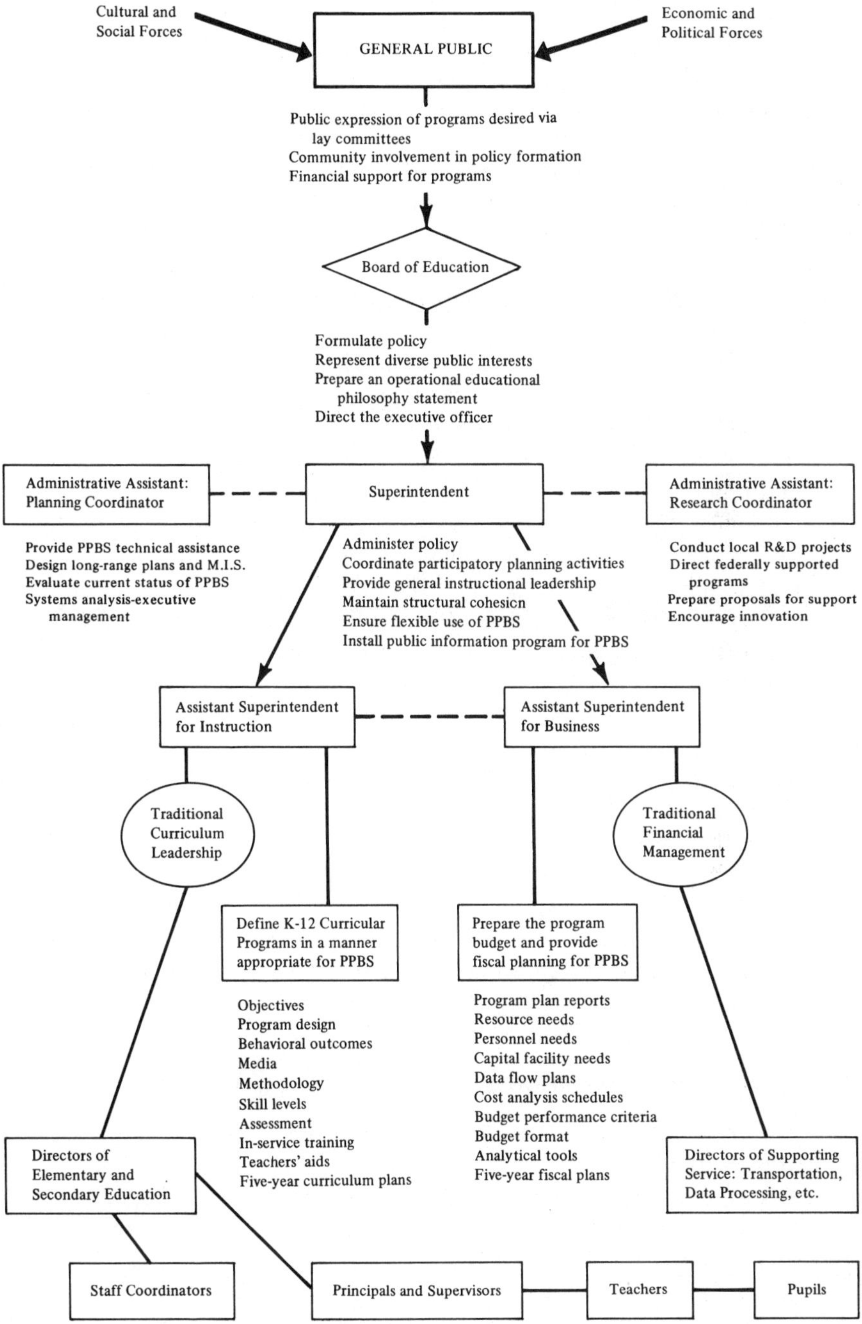

Figure 5. Simplified Pattern of Organizational Interactions for Existing Schools Seeking to Adopt PPBS.

such specialists, they should be employed considerably before the target date for full-scale PPBS installation. The early procurement of a specialist's services will increase the probability of *lead-time* in a project designed to result in program budgeting. Gradual phasing-in of systems procedures may be more desirable than complete transformation on a given date.

When properly established within a given school district, PPBS need not require a drastic departure from existing organizational patterns. Whether existing decision making is diffused or tightly centralized makes little difference, for the same pattern is likely to prevail, and the actual organizational chart will vary in response to local conditions and resources. Choices of leader styles, such as formal or informal, idiographic or nomothetic, proximate or remote, and other types will continue to reflect personal administrative discretion. With PPBS, the distance between the *leader* and the *led* may be reduced, and perhaps policy planning can be conducted less unilaterally.

Part of the conflict currently manifested most sharply in the urban school environment may be traced to outdated organizational structures and the lack of a rational framework within which diverse values and public demands can be transformed into school programs and resources. PPBS may provide a framework in which such a transformation takes place. In settings where the gulf is widening between the advantaged and disadvantaged members of the community, for instance, the program budget format may serve as a vehicle for residents of the community to express their needs in relation to policy formation and program offerings of the school. Incremental planning by power coalitions is inadequate for it often produces a kind of educational perfidy which spells doom for responsible public policy in urban schools.

Current organizational trends

Two of the most pronounced recent trends in the administrative organization of public schools are the reduction in the total number of school districts in the United States and the increased specialization within the administrative offices. Consolidation and other factors trimmed the figure from 117,000 in 1940 to fewer than 20,000 operating public school districts in less than three decades. The reorganization and merging of local schools, often spurred on by state mandates and financial incentives, resulted in a net loss in the number of schools but it also produced a sharp increase in the size and bureaucratic characteristics of many of the remaining districts. Present patterns of formal education mirror something analogous to an *organizational society,* and although the merits of the conceptual model of bureaucracy are well documented by students of organizational theory, the present educational structure may have become alien to the needs of the people served by it. Competing expectations of the public for its schools are symptoms of variability in societal values.

Implications for the chief school officer

The second trend noted above pertains to the increasing degree of specialization found at the administrative level. Such specialization places a greater burden upon the top level executive. Generally, the superintendent is the only person in a position to observe all specialized functions interacting, and upon him falls the responsibility of coordinating their activities and providing the best work environment and organizational control. If integrated at the responsible operating levels, PPBS facilitates dispersion of responsibilities through the administrative structure with the result that information should arrive at the top level in a more efficient, coordinated fashion. This will free the superintendent for time to devote to long-range planning and formulation of new program objectives. Also, it will help to minimize the tendency toward polarization of school functions into instructional and noninstructional groups and activities.

At the central office level, an administrative plan may be developed to project the policies, goals, and resources required to execute the various program plans. The initial format might consist of the five sections listed in Table 17: general administrative objectives; curricular program objectives; personnel requirements; facilities requirements; and fiscal requirements.

Board of Education and Community

Some of the causes of friction between professional educators, lay governing boards, and segments of the general public may be reduced with the installation of program budgeting. The premise is that present educational structures and school budgets are not serving the people as they were intended to serve. Developed by professional educators over a period of time with an eye upon convenience and cost-savings, they often fail to portray the aims and accomplishments of the schools. If the aims could be stated in programmatic terms at the time that the schools are asking for public support, it is likely that the schools would be brought closer to the community without a concomitant danger of community domination and loss of professional autonomy.

Observations of present practices indicate that board of education policy decisions are often made independent of budget development. Budgets are typically prepared by the professional staff and presented as a complete document to the board for its consideration. Then it is usually a matter of acceptance or rejection, in whole or in part. With PPBS, educational program decisions and fisçal decisions can be made concurrently when the budget is being developed. A number of people, including interested taxpayers, believe that the most important single work task performed by a board of education is to formulate a budget or establish a tax level. Therefore, a board's legally determined function, making policy, is most easily observed when it is doing its most prominent and painstaking work.

In the development and modification of budgets, PPBS can enable boards of education to operate more effectively. Traditional budgets, when presented as lists of objects, tend to encourage a quantitative frame of mind for board members. Budget deliberation becomes a search for excess quantities. In such an environment, persons may overlook the probability that reduction of input may result in a corresponding reduction of output. This is not to imply that no excess exists. Savings can be made without a reduction of output by a more efficient operation; however, this is generally accomplished by some sort of internal reform which lay governing boards may find difficult to achieve with present fiscal-planning devices. A reduction in output may be justified, and hence a budget reduction is in order, but it should be the result of a conscious, programmatic decision by the board made in response to consideration of the desired level of output and the input expenditures necessary to achieve it.

Some of these remarks might be interpreted to indicate that the power and influence of boards of education and participation of the community in school affairs may increase under PPBS. If such an increase occurs, it need not be viewed as a danger sign by the administrator. It is not a case of creating power sources that never existed; rather, it is unifying all power and influence in behalf of improved education. The intent is to mobilize power so as to devise better educational programs and not attack each other in a way which detracts from common objectives.

Suppositions for improved collective negotiations

Predictably, in the manner of nearly all bargaining conflicts, the key to resolving educational disputes of the decade of the 1960's was, for the most part, financial. However, the professional and union organizations representing teachers appear to be directing greater attention to demands for "better education," or to issues with similar global phrases, indicating that they seek improvements in instructional programs. Slogans such as "Teachers Want What Children Need" are persuasive, and would be more so if the needs of children could be made explicit through a vehicle such as the program budget. In an optimistic vein, it would appear that both sides in the negotiations process would benefit by the design of program structures that are acceptable to students, teachers, boards of education, administrators, and the general public.

Little change can be expected to take place in the behavioral-attitudinal-political factors of negotiations, bargaining, and other complex strategy contexts. However, program budgeting can lead to a revision of structural elements and provide a common ground for conflict resolution. With a convergence of research literature from the area of bargaining behavior [1] and that of program budget-

[1] Research literature is filled with empirical approaches to game theory and bargaining behavior. For example, the Society for General Systems Research recently published an extensive bibliography containing hundreds of research reports and allied publications pertaining to bargaining behavior: Charles G. McClintock and David M. Messick, "Empirical Approaches to Game Theory and Bargaining," *General Systems,* Yearbook for the Society for General Systems Research, XI (1966), 229–236.

ing, creative proposals for reforms in the present negotiations process might result.

Some teachers' organizations seem to be led by a belief that spending money makes good things happen and spending more money makes better things happen. Conversely, some boards of education appear to believe that spending more money of any amount is irresponsible. A common ground leading to programmatic contractual language may be needed. Instead of seeking only salary increases and similar benefits from the total reward system in a narrow, self-interested manner, teachers could, with a program budget, focus upon programs, or programmatic aspects of a school, and seek support for more resources for these programs.[2] It is likely that public support for teachers would be greater if the public could be shown that the various pupil programs would be the major beneficiaries of increased taxes, and not merely the salaries of teachers. Admittedly, the major component of most instructional programs from a budgetary standpoint is the salary of teachers, but the schools have done themselves a disservice with the manner in which they have seen fit to report to the public how their funds are appropriated. Object of expenditure budgets simply do not adequately describe how the operating budget supports programs.

After suitable program structures have been devised, and school budgets have been designed to show something more than items such as "inter-fund transfers" and "board of education costs," then educators can provide supportive evidence to show that their salaries and benefits are prime components of programs which public policy deems desirable. At that time, teachers and boards of education can engage in cooperative planning and negotiate more intelligently over the priorities, relative merits, and costs of issues such as smaller classes, team teaching, disruptive children, vocational schools, ghetto school problems, preparation periods, reduction in work hours, community involvement in school policy, and other issues that have educational program implications. Until then, educators may suffer from: internal power struggles; unionism-versus-professionalism frictions; constraining new legislation; resistance

[2] Some of the implications from including curricular programs as a topic of negotiations were described by Leslee J. Bishop, *Collective Negotiation in Curriculum and Instruction* (Washington, D.C.: Association for Supervision and Development, 1967), 22 pp.

from civil rights leaders and slum area residents; and, in general, decreasing community support for the needs of the schools.

If program budgeting proves successful in this arena, future collective negotiations may focus upon instructional programs, with teachers' salaries as a prime subsidiary, rather than vice versa. This remains a remote, but enticing, possibility.[3]

Arrangement and Use of Information

Administrative conduct and policy execution are dependent upon the information available to the officials of the school system. In a sense, information is a system's lifeblood. Data for general administrative purposes may be collected from all of the sources in the school system and transmitted to a central processing point where they are transformed into information.

Management information system (MIS)

The design of an integrated MIS consists of molding together a pattern of instructional-administrative activities and automated processes into a harmonious, efficient working arrangement. With the installation of an information exchange procedure, the system requirements should become more easily determined by means of analysis of existing data and organizational processes.

Although the terminology surrounding MIS may arouse suspicions of nonhumanism, this approach can enhance individualized instruction. To illustrate, one of the applications of the system is in teacher selection and assignment to particular students. The MIS source data for teacher placement would include training and experience records, location preference information, and specific data describing the instructor's performance and unique accomplishments relative to student groupings, specialized instructional methods, and subject matter areas. Pupil-teacher assignments could thus be improved, and personalized instruction attained. The process could

[3] This section is a revised portion of a paper presented by the author. See Harry J. Hartley, *Program Budgeting: Current Research and Possible Implications,* paper presented to a symposium on collective negotiations at the annual conference of the American Educational Research Association, Chicago, February 12–15, 1968.

be refined through continuous updating from supervisory reports, questionnaires, student records, student opinion data, training records, and informal discussions. Implied in the adoption of MIS is the tenet that its primary mission is to support the teaching-learning process.

All of the informational elements of PPBS, taken together, constitute an MIS that is designed to facilitate decision making. A hypothetical MIS structural planning calendar is presented in Figure 6. Intended to serve as a guide for local school systems, the elements shown are suggestive of what kind of planning might accompany the installation of such a system. The proposed dates for completion of each phase are merely suggestive, with variations to be expected according to local conditions. It is important that school officials consider designing a time-phased framework prior to undertaking a pilot project with systems procedures. Cost implications for each phase could be added. Figure 6 is called a GANTT Chart and serves a purpose similar to that gained by PERT networks or other planning diagrams. It includes the blending of *conceptual* elements (system specifications), *procedural* aspects (administrative plan), and the day-to-day, *operational* facets of collecting and utilizing the information. MIS is more than just record keeping. Although information will be received and recorded, it is classified in a manner consistent with programs and objectives; it is accessible for program reports and analysis.

MIS helps to systematize planning and provides greater assurance that interdependent activities are recognized and accounted for in the preparation of schedules and in resource allocation. Other applications of this concept are discussed in the sections on instructional and financial administration.

Reports and accounting

School districts are required to file budgets with their state department of education. In most cases, this ensures compliance with the various state laws. For example, some states mandate that total textbook expenditures be reported separately, while others require that salaries must exceed a fixed percentage of the operating budget. A number of local school budget items and functions are grouped together simply because of state aid formulas that reimburse some

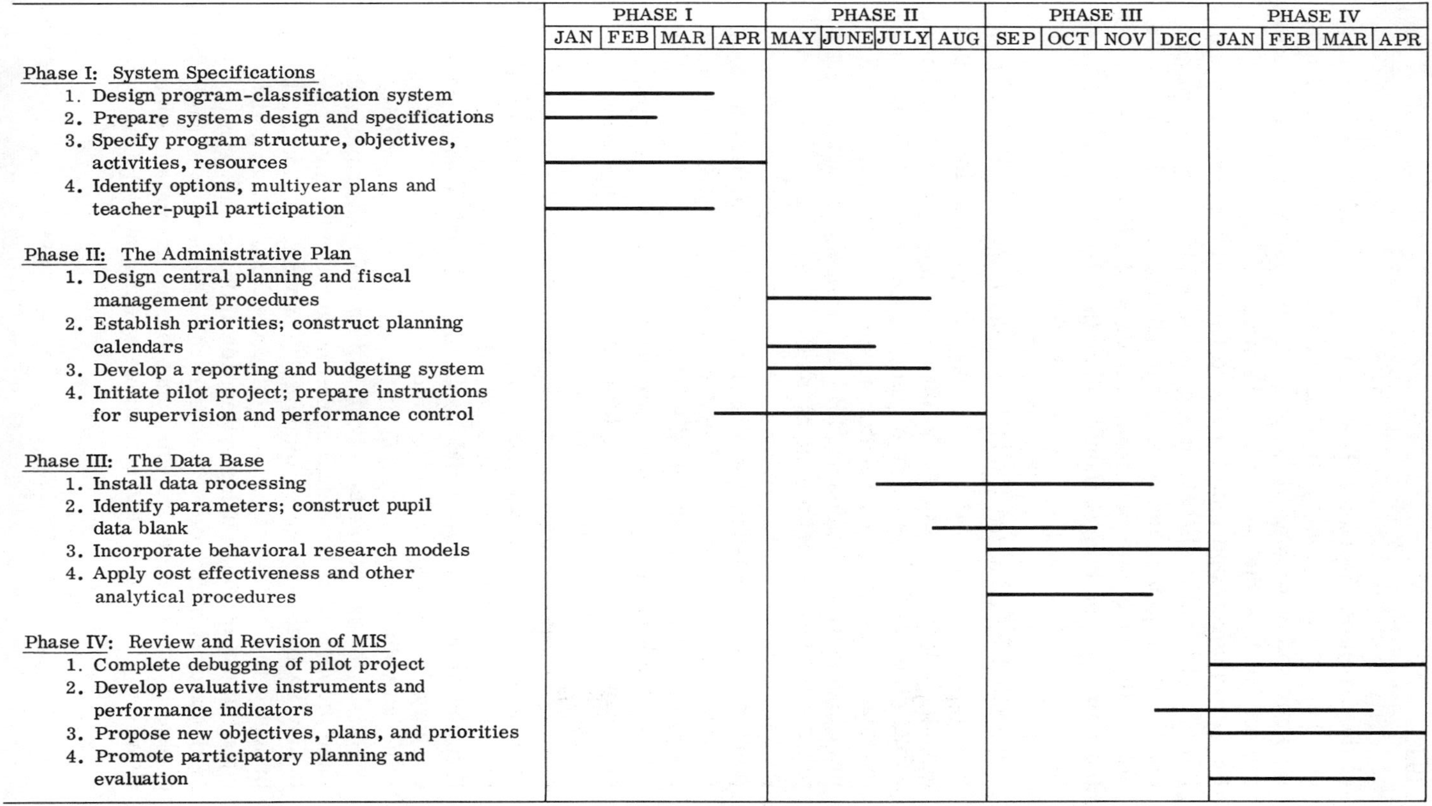

Figure 6. MIS Development Schedule and Planning Calendar for a School District.

of the expenses. Most state departments of education collect financial data and issue comparative expenditure reports. For these and numerous other reasons, there is generally a state-mandated form prescribing how the budget is to be reported and adopted. Thus, the local budgets and reports derived from budgets are fairly uniform for all school districts in a given state. However, the needs, objectives, programs, and resources of all school districts in a state are not the same. And because it is basic to the PPBS concept that the format of the budget should follow the objectives of a district, the formats for program budgets in a given state may not be uniform.

It should be admitted frankly that differences will occur which may result in some states developing compromise formulas that attempt to please all, but fail to please anyone. The task of translating program budgeting into state budget codes is not insurmountable, providing sufficient time and consideration are given prior to statewide adoption of PPBS. Regardless of how a budget is organized, the expenditure items remain the same: salaries; employee benefits; contract payments; equipment, supply and material purchases; professional and service contracts; and transfers of funds. Program budgeting provides a better way of relating these items to the programs they are designed to support.

The establishment of an accounting system follows the appropriation plan of the budget in the form in which it was officially approved. Concern should be given to the manner in which the budget is legally adopted. To avoid any legal difficulties and possible tax payer suits, it would be advisable, until states install PPBS, to adopt the budget in the state-specified general format, making it very clear that the appropriations would be so divided within each general category that a reclassification into a program format could be achieved without any alteration of the official appropriations.

The day-to-day accountability of a program budget presents the same problems that functional or performance budgeting presented. It may be that from an accountant's viewpoint, the ideal type of budget is the traditional listing of objects of expenditures. It facilitates the use of the voucher system for auditing and provides the most direct correspondence between the appropriations (as a list of objects) and the audited vouchers (as a list of the same objects). However, if it is true that accounting systems must follow appropriations, then program budget proponents argue that appropriations must follow programs.

PPBS probably will not require a great amount of information which is in addition to what a well-managed school district already possesses. The justification for retaining information is the use to which it is put. The media for use and transmittal are the reports (regular and special) that are required to measure the objectives sought, and no decision should be made concerning how information is to be retained or filed until the nature and content of these reports are clearly identified.

Reports that are descriptive or evaluative but that lack quantitative data may be satisfactory at the outset of program budgeting, but in full-scale PPBS operations, reports should contain both quantitative and nonquantitative information.[4] Far more common are reports that merely list column after column of figures without any analytical-evaluative framework. Financial reports are especially susceptible to this. A need exists for a kind of balance sheet for the programs in operation, but with the debits and credits replaced by an attempt to indicate the costs, benefits, effectiveness, and performance involved. Several administrative planning activities and representative reports needed by the management of the schools are depicted in Table 17.

Data processing and a data base

In future educational planning, electronic data processing (EDP) may become the core organizational component, by virtue of its ability to process large amounts of complex data and simulate the behavior of school systems, without a corresponding loss of individual identity. PPBS emphasizes long-range planning, or greater *lead time* than is customary, and electronic data processing can facilitate this procedure. Size of district, wealth, and staff expertise

[4] An example of types of output measures that were reported during one district's transition to PPBS procedures is shown by New York City Public Schools. Until other measures were agreed upon, building principals were asked to report the following: 1) test results (such as Metropolitan achievement tests in reading); 2) percentage of pupil attendance; 3) percentage of pupils participating in extracurricular activities; 4) number of diplomas and certificates granted; and 5) percentage of pupils promoted and passing New York State Regents examinations. A number of other output measures will be developed as the District gains more experience with PPBS.

TABLE 17

PPBS ADMINISTRATIVE PLAN AND PROGRAM REPORTS FOR A LOCAL SCHOOL DISTRICT [5]

I. General Administrative Objectives
   A. Central planning, systems procedures, and K–12 coordination;
   B. Integration of instructional program activities and fiscal management;
   C. Coordination of building-level administrators;
   D. School-community relations plan; and
   E. Board of education policy operationalized into program design.

II. Curricular Program Objectives
   A. K–12 program classification;
   B. Five-year master plan;
   C. Instructional activities transformed into program design; and
   D. Program changes (reconciliation with appropriations) and evaluation.

III. Personnel Requirements
   A. Staff recruitment, selection and appointment; possible retraining;
   B. Pupil projections to determine future needs;
   C. Workload information statements; and
   D. Staff needs specified in each program area for each year of the next five-year period.

IV. Facilities Requirements
   A. Needs projected for school site, plant and facilities;
   B. Time-phased construction master plan;
   C. Space utilization-environmental studies; and
   D. Transportation data.

V. Fiscal Requirements
   A. Revenue needs projected for a five-year period;
   B. Current economic data and forecasts analyzed;
   C. Budget dollars assigned to the program budget; and
   D. Program cost estimates related to appropriations.

VI. Control of Reports
   A. Reports on data requirements for the superintendent;
   B. Reports to and from agencies outside the school district;
   C. Emergency reports not repeated at periodic intervals;
   D. Operating documents and ledgers (orders, vouchers, authorizations, medical reports, requisitions, time sheets, etc.).

[5] This Administration Plan is somewhat similar in design to one used by New York State budget officials. See *Guidelines for Integrated Planning-Programming-Budgeting* (Albany: Executive Department, State of New York), p. 47.

will help to determine the scope of EDP operations.[6] Data processing is an important component of a Management Information System, particularly if it is related to a *data base* through which information is received, secured, accounted for, converted, and retrieved. The data base (or data bank, or unit record center) for a school district can be expanded over the years after the following basic system components have been provided:

1. data-collection devices and processing procedures
2. PPBS procedures and skilled personnel
3. utilization and documentation procedures
4. computer simulation models and computer programs (if possible)

School officials have always processed data, but now the approach is dramatized by the advent of machinery whose capacity and capability are nearly unlimited. The issue is not really whether a school district should or should not have data processing equipment; rather, it pertains to comparing the estimated benefits of a particular EDP installation with the costs and then judging the merits of the proposed project. A number of school officials appear to associate EDP with the cost savings, but it may be that data processing will bring about additional costs to the district.

It is dangerous to plan any proposed MIS around a particular type of hardware, or machinery, because doing so may involve a number of changes that do not move PPBS closer to program objectives, but merely attempt to keep the PPBS concept compatible with the hardware. Data processing equipment changes quite rapidly; ideas for handling information that developed when computers first received wide-scale usage remain vital today, whereas the hardware has long been obsolete. In the initial planning and design of EDP concepts for a district, there should be less concern over specific hardware and more attention devoted to the process desired. A worthwhile exercise might be to lay out the entire information process as if it were to be compiled manually. Then, if shortage of funds prohibits immediate installation of EDP, a plan for future

[6] EDP has brought an unprecedented boom to the management consulting field, with the number of consulting firms active in EDP services exceeding 3000 and predictions that by 1970, the total billing for EDP consulting assignments will surpass a billion dollars. See Arnold E. Keller, "EDP Consultants—Pro and Con," *Business Automation*, XIV, No. 11 (November, 1967), 34.

conversion is available and the benefits of the new procedures are more clearly determined.

Four issues should be considered in developing data processing procedures: forms design, accuracy of input data location, location and distribution of data, and time-sharing of computers:

1. *Forms design.* Attention should be devoted to choosing the sequence in which information is presented. Forms and reports should not only be readable, but information should be positioned so as to be easily extractable. Where the possible responses to an item requested are known and limited, a checking off system is superior to one that requires the respondent to supply the information. Related information should be blocked off so the selective reader can react faster.

2. *Accuracy of input data.* As a district moves toward EDP, accuracy becomes a potentially significant operating problem. The degree of accuracy required depends more upon the standards maintained by the district than upon the machines it uses. As long as humans are processing reports, the understanding that they can bring to the reading compensates for minor errors, especially omissions. They can make corrections and modifications as the information is developed and conveyed. The same is not true with EDP systems. Once information is secured in a data system, it takes time, money, and effort to modify it. Perhaps the greatest single problem in all data processing systems is maintaining high quality of the input data. Consideration given to this area prior to any hardware installation will be returned many-fold in the form of better output data.

3. *Location and distribution of data.* A data base that is expressed in a machine processing form (punched cards, tapes, etc.) can avoid a potential problem pertaining to the location of the important source documents. The basic documents concerning student achievement should remain close to the operating level at the individual schools. Curricular and other resources also should be decentralized. Unless the information is directly and immediately accessible to the principals and guidance counselors, it may never be used. Little value is gained by storing test scores and evaluative data in some geographically distant planning center. The source documents and detailed information on fiscal matters, however, are usually centrally located, and often where the payments are made.

To try to duplicate the educational information at the individual building level for the use of the central planning unit is an expensive and time-consuming process. It often tends to reduce the initiative of the individual schools and develops an unnecessary centralizing tendency that could not be justified by organizational theory or desired practice. The attempt to maintain individual accounting and fiscal records in a school building is likely to consume time and labor that could be spent more fruitfully in direct instructional support. EDP systems that possess the ability to transfer the selected data via machine can avoid this dilemma.

4. *Time-sharing.* Even though the number of possible applications of EDP is continuing to increase, it may be difficult for a local school district to justify installation of a complete system on its premises. Techniques have been developed to determine the amount of machine operation and time utilization that are required to justify EDP on an economic basis. To complicate matters, curricular-instructional models that expand computer application far beyond a record-keeping function are being developed; such models usually require greater computer capacity, which invariably increases costs. A possible solution is the notion of time-sharing of computers:

> At first thought, time-sharing seems simply a convenience: a means of allowing fuller use of the machine by more people and of saving time for the users. In practice, however, experiments with the technique have demonstrated a wide range of interesting possibilities. It enables the user to conduct a continuous dialogue with the machine and in effect makes the computer his intellectual assistant. Further, the system makes it possible for the users to carry on a discourse with one another through the machine, drawing on the large store of knowledge and its computing speed to do so. The time sharing system can unite a group of investigators in a co-operative search for the solution of a common problem, or it can serve as a community pool of knowledge and skill on which anyone can draw according to his needs. Projecting the concept on a large scale, one can conceive of such a facility as an extraordinarily powerful library serving the entire community—in short an intellectual public utility.[7]

In conclusion, the ultimate scope of the data base in program budgeting includes storage of *all* information relating to program

[7] R. M. Fano and F. J. Corbato, "Time Sharing on Computers," *Scientific American*, CCXV, No. 3 (September, 1966), 129.

areas and program elements. This subsumes the traditional functions of school business administration as well as curriculum content, library and instructional materials inventory, research results, test items, operations information, special projects, and the like. When fully developed, the data base can serve as the nucleus of a comprehensive MIS, which in turn, is a component of a PPBS system. However, the use of the computer in storing and retrieving information leads to an ethical issue over the invasion of human privacy. School officials should devise policies related to information gathering, disclosure, and confidentiality. Educational data banks, if improperly used, can convert the school into a transparency in which socioeconomic factors, IQ and achievement test data, physical characteristics, adolescent indiscretions, personal habits and citizenship records, and other records may be exposed to the most casual observer. The issue is similar to the one involving the proposed establishment of a National Data Center by Congress. Although the objective of the proposed center would be to bring together the scattered statistics in Government files on citizens, opponents argue that it might become an "intelligence center" rather than a purely statistical data bank and would thus detract from personal privacy.

Financial Administration

It is in the area of financial administration, which is already centralized, that the centralizing bias of PPBS is most pronounced. The entire operations within the domain of the fiscal officer may be centralized: fiscal planning, control, financial reporting and evaluation. The advantages of centralized record-keeping appear to outweigh the liabilities of centralization itself. Both the Management Information System and data processing can readily be applied to fiscal operations of a school district. At present, many districts administer procedures such as payroll or accounts payable through some data processing medium. In addition to the usual output of checks, registers, and warrants, many different analyses and program classifications of expenditures can be obtained. The payroll and bills are of a high volume output, relative to the capacity of the machines, and are among the first applications turned over to data processing machines. This procedure may be followed in an attempt to build up a high machine utilization from the outset in order to justify the costs incurred, even though an immediate pay-off may not be in the best interests of the district.

Transferring to EDP may produce initial problems. If it can be ascertained that the problems are restricted to machine and programming adjustments, they can be resolved through debugging in a reasonably short time. But if they are input problems that involve accuracy and sufficiency of data, the more complex machinery will make it difficult to remedy the situation. It is possible to obtain faster, newer and more diversified output, but never more accurate output than is initially fed into the system.[8]

Table 18 indicates some representative areas in which data processing may be utilized in school business administration. With EDP, the financial officer can better estimate the manpower, time, facilities, and fiscal resources necessary to carry out the specified program plans. References and technical manuals are generally available. For example, even in the somewhat less likely area of food management, programming techniques have been developed and applied to institutional menu planning. Menus were designed to satisfy specified criteria such as optimum nutrition, daily variety, and economic efficiency.[9]

Although the functional areas shown in Table 18 preceded the adoption of program budgeting-systems analysis procedures, some of the operations may be modified and streamlined with the installation of PPBS. If it should facilitate a centralized data base, the resulting efficiency of operations should be an improvement over present practices. Examples shown include the analysis of purchasing procedures by four methods and the tabulation of expenditures by vendors. Most school districts maintain a record of school-age populations and produce an age-grade breakdown. EDP can, in addition, supply information concerning mobility both within and outside of the district that may have some programmatic implications. In certain areas, the major problem is one of continually updating the information on hand.

[8] This is aptly expressed by the term GIGO, meaning "garbage in, garbage out."

[9] Ronald L. Gue, "Selective Menu Planning by Computer," *Proceedings*, American Society for the Advancement of Food Services Research, October 4, 1965. Professor Gue achieved optimal solutions to problems of menu planning in the context of hospitals.

TABLE 18

SPECIALIZED AREAS OF SCHOOL BUSINESS ADMINISTRATION THAT ARE SUSCEPTIBLE TO ELECTRONIC DATA PROCESSING APPLICATION

AREAS OF RESPONSIBILITY	APPLICATION
1. Accounting	analysis of expenditures by vendors, or budget code, or school buildings, or objects purchased
2. Budget preparation	multiyear budget preparation with possible variations on future projections
3. Capital facility planning	existing plant utilization with future projections
4. Capital fund management	evaluation of performance by actual investment and possible alternatives
5. Census and pupil projections	pupil mobility within and out of district
6. Construction of school plant	PERT network to meet time schedules and to signal pending delays
7. Debt service	formulation of new bond schedules for maximum fit with existing schedules
8. Equipment inventory control	utilization studies
9. Federal and special programs	benefit-cost comparisons
10. Food service	menu selection
11. In-service training programs	subject matter indexes relating training manuals to existing operations
12. Insurance	determination of insurable values of equipment and materials
13. Long-term fiscal planning	trends in expenses and revenues
14. Office personnel management	inventory of skills of present staff, especially those not being presently utilized
15. Purchasing	analysis by procedure: open bidding, invitational bidding, informal quotes, direct negotiations
16. Transportation	alternate bus routes and schedules

Inventory control, insurable values for equipment, and personnel skills are other noteworthy examples. Many conventional business procedures will continue to be used within a PPBS framework, although present systems for each of the functional areas could be recorded in flow charts, showing where each document is prepared and to whom it is distributed. Data pertaining to the average and peak workloads for all business procedures and cost comparisons for present and proposed work methods could be prepared. The unit record center might be developed after consideration is given to its possible scope of operations, anticipated benefits, desired systems procedures, staffing, costs, and its relation to the organization chart of the school system.

Instructional Administration and Supervision

The implications of PPBS for curriculum administrators and supervisors of instruction perhaps are not quite as clear-cut as for financial administrators. Depending upon the degree of centralization in the school system, central office administration of the future will probably become more supportive of instructional programs and less despotically commanding. The existing role of "teacher" will generate an even greater variety of specializations with well-defined responsibilities such as program chairman, team leader, prescriptive specialist, measurement specialist, and numerous other roles that require substantial graduate-level study. The number of paraprofessional employees in the schools will increase in order to relieve teachers of nonteaching and quasiteaching duties. Many of the paraprofessionals will possess technical skills in systems design, data processing, programming, instructional media equipment, and other similar areas.

With the advent of systems procedures in local schools, the introduction of innovations and the process of change in instructional activities can take place in a planned manner. Computer simulation models may be devised to permit the testing of proposed changes without upsetting the normal school routine. This would allow only "tested" changes to be introduced on a districtwide or statewide basis, and would offset the bandwagon approach to educational innovation that equates any change with improvement. Some liberal educators seem to advocate change for the sake of change, whereas among the conservative group, there may be an enduring allegiance to curriculum content that is being rendered obsolete and irrelevant as today's popular media daily document the velocity of change of our age.

As mediators of these extreme positions, supervisory specialists might provide leadership in computer-simulated construction of detailed, dynamic models of the schools that furnish a vehicle for testing hypothetical instructional changes. A model of a school should possess the dynamic capability to: (1) represent diverse curricular design configurations; (2) depict events which occur during simulation; (3) analyze events in relation to time; and (4) produce observable output data that reflect the effects of various program design changes within the model.

With the adoption of PPBS, supervisors of instruction would provide leadership and assistance to teachers in the following ways:

1. Construct K-12 curricular program designs, that specify the implicit assumptions of the school system.
2. Define programs in explicit terms.
3. Devise alternative means of achieving objectives and establish a priority for all options.
4. Assign the components for each program; the desired attitudinal-behavioral outcomes for each curricular program should be stipulated, as much as possible.
5. Make organizational arrangements to support the program design; these include assistance in planning class schedules, grouping pupils, staffing, providing facilities and materials, and conducting in-service programs.
6. Diagnose overall system performance with periodic evaluation and revision of programs, objectives, and methodology.
7. Assess teacher performance on the basis of program accomplishments and performance criteria devised by the school system.
8. Compile the data base elements for a centralized pupil information file.
9. Make available to teachers the results of recent research projects and similar professional contributions designed to improve instruction.
10. Promote long-range planning for each program area, conducted both formally and informally, with the aid of planning calendars.

A districtwide cumulative data base could be of great assistance to teachers and would also improve the coordination of curricular and financial planning. In addition to data files pertaining to teachers, programs, and school facilities, there might be a pupil information file, the elements of which would vary in response to the needs of the school system. Each year, the teacher, counselor, or supervisor would have access to well-organized and recently updated files of cumulative individual student records of grades, attendance, standardized test results, and so forth, for each student under his supervision. Student aptitudes, interests, preferences, and abilities would be recorded, along with relevant socioeconomic data. A descriptive analysis of the student body, the *school profile,* could be provided, and the data file might serve as a clearing house for requests for information about students or the schools within the system.

Computer-assisted instruction

Instructional administrators may wish to use computer-assisted instruction (CAI) techniques in conjunction with program budgeting. There are at least three kinds of CAI: (1) drill and practice; (2) tutorial (computer does the teaching, in effect); and (3) the dialogue system (student and machine interact and converse). It is difficult enough to assess the worth of existing teaching methods, and it may be even more difficult to verify the efficacy of CAI. The literature describing this concept is increasing at an impressive rate and thus the pros and cons are not repeated here.

Instructional planning council

The school district may wish to create an Instructional Planning Council (IPC), to coordinate and develop curricular activities within a systems framework. A number of school districts have councils of this type, although the functions and membership vary. IPC will examine needs, encourage instructional proposals, define objectives, make recommendations to the superintendent, evaluate programs, and serve as a quality-control unit for the entire district.

Citing an urban example, the Seattle Public School System has the equivalent of an IPC. (See Appendix I.) Its duties and responsibilities include reviewing instructional plans, proposals, and ideas to assure adherence to the systems procedure. Plans are considered in terms of districtwide objectives for grades K-14, personnel, feasibility, available materials and teaching facilities, pedogogical soundness, auxiliary services required, evaluation, long-range implications, and of course financing. The IPC-type of organization in Seattle is responsible also for proposing new emphases, and it does this by raising questions: (1) How rapidly should we move in new directions and with new programs? (2) What are the areas of deficiency in our present programs that need bolstering? (3) What are some new dimensions in education that should be explored and what innovations and pilot projects might be feasible? [10]

Instructional usage of MIS

It is unfortunate that when university or private management consultants are engaged by schools, they usually restrict their scope of operations to fringe areas of cost savings, such as pupil bus service, food service, or maintenance. The actual teaching process is seldom analyzed sufficiently. With MIS, greater attention could be devoted to analyzing actual classroom events. A recent study by a private concern of a junior high school of 1500 pupils contained an interesting profile of activities and time allocation of the teachers. Factors such as the instructional activity, teaching method, equipment, group size and skill level of pupils were classified by means of a six-digit coding system. The objective was to improve the utilization of teachers' competence, and several provocative observations emerged from the data collection and analysis:

1. Only about 53 per cent of the teachers' time was spent on instruction, of which 13 per cent was devoted to teaching new material and 40 per cent to practice, repetition, and testing.
2. The actual planning phase of the preparation of lessons accounted for only 3.1 per cent of the teachers' time.
3. Thirty-six per cent of the teachers' time was spent on nonprofessional or nonproductive tasks, such as clerical duties and monitoring of student work.
4. Audio-visual equipment was used during 29 per cent of lessons, and the net use was 5 per cent of the total lesson time.
5. Forty per cent of the teachers' activities were found to be suitable for delegation to assistants or teacher aids, and 27 per cent for transfer to some form of instructional media.
6. Although the school claimed to be overcrowded, the net utilization of the classrooms amounted to only 45 per cent. Thirty-eight per cent of the classrooms were unused, and 17 per cent of the desks were vacant, indicating unused capacity.[11]

[10] *A Guide to Systems Planning* (Seattle, Wash.: Public Schools of Seattle, February 6, 1966), p. 12.

[11] Fred C. Manasse, *Crisis in School Finance*, paper prepared for, and distributed by, H. B. Maynard and Co., Inc., Management Research Division, New York, 1967, Mimeograph, pp. 6–7.

Other areas of the teaching process can be examined and graphically displayed on a master plan with a MIS. In supporting the teacher, the objective is to pinpoint sources of potential improvement that will lead to better utilization of limited funds, materials, and personnel in the teaching-learning process.

Informing staff and community

In most school districts that are presently attempting to develop program budgeting, the superintendent was the key figure in the decision to introduce the planning innovation. It is assumed that this pattern will continue, and that chief school officers will be well advised to "sell" PPBS to boards of education, central office and building level administrators, teachers, and the general public.[12] It is essential to make a special effort to describe the merits of program budgeting, to dispel the fears of thoughtful critics who foresee some of the shortcomings of this approach, and to consider the advantages that will accrue to each of the persons in these roles.

Staff-public relations

The superintendent might stress the advantages for each role as follows: (1) board of education—a better basis for making policy, assessing performance, determining future year costs of present decisions, and reporting budgets to the public; (2) administrators—a comprehensive executive tool for engaging in long-range planning, utilizing systems analysis procedures in defining objectives, weighing alternatives, evaluating programs, and allocating human and material resources; (3) teachers—a means of involving instructional personnel in policy formulation, curricular program design, long-range planning, and providing greater assistance to teachers with data processing and other supportive services; and (4) general public—furnishing a means by which the schools report their expenditures on the basis of programs and offering a framework for

[12] Pupils are not being overlooked, inasmuch as they should be the prime beneficiaries of the ultimate benefits of program budgeting. However, at this stage, it is difficult to ascertain just how, or whether, to inform them of how they can be involved in school planning with PPBS. Perhaps they can be introduced to planning avenues at a later stage without using technical terminology.

transforming public preferences first into public school policy and then into school programs.

The extent of success in the campaign to promote program budgeting may mean the difference between enthusiastic reception for a new approach to supporting instructional improvement or outright disdain for another example of administratively imposed red tape. The reaction of individuals at all levels within a school system can be expected to vary greatly. At least four distinct types of persons (in terms of reaction) may be found: (1) the *advocate*, who believes that PPBS represents a substantial improvement over existing approaches and should be adopted; (2) the *ambivalent*, whose conflicting feelings about the advantages and disadvantages of the new framework prevent him from taking a consistent pro or con position; (3) the *apathetic*, who shows indifference towards the issue of improving educational planning; and (4) the *opponent*, who perceives program budgeting as an untested, threatening, potentially dangerous device that places supreme confidence in analytical tools which cannot be applied to the context of education.

In preparing his campaign to familiarize persons with program budgeting and systems procedures, the administrator should consider the anticipated consequences of correspondence and meetings with members of the school and community. He should, therefore, acknowledge that there may be some unanticipated consequences from the new planning approach. Past experience indicates that many educators react negatively, or at best in a neutral manner, to the topic of PPBS on the initial occasion in which it is described. A "soft-sell" approach that utilizes visual media and minimizes quantitative analysis may result in more enthusiastic support for the concept in districts where innovations are accepted on a highly selective basis. After careful planning of a campaign to gather support for PPBS, formal and informal means can be employed in utilizing the media of press, broadcasting, brochures, letters, bulletins, speeches at staff meetings, luncheon groups, parents groups, and other means.

Communications

An important part of the installation phase of PPBS involves correspondence with administrators and teachers that provides background information, objectives of the new program, illustrative program structures, technical manuals, and directions for completing forms pertaining to programs, objectives, output measures, facilities, materials, personnel, future plans, and so forth. Preparation of written narrative-style guidelines is improved with the usage of several rules:

1. *Use simple words* to improve clarity and understanding.
2. *Use short sentences* to increase the attention span.
3. *Use present tense* to avoid complex sentence structure.
4. *Use straight order,* that is, subject, verb, object, to make reading easier.

Another technique that may be used to write formal procedures is called "playscript." Borrowed from the style of stagecraft, the playscript style identifies responsibility of each actor (or member of an organization) in logical sequence. It tells WHO does WHAT, WHEN. Each activity begins with a verb that propels action forward in a readable, understandable manner. Matthies[13] helped to develop this approach after his research of numerous business firms convinced him of the need for improved techniques of procedures writing. Table 19 contains an illustration of playscript usage with PPBS procedures.

TABLE 19

ILLUSTRATION OF PLAYSCRIPT STYLE FOR PREPARING PPBS GUIDELINES

RESPONSIBILITY	ACTION	DATE
Superintendent	Establishes PPB cycle for the coming school year.	August 1
Building Principal	Prepares Program Element Summary Data (PESD) sheet.	October 1
Program Chairman	Prepares Program Memorandum Cost Data (PM–6) form.	March 1
Classroom Teacher	Reviews program structure, objectives and performance indicators, and makes recommendations for changes to program chairman.	June 1

[13] Leslie Matthies, *Systemation: A Semi-Monthly Letter on Systems Trends and Techniques,* Nos. 114 and 115 (1963). See also Chester Kiser, *Communication in a Program Budgeting System,* paper presented at Section Meeting, national convention of Association for Educational Data Systems, Detroit, Mich., May 1–3, 1967, Mimeograph, 10 pp.

Designing technical manuals

The installation of PPBS can be expected to arouse some resistance from personnel who doubt the merits of the approach for one reason or another. In order to minimize this opposition, and to ensure fairly smooth adoption of the new procedures, it would be desirable to prepare technical manuals that describe in concise terms the operational procedures for central-office financial and curriculum administrators, principals, supervisors, department or program chairmen, and other personnel. These manuals should not be too extensive or abstruse, but they should delimit the responsibilities and procedural activities for each member participating in the planning process. Primary consideration should be given to the development of guidelines for teachers that clearly describe the overall program design for each teacher's area of specialization and his role in program planning. Teachers' manuals should also include descriptions of objectives, resources and facilities available, long-range planning, evaluative criteria, the process of invoking innovations, determination of priorities, and administrative assistance available with MIS and PPBS.

The kinds of manuals needed will vary among schools, but the topics might include program design, preparation of program reports, analyses of accomplishments, multiyear planning calendars, budget preparation, cost accounting procedures, data processing and information management, and special studies, among others. Manuals have been developed, although they are not reproduced here, for many of the organizations that have adopted program budgeting and are mentioned elsewhere in this text. The entire system should operate within the framework of overall policy guidance and dialogue between teachers and the central administrative staff. Formal planning may be unpalatable to some, and PPBS is not likely to alter this kind of outlook. Furthermore, some administrators may misuse the concept and treat PPBS as an end in itself and not as a supportive means for improving the teaching-learning process in the classroom.

Preparing the popularized budget document

The detailed budget document that is prepared for internal planning purposes by a school district may be considered too comprehensive for general distribution. In such a case, it might be desirable to prepare a popularized, or general presentation, budget that contains extractions of salient portions from the detailed document and that reports expenditures on the basis of programs. Sound fisco-educational planning requires the design of an overall educational plan, and its transformation into programs, as prerequisites to devising a composite financial plan. During at least the first several years in which an organization attempts to develop PPBS procedures, it is desirable to report expenditures by means of two types of budget: the conventional object of expenditure type, and the program-budget format. Such reporting would minimize confusion for lay persons, and would provide ample time for the program budget to prove its worth. It is likely that organizations will wish to maintain both budgets for an indefinite time. The traditional function-object budget would be used to report inputs, the program budget to report outputs; thus each would complement the other. There is much variation among school districts as to the content and format of the document that may be distributed to the public. General guidelines are offered below for the construction of the budget document for districts that adopt program budgeting for the first time.[14] The program budget publication will retain some of the contents of traditional, line-item school budgets.

General Contents

1. Letter of transmittal: briefly and concisely describes issues of basic concern to taxpayers.
2. Statement of explanation: describes PPBS, and outlines the advantages of this approach for the school system.
3. A table of contents: pages should be numbered.
4. Traditional budget: report of proposed expenditures, by function.
5. Program budget: report of proposed expenditures, by program (the totals for this and the traditional budget are equal).

[14] A number of authors have provided suggestions to school business administrators in the preparation of conventional budgets. Among these are: Cris A. DeYoung, *Budgeting in Public Schools* (Chicago: John S. Swift Co., revised 1950); Frederick W. Hill and James W. Colmey, *School Business Administration* (Minneapolis: Denison, 1964), Chapter 6; Stephen J. Knezovich and John Guy Fowlkes, *Business Management of Local School Systems* (New York: Harper and Brothers, 1960), Chapter 2; Leon Ovsiew and William B. Castetter, *Budgeting for Better Schools* (Englewood Cliffs, N.J.: Prentice-Hall, 1960); and some state education departments prepare handbooks on budget preparation.

6. Summary of anticipated receipts: detailed on the basis of source.
7. Program accomplishments: make use of performance indicators.
8. Long-range plans: projections of programs and costs.
9. Descriptive data and comparative analyses: report of pupil projections, general growth patterns, and other observed trends.
10. Tax information: full and assessed valuation data, required tax rate compared with past rates, equalization data, clear explanation of reasons for changes in tax rates.
11. Detailed report of budget appropriations: breakdown of account items in sufficient detail.
12. Explanation of changes: describes why there were increases or decreases in general fund accounts.
13. Glossary of terms: defines important terms used in the documents.
14. Appendices: supportive information, such as bonded indebtedness schedules, salary schedules, unit cost analyses, organization charts, notices of public meetings, and voting requirements.

General Format

1. Cover: simple but effective.
2. Size of pages: easily handled.
3. Typing: reproduced on reasonably good paper.
4. Editing: checked for errors of content and style.
5. Graphic presentation: statistical charting for summarization.
6. Binding: attractive, durable and economical.
7. Length: this will vary, but a suggested maximum is fifty pages; the reader should not be overwhelmed by myriad details, and excessive details and verbiage should be omitted.
8. Numbering: pages numbered (accounts should be coded and there should be a table of contents and index).
9. Authority: legal name of school district and identification of persons responsible for budget preparation.
10. Media for distribution: radio, television, newspapers, display windows of community stores, newsletters, periodic bulletins, citizens committees, and public forums.

Program review and budget preparation is a year-round process of reevaluating and updating program objectives, performance and costs. With PPBS, program review is related to the budget cycle, which in turn is affected by state regulations and other factors. In preparing the budget document for the public, the administrator should take full advantage of the informational assets of PPBS. With the program budget, he can show how public funds are supporting programs, and these programs are expressed in understandable terms, rather than in the technical jargon found in most present school budgets. Improved public support for the schools may result from this approach. Appendix G contains a function-object budget format and a program budget format for a small local school district.

Conclusion

This chapter dealt with some of the operational issues which school administrators might face in developing program budgeting, systems procedures, and data processing. Discussion areas were selected that appeared to highlight the concepts introduced, but it should not be implied that these would be the only areas involved in an actual installation process. The roles of the various participants in local school planning would be modified as a district develops a full-scale forward thrust with PPBS; thus it is imperative that the staff and public be well-informed about new approaches to instructional and fiscal planning.

Exhortations to spend more money, develop better instruments and more materials, increase responsiveness and tractability, and employ more people may be one of the results obtained from a systems approach to educational planning, but if it is the only consequence, PPBS is not likely to engender much enthusiasm. Likewise, utterances of "what we need is . . . ," followed by a list of items such as "more resources, better teachers, smaller classes . . . ," are of little value to school officials who are already well aware of such shortcomings. If it is indeed possible to offer a single comprehensive framework for organizing all of the activities of a school system, PPBS comes closer to such a model than any other existing format. Although it has limitations, the program budgeting process appears to represent a substantial improvement over conventional planning and budgeting practices in education. When one considers that, using a generalization, *budgets did not exist prior to the 1920's,* considerable progress has been made in refining budgetary practices within the past fifty years.

Suggestion for Discussion

Describe the activities of the various central-office administrators in creating, executing, supporting, reporting, and evaluating PPBS and MIS procedures in a local school district.

Selected References

American Association of School Administrators, *Electronic Data Processing and the School Administrator.* Washington, D.C.: American Association of School Administrators, 1967.

Costa, Arthur L. "Synergism: Administrative Involvement of the Curriculum Worker," *Educational Leadership,* XXV, No. 5 (February, 1968), 418-422.

Dade County Public Schools, *A Program Budget Research Proposal.* Miami, Florida: Dade County Board of Public Instruction, November, 1966, Mimeograph, 79 pp. A bibliography of 86 references is included.

State of California, *Programming and Budgeting System.* Sacramento: Department of Finance, May 1, 1967. 70 pp.

State of New York, *Guidelines for Integrated Planning-Programming-Budgeting.* Albany: Office of Planning Coordination and Division of the Budget, 1967. 64 pp.

United States Civil Service Commission, Instructional materials used for internal orientation and government-sponsored training courses in PPBS.

The principal objective of PPBS is to improve the basis for major program decisions.

Charles S. Schultze

Chapter Nine

PROGRAM BUDGETING IN HIGHER EDUCATION

by Robert Pavese *

In recent years tremendous demands have been placed upon public and private institutions of higher education for improved services in instruction and research and for social, cultural, and economic improvements in the urban community. Factors that add to these critical demands are an increased population, a larger proportion of high school students entering college, projections that student enrollments will double between 1960 and 1970 and triple by 1985,[1] and changes in social and technological areas.

The warnings of red ink on university ledgers reflect the serious strain on their resources. Private colleges and universities are facing particularly difficult financial prospects, and the less well-endowed institutions are hard-pressed as they attempt to compete for faculty, programs, and facilities. The cost of higher education is rising much faster than academic revenue, and a number of prestigious institutions have sizeable annual operating deficits. Although two thirds of the nation's 2200 colleges and universities are private, their share of student enrollment slipped from 50 per cent in 1950 to approximately 34 per cent in 1968. The injection of new funds,

* Mr. Pavese is the Budget Director of Long Island University.

[1] United States Bureau of the Census, "Projections of School and College Enrollment in the United States to 1985," *Population Estimates* (Washington, D.C.: U.S. Government Printing Office, May 21, 1966), pp. 1–8.

from state and federal governments, expanded endowment funds, and other sources will be needed to keep pace with rapidly expanding staff salaries and costly research, library, and computer facilities. In view of these forces, one of the perennial dilemmas facing higher education is how to obtain sufficient financial support. It is imperative that these educational institutions employ all available tools to allocate scarce resources efficiently for those present and future programs demanded by their rapidly growing and changing clientele. The program budget structure presented later is appropriate for junior-community colleges, four-year colleges, and universities.

To maximize efficient use of limited human and nonhuman resources, an institution of higher education should first prepare a long-range financial plan to use as a guide in reaching its goals and objectives. Far-sighted planning is an essential requisite for current decisions that may require permanent investments in personnel, plant, and educational programs. Before a financial plan is devised, the objectives and general purposes of the institution are to be identified, analyzed, and evaluated in relation to its desired educational role.

> Since no educational institution can possibly do everything that there is to be done—be "all things to all people," as the saying goes—it has an obligation both to itself and to its contributors to develop carefully its notion of itself, to decide what part it is to play in the total educational effort of the nation, region, and state, what quality and variety of educational programs it is to sponsor, and which among its existing activities it will augment, diminish, or do away with entirely.[2]

A number of universities have pioneered in the development of new ways to plan for and finance university growth. To cite one, Yale University announced the largest fund-raising goal ever established by a university, 388 million dollars between 1968 and 1977. This program has implications for all private institutions, more and more of which will face deficits. The basic reason for such an ambitious program is that Yale's educational costs were rising at about 8.5 per cent annually, but its income was rising at about 7 per cent. To close this gap, the University created a new man-

[2] Frank Dilley, "Program Budgeting in the University Setting," *The Educational Record,* XLVII (Fall, 1966), 475.

agement team, established an investment firm with the objective of higher investment return, and instituted accounting and budgeting systems designed to promote efficiency. Program budgeting will not solve the problem of how to obtain more dollars, but it will facilitate better management of the funds available.

Determination of Objectives

The basic purpose, or mission, of most higher educational institutions is to advance knowledge by means of demonstrated scholarship; every dollar spent and each operational plan should lead toward the realization of this mission. Listed below are some items to be used as a basis for determining the desired long-range objectives:

1. The courses taught presently and those proposed during the next ten years.
2. The degrees granted and new degrees proposed for the future.
3. A profile of the students currently enrolled and an indication of the profile of students to attend in future years.
4. Requirements for admissions to the degree programs.
5. The time allotted to complete degree programs.
6. The role of the institution in the community.
7. The results expected and required of faculty in teaching, training, research, and scholarly publications.
8. The expected benefits the student may receive after completing a degree program.
9. The role of the trustees and administration.
10. Federal, state, and private financial support for the institution.
11. Educational plans of other public and private institutions, with particular emphasis placed on those in the same community.
12. Plans for cooperation with neighboring institutions.

The information required may be contained in the formal charter of the institution, the minutes of the board of trustees, internal academic and financial plans, faculty committee reports, evaluation committee reports, consultant's recommendations, federal and state studies, and research findings. It is important that all of this information be compiled and written in one document to guide the institution in establishing and approving policies and procedures that will result in the accomplishment of its objectives. There should be a continuing review of present and proposed programs to determine whether they are in agreement with the accepted purposes and objectives. The energies of all members of the institution of higher education should be devoted to programs that promote the established goals.

The institution should also determine the level of enrollment expected in each year for the next ten years and base the financial plan on this projected enrollment. This plan should be continuously reviewed and revised as necessary. There are times when an institution finds enrollment far in excess of available space. Even after maximum utilization of classrooms, the institution may be faced with overcrowding. Space in the immediate area may be rented, temporary buildings may be erected, premiums may be paid to speed up work on buildings under construction, furniture orders may be rushed at the expense of quality and cost, and money may be borrowed to pay the increased costs of construction. The result is that resources available for the basic mission of teaching diminish. Comprehensive enrollment projections for the next ten years should be available, giving totals not only of the sum enrollment of full-time and part-time students, but also totals of each of the programs of the institution. Enrollment projections will not only assist planners in allocating space but also in planning for personnel, library, equipment, and supplies. Reviewing publications on enrollment of the Bureau of the Census; Department of Health, Education, and Welfare; state; city; and other institutions of higher education may be helpful.

The faculty-student ratio should also be determined in both the academic and research areas for the total institution and for each of its program areas.

The Financial Plan: Current Budgetary Practices

After the general purposes and objectives are defined, a financial plan is formulated to guide and control the educational programs of the institution. Presently, a budget is the instrument used in planning and control. As stated by the American Council on Education:

> Budgets are statements of estimated income and expenditures for fixed periods or for specific projects. They express in terms of dollars the educational program of the institution. Their approval by proper authorities constitutes authorization to incur the expenditure set forth therein and to collect the anticipated income. One of the purposes of budgets is to insure that an institution does not obligate itself in excess of available resources. The approved budgets of an educational institution are the primary instruments of fiscal control.[3]

A review of current budgetary practices in higher education indicates that the budget is designed for short periods, usually one year. The long-range costs for commitments approved in the one year budget may be overlooked. Costs for a particular program may be distributed among many different budget line-items; the actual cost may be difficult and at times almost impossible to obtain. In many instances a budget line-item is prepared by adding an increment to a base obtained from the prior year's results. Possibly, an evaluation is made of an addition of a new program, new construction, and new members of the staff.

Usually there is a lack of participatory planning by all personnel involved in the educational program. Budgets in many institutions are prepared by the head of a department, with or without consultation of other members of the department; then go through the normal chain of command for review and approval. It is possible for any link in this chain to take a pencil in hand and alter the budget without necessary evaluation of existing and proposed programs. At times, there may be no relation, or only a weak relation, of an approved budget item to the stated objectives of the institution.

For efficient use of available resources, the whole budget is to be analyzed to compare all the possible means of carrying out the functions determined by the objectives of the institution. In this respect, and in the absence of long range projections, participatory planning, cost analysis and program analysis, the current budgetary practices are limited as a tool for fact-finding, planning, and reporting to the decision makers of the institution. In addition to the fiscal control of the present input-oriented budget, there is a need

[3] National Committee on the Preparation of a Manual on College and University Business Administration, *College and University Business Administration,* I (Washington, D.C.: American Council on Education, 1952), 23.

for an output-oriented financial planning tool known as a *program budget.*

The Program Budget and Analytical Techniques

As defined in Chapter Four, a program budget is organized in terms of the explicitly stated objectives of the institution of higher education, contains alternative ways to achieve the objective, has means for measuring the resources used and the results or output of the operation, facilitates the making of decisions, cuts across departmental lines, and is organized for longer planning periods (five to ten years) to provide full cost implications of present decisions.

> A budget is undeniably a primary instrument of fiscal control. But it is more than that. A budget should also lay bare the efficiency (or lack thereof) with which a university is combining its available resources to achieve results that promote the goals and objectives of that university. A university budget should not only reflect fiduciary responsibilities but should reflect, in a manner of speaking, the economic responsibilities of that university.[4]

The primary services to be performed may be listed under eight program areas: division of humanities; division of life and physical sciences; division of social sciences; services to the divisions of instruction; student, faculty, and staff services; public services; research and development; and general support. Dilley cited an English department as a program and provided the following definition:

> An English department is a program, for it has specific objectives and functions, it has measurable inputs and outputs (even though aspects of output may be difficult to quantify), it makes policy decisions both as to objectives and as to allocation of resources to meet those objectives, and it is a part of larger programs, and college and the university.[5]

In measuring the programs quantitatively, a wide variety of analytical techniques are available such as management information

[4] Harry Williams, *Planning for Effective Resource Allocation in Universities* (Washington, D.C.: American Council on Education, 1966), p. 14.

[5] Frank Dilley, "Program Budgeting in the University Setting," *The Educational Record,* XLVII (Fall, 1966), 478.

systems, operations research, input-output analysis, cost-effectiveness analysis, tradeoff analysis, and PERT. Not surprisingly, an increasing number of colleges and universities are attempting to systematize their fiscal and curricular planning efforts by means of some of these emerging planning strategies. Several recent seminars that were devoted to systems procedures, including program budgeting, are indicative of the growing interest in better planning. One seminar, entitled "Computer Assisted Planning for Colleges and Universities,"[6] introduced college and university personnel to new methods in the use of the computer in long-range planning. Information requested by a planner was fed into a time sharing computer miles away, calculated rapidly, and fed back within ten to fifteen minutes. It was possible for a planner to see, within minutes, the effect his decisions would have on the institution's planning for the next ten years. Another session on the use of models in higher education was sponsored by the United States Office of Education in late 1967. Although the topics ranged from endowment management and portfolio turnover to budget models and capital expenditure projections, the symposium reflected the efforts of numerous institutions, including Yale, California, Toronto, and Michigan State, to devise conceptual management techniques.[7]

Any of these techniques or a combination of them may be used. For example, cost-benefit analysis may be used as a tool in determining the feasibility of a new program, part of which may call for the construction of a new building. The construction superintendent may then use a PERT network during construction of the building. These analytical techniques help the decision maker examine and compare the alternative courses of action in terms of costs, benefits, and time.

> In practically no case should it be assumed that the results of the analysis will *make* the decision. The really interesting problems are just too difficult, and there are too many intangibles (e.g., political,

[6] Conducted by Peat, Marwick, Mitchell and Company and Peat, Marwick, Livingston and Company, Boston, Mass., June 18–20, 1967.

[7] "College and University Systems," a subsection of the "Symposium on Operations Analysis of Education," sponsored by Division of Operations Analysis, National Center for Educational Statistics, Office of Education, United States Department of Health, Education and Welfare, Washington, D.C., November 19–22. The results of this symposium will be published in late 1968.

psychological, and sociological) considerations that cannot be taken into account in the analytical process, especially in a quantitative sense. In sum, the analytical process should be directed toward assisting the decisionmaker in such a way that [hopefully!] his intuition and judgment are better than they would be without the results of the analysis.[8]

Devising a Program Budget for a College

After determining the long range objectives and purposes and defining a program along with the measurement criteria, the next step is to devise a program budget. The number and types of the proposed programs will be listed; a statement will be made of the objectives of each program; the resources and output characteristics will be identified; the sources of income generated within each program will be identified; the time dimensions constructed; and some budget formats will be displayed.

As an illustration of programs, the subsequent discussions will focus upon an exemplary undergraduate liberal arts and science college. Eight programs and their objectives will be listed.

The list of eight general program areas is in line with the definition of systems analysis presented in Chapter Two; the sequence begins with general, undifferentiated components and concludes with specific, differentiated parts. These illustrative programs are generalized, but each eventually can be shown to have many subprograms and program elements.

Program I, division of humanities

This is a direct instructional area involving teachers and students. The major courses offered are English, foreign languages, art, philosophy, speech, and theatre arts; they are designed to develop independent thinking; fundamental skills; student intellectual, moral, and cultural growth; and an appreciation and enjoyment of the arts. The degree of Bachelor of Arts will be granted upon completion of 128 credit hours with a quality point ratio of at least 2.0 (C) in all academic work.

[8] David Novick, editor, *Program Budgeting: Program Analysis and the Federal Government* (Cambridge: Harvard University Press, 1965), p. 67.

Program II, division of life and physical sciences

This is a direct instructional area involving teachers and students. The major courses offered are biology, chemistry, mathematics, and physics—all of which are designed to contain the principles underlying the sciences. The primary objective of this division is to prepare students for advanced work in the sciences. The degree of Bachelor of Science will be granted upon completion of 128 credit hours with a quality point ratio of at least 2.0 (C) in all academic work.

Program III, division of social sciences

This is a direct instructional area involving teachers and students. The major courses offered are economics, history, political science, sociology, and psychology. Each course is designed to provide the foundations and principles for the student to study concepts concerning the individual, group, organizational, and cultural behavior. Relationships of social science principles to the humanities, and to the life and physical sciences are emphasized. The degree of Bachelor of Arts will be granted upon completion of 128 credit hours with a quality point ratio of at least 2.0 (C) in all academic work.

Program IV, services to the divisions of instruction

This service function to the instructional units has six subclassifications—admissions, registrar, bursar, counseling, library, and data processing.

In admissions, the activities are recruiting, interviewing, evaluating, selecting, and admitting students for instruction.

In the registrar's office, the activities are registering students, classroom scheduling, recording of grades, granting of degrees and transmitting of students' records to other institutions of higher education and to employers.

In the bursar's office, the activities are collecting tuition and fees from students, maintaining and controlling student financial records.

In counseling, the activity is consulting with students by faculty, professional staff, and religious leaders concerning academic programs, progress of the student, personal problems, and moral and spiritual guidance.

The activities of the sixth subclassification, data processing, include providing assistance to the admissions department, registrar, bursar, and counseling center in performing their jobs, and assistance to the instructional divisions in teaching and research.

The final unit, the library, has as its activities acquisition, preparation, and circulation of books, periodicals, pamphlets, government publications, and audio-visual material.

Program V, student, faculty, and staff services

This is a personal service to students, faculty, and staff in providing food services, housing, financial aid, recreation, health services, parking, and entertainment.

Program VI, public services

This is a service provided to people other than the faculty, staff, and degree credit students. One example is instruction given to students in subjects that do not carry credit toward a degree. The noncredit courses are listed as adult studies, workshops, institutes, and conferences. Instruction is also made available to the public through radio and television programs, a college or university press, and in lectures, art exhibits, cultural events, and consulting services.

Service is also provided to people through participation in community projects.

Program VII, research and development

This service involving students, faculty, and staff has three subclassifications: (1) institutional research and planning, (2) professional development, and (3) sponsored research.

Institutional research and planning contains activities that involve the continual investigation, experimentation, review, and revision of new and accepted facts, theories, and policies affecting the development of the institution.

Professional development involves assistance to the staff for independent research, writing, traveling, and schooling.

In sponsored research, financed by private and public agencies, the activities involve investigation, experimentation, review, and reporting of new and accepted facts.

Program VIII, general support

This category encompasses activities that render supportive services to all the other programs. It is a kind of residual classification.

The support units are as follows:

1. Board of Trustees
2. President
3. Vice President, Financial Administration
4. Fund Raising
5. Alumni Relations
6. Personnel Administration
7. Public Relations
8. Institutional Memberships
9. Professional Fees
10. Plant Operation and Maintenance (for Support Units)
11. Fringe Benefits (for Support Units)
12. Debt Service (portion not directly charged to other programs)

These constitute the eight general programs for our illustrative undergraduate liberal arts and science college. The same format could easily be applied to a junior college or university.

Program Resources, or Input

The input, or financial and nonfinancial resources for each of the eight programs can be distributed among six categories as follows:

1. Personnel Employed: the number and type of positions required for each program and the average salary and work load in each position; examples of some of the positions are:
   a. Professors (Full, Associate, Assistant)

   b. Instructors
   c. Lecturers
   d. Teaching Fellows, Graduate Assistants
   e. Administrators
   f. Secretaries
   g. Librarians
   h. Building and Grounds Workers

2. Students: the number in each of the instructional programs, including full-time and part-time (stated as full-time equivalent).
3. Class size ratios: the average class size for each of the instructional programs.
4. Instructional courses: the number and description of the courses in each of the instructional programs.
5. Supplies, equipment, and furnishings: an inventory of materials and a listing of items requested to be purchased for each of the programs.
6. Physical facilities: an inventory listing of the number, square feet, and utilization of classrooms, offices, laboratories, and libraries.

Program Output

The output for the programs can be identified as follows:

1. Degrees: the number and type of degrees granted.
2. Degree courses: the number of students in each major and elective course; the number of student credit and class hours provided.
3. Library growth: the number of volumes in the library.
4. Research and scholarly publications: expressed in terms of research grants and research publications.
5. Contributions of the institution to the community: expressed in terms of lectures, cultural events, art exhibits, and urban and community projects.
6. Standardized test results: performance of students on standardized tests given in the freshman and senior years and on graduate admissions tests.
7. The number of seniors admitted to graduate schools.
8. Alumni: questionnaires filled out by alumni giving a personal history after receiving their degrees, listing positions, salaries, partici-

pation in community affairs, graduate studies, and their evaluation of the institution.

9. Evaluations of programs by college and university accrediting associations.
10. Self-evaluation by college and university committees.

Sources of Income

The sources of income generated for each program will be identified and applied to the program earning the income.

Programs I, II, III, IV, divisions of humanities, life and physical sciences, social sciences, and service to the divisions of instruction:

1. tuition income
2. laboratory fees
3. application fees
4. state appropriations
5. gifts
6. endowment income
7. grants

Program V, student, faculty, and staff services:

1. student activity fees
2. athletic income
3. room and board fees
4. food services, cafeteria sales
5. gifts
6. parking fees
7. health service fees
8. government grants
9. library fines

Program VI, public services:

1. admission fees to cultural events
2. fees for noncredit courses
3. book sales

Program VII, research and development:

1. government gifts and grants
2. industry grants
3. gifts

Program VIII, general support

1. unrestricted gifts
2. endowment income

Suggestive budget formats[9] to support the eight general programs of the illustrative college are shown in Tables 20, 21, and 22.

Summary and Conclusions

The procedures described and recommended above for program budgeting are additional tools to be used with the basic input-oriented conventional budget and accounting system. They are not designed to replace the line-item budgets. The program budget is a comprehensive, output-oriented policy and planning budget, and is thus not restricted to the fiscal control functions of a conventional budget.

Summarized are some of the advantages of using a program budget in higher education:

1. The programs of a college are organized on the basis of systems analysis rationality.
2. Actual, total costs of a program are obtained. The budget cuts across traditional departmental lines and gives the cost, in both financial and nonfinancial resources, for extended time horizons (five to ten years).
3. Direction is given to everyone in the junior college, college, or university family, as to the general objectives and goals of the institution and to the explicit objectives of each program. Input-oriented conventional budgets may not make available the future plans of other programs within the institution.
4. Participatory planning is encouraged.
5. Allocation of resources is made on a more rational basis. Evaluation of programs is made by means of a wide variety of analytical techniques.
6. There is an emphasis on outputs or desired results, and all resources are directed to these outputs.
7. All programs, existing and new, are continually reviewed and revised on both a formal and informal basis.
8. Fund-raising activities may be coordinated with the long-term planning objectives of the program budget.
9. A Management Information System (MIS) can be developed around a program budget structure in order to provide data for progress reporting and program planning and control.

[9] See, for other examples, Harry Williams, *Planning for Effective Resource Allocation in Universities* (Washington, D.C.: American Council on Education, 1952), pp. 8, 22–24, 67, 71–73.

TABLE 20

PROGRAM BUDGET FORMAT FOR A SPECIFIC PROGRAM
PROGRAM I, DIVISION OF HUMANITIES

	1970		1971	1972	1973	1974	1975	1976	1977	1978	1979
	Number or Unit Cost	Total									
I. Revenue											
A. Tuition											
1. Students (full time equivalent)											
a. Number											
b. Average class size											
c. Tuition per year	$										
d. Tuition income		$									
B. Fees		$									
C. Gifts and grants		$									
D. Endowment		$									
TOTAL REVENUE		$									
II. Expenditures											
A. Personnel											
1. Full Professors											
a. Number											
b. Average salary	$										
c. Total salaries - Full Professor (a times b)		$									
2. Associate Professors		$									
3. Assistant Professors		$									
4. Instructors		$									
5. Clerical		$									
6. Student Faculty Ratio											
B. Physical Facilities											
1. Classrooms											
a. Number											
b. Average square feet per room											
c. Maintenance cost per square foot	$										
d. Cost of maintenance (a times b times c)		$									
e. Debt service per square foot											
f. Cost of debt service		$									
2. Offices		$									
C. Fringe benefits		$									
D. Supplies		$									
E. Equipment		$									
F. Furniture		$									
TOTAL EXPENDITURES		$									

TABLE 21

PROGRAM BUDGET FORMAT: A SUMMARY OF ALL PROGRAMS FOR ONE YEAR COLLEGE OF LIBERAL ARTS AND SCIENCE—1970

	Program I		Program II	Program III	Program IV	Program V	Program VI	Program VII	Program VIII	Total
	Number or Unit Cost	Total								
I. Revenue										
A. Tuition										
1. Students										
a. Number										
b. Tuition per year	$									
c. Class size										
d. Tuition income (a times b)		$								
B. Fees		$								
C. Gifts		$								
D. Endowment		$								
E. Dormitory fees		$								
F. Fees for noncredit courses		$								
TOTAL REVENUE		$								
II. Expenditures										
A. Personnel										
1. Full Professors										
a. Number										
b. Average salary	$									
c. Total salary		$								
2. Associate Professors		$								
3. Assistant Professors		$								
4. Instructors		$								
5. Student Faculty Ratio										
6. Clerical		$								
B. Physical Facilities		$								
1. Classrooms		$								
2. Offices		$								
3. Laboratories		$								
4. Dormitory rooms		$								
C. Fringe benefits		$								
D. Supplies		$								
E. Equipment		$								
TOTAL EXPENDITURES		$								

TABLE 22

PROGRAM BUDGET FORMAT FOR TEN-YEAR PERIOD COLLEGE OF LIBERAL ARTS AND SCIENCE, 1970–1979

	1970		1971	1972	1973	1974	1975	1976	1977	1978	1979
	Number or Unit Cost	Total									
I. Revenue											
A. Tuition											
1. Students											
a. Number											
b. Class size											
c. Tuition per year	$										
d. Tuition income		$									
B. Fees		$									
C. Gifts		$									
D. Endowment		$									
E. Dormitory fees		$									
F. Fees for noncredit courses		$									
TOTAL REVENUE		$									
II. Expenditures											
A. Personnel											
1. Full Professors											
a. Number											
b. Average salary	$										
c. Total salary		$									
2. Associate Professors		$									
3. Assistant Professors		$									
4. Instructors		$									
5. Student faculty ratio											
6. Clerical		$									
B. Physical Facilities											
1. Classrooms		$									
2. Offices		$									
3. Laboratories		$									
4. Dormitory rooms		$									
C. Fringe benefits		$									
D. Supplies		$									
E. Equipment		$									
III. Surplus or Deficiency of Revenue over Expenditures		$									

10. The interrelated procedures of planning-programming-budgeting systems (PPBS) can be used to improve the administration of higher education.

There will be difficulties in implementing program budgeting in the junior college, college, or university. Usually, any major proposed change in the operations of the institution is met with some resistance and skepticism. The program administrator must meet this resistance and prove to the faculty and staff that the new system is a substantial improvement over the old system. The cost in dollars and time of administrators and faculty may be high at inception. There will also be problems in collecting and analyzing data, in designing new systems and in administering the program by the present administrators. Perhaps some new planning staff members will be needed, adding to costs.

However, the usefulness of program budgeting, in terms of maximizing the efficient usage of resources and the promotion of well-defined objectives should more than offset the additional costs and problems of inception. Its success in other forms of organization is cited as evidence of its unlimited potential success in the complex arena of higher education. The shortcomings of program budgeting were not considered, inasmuch as the next chapter describes in detail some of the limitations of PPBS in education.

Suggestion for Discussion

Consider alternative program structures that would be appropriate for junior colleges, four-year colleges, and universities.

Selected References

Daniere, Andre, *Higher Education in the American Economy*. New York: Random House, 1964. 220 pp.

Dilley, Frank B., "Program Budgeting in the University Setting," *The Educational Record,* XLVII (Fall, 1966), 474–489.

Harris, Seymour E., *Challenge and Change in American Education*. Berkeley, Calif.: McCutchen, 1965.

———, *Education and Public Policy*. Berkeley, Calif.: McCutchen, 1965.

Hirsch, Werner Z., *The Budget as an Instrument for Medium- and Long-Range Planning and Programming of Education*. Paris: Organization for Economic Cooperation and Development, Directorate for Scientific Affairs, April 3, 1968, Mimeograph, 30 pp.

Judy, Richard W., *et al., Systems Analysis of Alternative Designs of a Faculty*. Paris: Organization for Economic Cooperation and Development, Directorate for Scientific Affairs, April 5, 1968, Mimeograph, 57 pp.

Novick, David, editor, *Program Budgeting: Program Analysis and the Federal Government*. Cambridge: Harvard University Press, 1965. 382 pp.

Williams, Harry, *Planning for Effective Resource Allocation in Universities*. Washington, D.C.: American Council on Education, 1966. 310 pp.

The pathetic fallacy of the expert is to believe that his technical concepts and language can be used to explain the universe.

Meno Lovenstein

Chapter Ten

LIMITATIONS OF PPBS AND RESEARCH NEEDS

The focus upon existing shortcomings of program budgeting is not designed to foster incredulity or to provide a self-defeating detraction from its application to education. Rather, it would seem to call for wider usage of this concept. Even after schools are able to develop appropriate program structures, a good deal of "debugging" of the systems probably will be needed. Before rejecting this new approach on the basis of its present limitations, one should consider the alternatives: incremental planning and conventional, line-item budgets that make no attempt to relate input-oriented expenditures to output-oriented programs. Keep in mind that the very notion of budgeting of any kind is of fairly recent origin. Refinements and improvements of this evolving control and planning technique should be welcome.

If this text appears to encroach upon the borders of administrative and organizational theory at times, no apology is offered. Administrative practice should be rooted in, and logically implied from management science-behavioral systems theory. This distinction between practice and theory is largely one of differing levels of abstraction. Emphasis in contemporary educational administration preparatory programs is away from the "cookbook" study of recipes for specific acts and toward conceptual models that facilitate a transfer of generalized knowledge to specific problems. The program budgets proposed in previous chapters were intended to be generalized models, the structured patterns of which could be transferred, with modifications, to specific educational institutions. Subsequent paragraphs describe controversial issues, liabilities, potential areas of research, and sources of opposition to this conceptual approach to budgeting.

Limitations of the Program Budget Format

Organizational strains are not eliminated

Far from being a panacea, the process of program budgeting will not abolish human conflicts that inevitably seem to accompany human groupings. Capozzola, a specialist in public administration, suggested that the analytical approach of PPBS sets in motion certain forces that may create severe organizational pressures and strains. "Measuring organizational performance quantitatively irritates those who are value-oriented, emotionally oriented, politically oriented, or just do not understand."[1] Program budgeting may initially serve to accentuate conflicts and engender antagonisms as organizational objectives and priorities are exposed in the cold, bold figures of the dollar. It can be anticipated that with the introduction of PPBS, ". . . bureaucratic inertia, vested interests, old prides, honest differences of opinion, and politics do not suddenly disappear."[2]

Program budgeting puts organizational dynamics into the spotlight, and this may foster some discord. Conflicts in schools occur because of disparity between an institution's organizational and *stable functions* (bureaucratic-formal) and its disorganizational and *forward-moving functions* (creative-informal). To illustrate, administrators rely on sanctions, but encourage brainstorming. Or to put it another way, one may observe a high degree of routinization within the very schools that profess to promote innovation. Bureaucracy sometimes tends to preserve and institutionalize the status quo in large schools, and program budgeting can help to reduce, but not

[1] John M. Capozzola, "PPBS: Systemization or Revolution in Government Management," *Governmental Research Association Reporter*, XVIII, No. 1 (First Quarter, 1966), 4.

[2] *Ibid.*

eliminate, this condition. Traditional budget preparation procedures sometimes are devised by entrenched, special interest groups who may not be anxious to encourage the adoption or expansion of PPBS. This can lead to political strains and conflicts within an organization.

Political elements may act as a barrier to PPBS

PPBS is basically an economic concept for budgeting, but in the earthy reality of school districts, the entire budgetary process is more likely to take place in the political arena. The politics of education as a field of study is still in its embryonic stage. Policy formulation in the area of budget planning is rooted in such political elements as persuasion, authority, power, coalitions, coercion, timing, compromise, bargaining, strategy, and many others. Certain members of the educational power structure may view the economic rationality of program budgeting as an infringement upon their domain. Even so, educational planning should be amenable to some amount of economic analysis. One writer even contends that program budgeting can become an integral part of system politics.[3] Whether this happens or not, the fact remains that political influence of some type is exerted throughout most of the budget-making process for education, whether it be at the local, state, or federal level. If the program analyst is a consultant to the school district, he may find that local administrators are not anxious to abandon their power to make decisions in favor of systems procedures. Educational leadership positions are transitory. With high turnover rates in career positions facing them, many administrators are not secure in their leadership positions. Hence, occasionally the attitude toward consulting analysts may be hostile or even envious (if the consultant's salary is quite high). At the local level, PPBS must gain acceptance from those who might be less than enthusiastic over its initial adoption. The case for political rationality and preservation of existing decision structures is stated thus: "A course of action that corrects economic or social deficiencies but increases political

[3] Aaron Wildavsky, "The Political Economy of Efficiency: Cost-Benefit Analysis, Systems Analysis, and Program Budgeting," *Public Administration Review,* XXVI, No. 4 (December, 1966), 305.

difficulties must be rejected, while an action which contributes to political improvement is desirable even if it is not entirely sound from an economic or social standpoint."[4] This idea, which is not a new one, embraces some controversial value positions.

Degree of centralization of authority is not clear

Participatory planning succeeds when all of the members of a school system have an opportunity to share in policy formulation. What are not clear are the relative merits of a highly centralized administrative structure versus a decentralized system. Program budgeting probably can be implemented successfully in either type of setting, although its critics can be expected to accuse PPBS of contributing to the evils of the authority system because of its centralizing bias. Substantial literature on the topics of bureaucracy and formal organizations is available for one who wishes to examine the structural context of educational institutions more thoroughly. It is apparent that consolidation in a number of states resulted in the transformation of many small, local school districts into large, centralized districts. Human life is increasingly becoming organizational life, and the trend in schools seems to be toward greater centralization of authority.[5] Size of schools might conceivably conflict with the human psyche, because employees and clients surrender their identity to the goals of the organization. On the other hand, it may be that large-scale organizations serve to liberate the individual.

The traditional approach in school systems has been to use central budget formulation and central budget administration as a means of unifying the objectives and activities of teachers in a group of elementary and secondary buildings. This approach is not unique to schools, because private enterprises and other public institutions

[4] Paul Diesing, *Reason in Society* (Urbana, Ill.: University of Illinois Press, 1962), p. 228.

[5] For a report of an attempt to construct an operational measure of bureaucracy in education, see Harry J. Hartley, "Educational Bureaucracy, Teacher Orientation, and Selected Criterion Variables," *Journal of Educational Research*, LX, No. 10 (October, 1966), 54–57. The opposing viewpoint holding that bureaucracy is antithetical to creative organizations is expressed well by Warren G. Bennis, "The Coming Death of Bureaucracy," *Think* (November–December, 1966), pp. 30–35.

also tend to use central budget administrations as a means of integrating and controlling the diverse activities of complex organizations. It is possible that program budgeting may, in some cases, accelerate this centralizing bias. An official of the New York City schools, with 1.1 million pupils, described one reason why this could happen: "The developing use of central data banks and computerized decision making all tend to bring decision making closer and closer to the information center. As this decision making occurs at the central logistics and information control points, local administrative personnel seem to assume less significance in the decision making process, the chain of command becomes tighter, and local initiative and responsibility become curtailed." [6] Excess centralization, a relative condition that must be defined by individual local districts, can be as dysfunctional as an insufficient degree of centralization. Educators often express a dislike for centralization (many also dislike administration) and seek some sort of colleagial model in which persons of different ranks are treated as colleagues and decisions are arrived at in a relatively decentralized manner. Although this is not yet a generally observable trend, some persons such as Hill hope to decentralize many of the operations of large school systems. "Controvening this centralizing tendency, there is an increasing awareness that individual identity becomes lost in the mass, and that if democratic government is to be preserved, a way must be found to protect the individual's rights of decision, dissent, and deviation." [7]

Hill's comments were made considerably before the controversial study on decentralization of the nation's largest school district. McGeorge Bundy served as chairman of the 1967 study which recommended that the public schools of New York City should be organized into a Community School System, consisting of a federation of largely autonomous school districts and a central education agency. Bundy's study proposed that from the present thirty, no more than sixty Community School Districts should be created, ranging in size from about 12,000 to 40,000 pupils. This size range was considered large enough to offer ". . . a full range of educa-

[6] Letter from Frederick W. Hill, Deputy Superintendent of Schools, Board of Education, The City of New York, March 1, 1967.

[7] *Ibid.*

tional services and yet small enough to promote administrative flexibility and proximity to community needs and diversity."[8]

New York City is obviously not an appropriate paradigm for small school districts. Thus, the task of determining the appropriate degree of central control should be performed by each school district. In some cases, existing organizational patterns would not have to be disrupted to accommodate the program budget concept.

USOE program structure is not applicable to local schools

The preliminary program classifications developed for the United States Office of Education will be of little value for local districts seeking guidelines. The programs supported by the USOE are quite unlike the instructional programs offered by schools. This lack of transfer of the federal program structure to a local setting may be good, because local districts will be encouraged to devise unique program structures independently. They need not accept a general format from Washington. If local autonomy is worth preserving in education, local school officials have the opportunity to use program budgeting to show how their system differs from other local schools on the basis of programs, operational objectives, and accomplishments. An idealized program budget was constructed several years ago for the USOE. It consisted of seven major programs that are shown in Table 23. The Office of Education supports these programs through grants and loans.

Cost Analysis Methods Have Limitations

One of the features of PPBS is the analytical process that permits a systematic examination of alternative courses of action and their implications. This may be called benefit-cost analysis, cost-effectiveness analysis, cost-utility analysis or by the name of some other offspring of systems analysis. The concepts overlap in meaning, and their virtues have been described elsewhere. Some sage might one day suggest that the technique of benefit-cost analysis itself should

[8] McGeorge Bundy, *et al.*, *Reconnection for Learning: A Community School System for New York City*, New York: Mayor's Advisory Panel on Decentralization of the New York City Schools, 1967, Part VI, Sec. 3.

TABLE 23

MAJOR PROGRAMS OF THE UNITED STATES OFFICE OF EDUCATION

I.	Primary Education
II.	Secondary Education (college preparatory and vocational)
III.	Higher Education (junior college through postgraduate)
IV.	Adult Education (retraining and continued education)
V.	Library Services
VI.	Research and Development
VII.	International Education

be the target of a benefit-cost study. Is the technique worth the bother of using it? Assessing the limitations of cost analysis methods, Quade admitted that ". . . every systems analysis has defects. Some of these are limitations inherent in all analyses of choice. Others are a consequence of the difficulties and complexities of the question. Still others are blunders or errors in thinking which hopefully will disappear as we learn to do better and more complete analyses." [9] The computation of educational, political and social value choices is impeded by surrounding uncertainties. Compounding this problem is the fact that educational benefits are not unequivocally measurable.

One objective of PPBS is to make cost comparisons of competing programs over a time horizon. An inherent danger is that one might judge the merits in terms of cost alone, rather than in comparison with benefits. A well-known critic of American education, Admiral Hyman Rickover, told members of Congress that America too often was measuring the worth of goals by a cost-effectiveness ratio. He indicated that perhaps effectiveness, instead of cost, should be the main ingredient of the ratio or formula. Directing his criticism at modern business management, Rickover expressed a fear that the high art of business efficiency might go more into cutting costs than

[9] E. S. Quade, *Systems Analysis Techniques for Planning-Programming-Budgeting*, P-3322 (Santa Monica, Calif.: RAND Corporation, March, 1966), p. 19.

in improving quality. This religion of efficiency, or "fog bomb," as he called cost analysis, ". . . cannot take account of human life. It is a limited tool in that it maintains the economic element is fundamental, and all other factors, social, cultural and political, are derivative." [10]

This distrust of cost-effectiveness techniques is somewhat justified, but the shortcomings of these approaches are frequently cited by their creators in the literature of systems analysis. Education can benefit greatly by some application of cost analysis, provided decisions are not made solely on the basis of cost considerations. Using benefit-cost analysis as an example, educational costs can be measured rather accurately, but the benefits do not easily lend themselves to quantification. Education has a long pay-off period, for the benefits of schooling are likely to last for a lifetime. There are both individual and social benefits (spillover effect), and there are other factors which might seem to make it correct to assert that educational benefits, or returns to investment in human capital, are not susceptible to precise economic analysis. Such is not the case. These economic concepts provide a framework for comparison which should reduce uncertainty and improve current vague qualitative judgments or personal hunches. The limitation should become apparent to those who prematurely attempt to formulate total educational policy on the basis of operations research and other mathematically derived procedures.[11] The greatest difficulty is in obtaining *adequate* measures of school output that can be related to costs.

[10] Hyman Rickover's testimony before a House Defense Appropriations subcommittee was reported in *The San Juan Star,* June 12, 1967, pp. 35–36. On another occasion, Rickover scoffed that on a cost-effectiveness basis, the colonists would not have revolted against King George III and John Paul Jones would not have engaged an inferior ship against *The Serapis.*

[11] A recent industrial study revealed the limited impact that computer procedures have had upon top-level management, even though these techniques have been used in industry for a number of years. In a sample of twelve large manufacturing companies, "The research yielded no instance of direct use of the computer by top management for decision making. In fact, I rarely found a top manager who received information of any kind in the format produced directly by the computer. . . ." Rodney H. Bradey, "Computers in Top-Level Decision Making," *Harvard Business Review,* XLV, No. 4 (July–August, 1967), 68–69.

Projecting long-range programs and costs is hazardous

PPBS should provide multiyear programs and financial plans if it is appropriately implemented. For the Federal Government, the programs are planned on the basis of five-year periods. Elaboration on the perils of making long-run forecasts in education is not needed. At the present time, the most sophisticated forecasting procedures of local schools have been developed to make pupil enrollment projections and to provide estimates of building needs. Very little has been done in the way of forecasting long-range curricular needs and objectives. The lack of long-range planning is quite evident if one critically examines an annual local school budget document or other materials prepared by central office administrators. With very few exceptions, the budget document reports only current revenues and expenditures, and makes no attempt to show future costs of present programs or to portray future planning and cost trends. This procedure minimizes the risk of making cost estimates which may not be completely accurate, but it is a very shortsighted approach. Program budgeting helps to clarify the future direction of a school and provides total cost implications of current decisions. The accuracy of such estimates is dependent upon the reliability of available data, human judgment, and intervening variables that produce uncertainties. Planning is always fraught with risks, but its major virtue is that it compels a long view.

Opposition to planned change exists in education

Another of the limitations of PPBS results from the simple fact that it is new and represents a departure from tradition. The literature on the topics of educational change and innovation is increasing rapidly and provides thoughtful analyses of how to bring about desired changes in the schools.[12] It is apparent that there are many barriers to change which result in the lack of implementation of

[12] Among the major contributors to the growing literature of educational change are Professors K. D. Benne, W. G. Bennis, R. Carlson, R. Chin, D. Clark, E. Guba, R. Lippitt, and M. B. Miles.

reasonable proposals. The strategy for effecting change consists of at least four distinct stages:

1. *development,* including conception and design of a process such as PPBS;
2. *demonstration,* including dissemination;
3. *adoption,* including installation and policy execution; and
4. *review,* including review and revision of the concept.

Program budgeting in education generally is still in its developmental stage, with notable exceptions, and it will probably encounter a good deal of opposition at the third stage, adoption. Indicative of this reluctance to consider the innovative approach to planning and budgeting are some comments attributed to several local board of education members. As these school leaders see it, PPBS is "a new and unproved tool" in education which ". . . might have value if used as one of many yardsticks for judging the worth of educational programs, but might be dangerous if depended on exclusively, especially when used for purposes initiated at the federal rather than the state or local level."[13] School board conservatism and aversion to innovations are not recent developments, but the stated rationale for not embracing program budgeting is interesting. To single out PPBS as the "one best way" to achieve more efficient operation of schools, in the opinion of a few board members, ". . . does a disservice to school boards and is not in the interests of scholarship."[14] Apparently, these persons view PPBS as merely an efficiency device used by the educational technostructure to enhance a cult of planning. This would be a self-defeating misuse of the concept. Some teachers may also resist change, not because they are stubborn, but because they are afraid of failing at something new.

Perhaps the barriers to new concepts and changes in schools are to be expected. Although some may question his view of social systems, social psychologist Raymond Hunt postulated that ". . . all social systems tend toward equilibrium, even if they may never achieve it and that in the face of disequilibrium, systems will be

[13] Elaine Exton, "State Legislators Urged to Install PPBS," *American School Board Journal,* CLIV, No. 2 (February, 1967), 13.
[14] *Ibid.*

constrained in the direction of accommodative change in form."[15] Organizational change is partially related to the value systems of the parties involved. Boards of education often neglect questions about program commitments or long-term budget implications that are shown as line-item amounts. They concentrate their efforts on the approval of capital expenditures for specific project proposals rather than on long-term program direction. There should be more concern over strategic commitments of resources for the long term.

It is well to consider whose interests are best served by an innovation such as PPBS. Students and teachers will benefit if the quality of programs is upgraded. The board of education will have an improved basis for policy making, and the public will be better informed about program plans and accomplishments of the schools it supports with taxes. Building level administrators will gain a better understanding of how to allocate resources and plan program packages within their budgets. Finally, because of the centralizing bias in school budget preparation, the program budget should serve the needs of the superintendent if it is to be viable. Burkhead goes so far as to claim that ". . . program and performance concepts must be so structured as to make this the primary objective."[16]

PPBS serves each of these parties. The sword of Damocles hanging over this concept is the threat that unimaginative minds will accept program plans as rigid commitments. Program budgeting must not be treated as an end in itself, but as a means to provide better information to educators.

Evaluative measurement of educational programs is rather primitive

The fact that advanced technical procedures are used in PPBS does not ensure valid results. Poor instruments, incorrectly inter-

[15] Raymond G. Hunt, "Role and Role Conflict," *Focus on Change and the School Administrator,* Harry J. Hartley and George E. Holloway, editors (Buffalo: State University of New York at Buffalo, School of Education, 1965), p. 45.

[16] Jesse Burkhead, "The Theory and Application of Program Budgeting to Education," *Trends in Financing Public Education* (Washington, D.C.: National Education Association Committee for Educational Finance, 1965), p. 185.

preted data, and purposely manipulated data can offset the advantages afforded by the program budget process.

The core of the system one is analyzing is human learning, and the ultimate success of PPBS is dependent upon more definitive research on the process and measurement of this evasive concept. Strong attacks on testing programs by educators are not uncommon, although there is enough blame around for everyone to share. In a recent annual conference of the Association for Supervision and Curriculum Development (ASCD), a substantial amount of criticism was directed at technology, big business, and national assessment. The mood of the ASCD conference was one of concern for the individual student in the depersonalized environment that seems to exist in many schools today.[17] A University of Wisconsin professor called present evaluation methods a "disaster area in education" and described most educational measurement as a "fraud or at least a misplaced effort." Furthermore, he saw a danger in the efforts of those attempting to organize education in terms of the economic theory of input and output at a time when the evaluation methods are so primitive. "One outcome of such an approach is the reduction of all the significant school activities, especially in the aesthetic and moral realm, that do not lend themselves to evaluation by the crude instruments now available for testing." [18]

The degree of controversy surrounding this hotly contested area was quite evident in the dialogue prompted by the proposed National Assessment of Educational Progress. The assessment is purported to take stock of American educational performance and to provide the first comprehensive measure of the nation's gross educational product. Designed to measure what the level of comprehension is for groups of people in certain regions, the assessment received early opposition from the 16,000-member American Association of School Administrators who ". . . opposed any act which would in effect establish a national testing system or a national curriculum." [19] It is possible that the initial resistance by the administrators may have minimized the potential benefits and exag-

[17] The Twenty-Second Annual Conference of ASCD was held in Dallas, Texas, March 12–16, 1967.

[18] James Macdonald's statement was cited in *News Trails*, XIV, No. 10 (April 14, 1967), 2.

[19] Leonard Buder, "Are Comparisons Odious?" *New York Times*, February 12, 1967, Sec. E, p. 9.

gerated some of the possible misuses. Regardless, it is apparent that powerful professional organizations such as AASA and ASCD are sometimes quite critical of existing and proposed procedures for evaluating instructional programs. If supervisors, administrators, and curriculum specialists disagree as to appropriate evaluative criteria, it is obvious that the program budgeting specialist and systems analyst who seek identifiable results would be well advised to tread lightly in this context. To do otherwise would be to encourage critics to view PPBS as a waste of resources in attempting to measure the unmeasurable.

It is also possible that an innovation such as PPBS may be "doomed to success." That is, if evaluation of this concept is made by the same administrators who introduce it into a school district (as is the case with many innovations), it is unlikely that they will claim that it is anything less than a smashing success.

Program structures will not be uniform

Lack of uniformity is actually a virtue of PPBS, but some might view it as a limitation of the approach. There may be similarity among the general programs designed by various state education departments and local school systems, but if PPBS is to serve local officials as it is intended, each state or district should develop programs and objectives to serve its unique needs. An important factor that will influence program structures is the curriculum mandated or recommended by particular states for their local schools. Usually, some minimal standards are established, but these serve as guidelines within which individual schools may exercise discretionary judgment. Programs vary greatly from state to state. Other factors that could help to determine the type of program structure a school may devise are indicated by these kinds of questions:

1. What specific educational services are offered?
2. What are the suggestions of the professional personnel and community?
3. What are the available facilities, materials, and tax revenues?
4. Does the district plan to operate a middle school?
5. Are procedures such as team teaching, modular scheduling, nongradedness, and other innovations desired?
6. Is the educational park concept appropriate?

7. What programs might be supported by the state and federal governments?
8. Does the program structure enhance individualized instruction?
9. Is the educational program flexible?
10. What shall be the program structure in five years?
11. Should the organization structure be revised to conform to the program structure?
12. What constitutes a suitable time horizon for long-range planning?
13. What measurements of output are appropriate for each program?
14. Should the roles of the assistant superintendents for business and instruction be altered?
15. Can education be optimized?
16. How will the community react to an analytical model of the school?
17. Should interdistrict and intradistrict comparative analyses be made?
18. Should budget categories emphasize process or expected product?
19. What budget documents and financial reports should be prepared?
20. Who has authority to transfer funds between and within programs?

A great many other questions should be raised and issues resolved by a school district as it embarks upon PPBS development. As it masters these problems, the limitations of the planning concept are reduced.

An example is given of how two school districts that operate similar instructional programs might devise different program structures. Let us assume that the curricular area involved is mathematics. District A decides that mathematics is in itself one of the major program areas that contains specific programs and subprograms subdivided according to grade level and particular courses in mathematics. A hypothetical, abbreviated set of program budgeting categories for District A is shown in Table 24.

By contrast, District B may devise its program structure on a grade level basis rather than on a disciplinary basis. In this case, mathematics is not a general program area, but is a component part of specified grade-level general-program areas, as is indicated in the hypothetical program budget format contained in Table 25.

In this illustration, the subprograms and program elements of Districts A and B are quite similar, but the difference lies in the priorities assigned to their program areas and programs. Each approach, discipline-oriented and organization-oriented, is feasible. Regardless of approach, the objective is to design a suitable number

TABLE 24

DISTRICT A: PROGRAM-BUDGET STRUCTURE BASED UPON CURRICULAR EMPHASIS

CODE	PROGRAM STRUCTURE	TYPE OF COMPONENT
100	Mathematics Instruction	(Program Area)
01	Elementary Arithmetic	(Program)
001	Fourth Grade (Multiplication and Division)	(Subprogram)
0001	Teachers' Salaries (Prorated)	(Program Element)
0002	Supplies	(Program Element)
02	Junior High School Mathematics, 7–9	(Program)
001	First year algebra	(Subprogram)
03	Senior High School Mathematics	(Program)
001	Calculus	(Subprogram)
0001	Teachers' Salaries	(Program Element)
0002	Supplies	(Program Element)
200	Science Instruction	(Program Area)

TABLE 25

DISTRICT B: PROGRAM-BUDGET STRUCTURE BASED UPON GRADE-LEVEL EMPHASIS

CODE	PROGRAM STRUCTURE	TYPE OF COMPONENT
100	Primary Grades Instruction, K–4	(Program Area)
01	Instruction in Mathematics	(Program)
001	Fourth Grade (SMSG approach)	(Subprogram)
0001	Teachers' Salaries (Prorated)	(Program Element)
0002	Instructional Materials	(Program Element)
02	Instruction in Language Arts	(Program)
03	Instruction in Science	(Program)
200	Middle School Grades Instructions, 5–8	(Program Area)

of program areas, perhaps ten or twelve, which are comprehensive enough to include all of the funds to be spent on the schools each year as shown in the annual budget. The emphasis is upon instructional programs, and the intent is to show how traditional input items such as teachers' salaries and materials are supporting specified programs. More detailed program structures are shown in Chapter Seven.

Local schools have inadequate staffs for systems planning

The success of PPBS in education will be dependent upon obtaining competent persons to implement the system at the state and local levels. Systems analysis in education, including even micro- and mini-analysis, emphasizes the importance of defining and incorporating into the systemic model any elements which will influence system behavior. Complex information transfer processes serve as central elements of this approach and the entire PPBS design requires careful research, analysis, and execution. The number of analysts required for any given school system is quite small, but the need for them is great. Presently, most local districts are not staffed for the type of planning required with program budgeting. Deficiencies exist in the training programs of administrators, in the number of central office administrative personnel, in the usage of electronic data processing, and in the desire to innovate or experiment in a program that is not mandated by a state department of education. In larger school districts, systems planning units can be created to provide leadership, to coordinate the program planning activities of curriculum and financial administrators, and to provide general support for the instructional activities of classroom teachers. In smaller schools, incumbent administrators may wish to become familiar with the notion of PPBS through the use of university and government workshops, consultants, and a review of related literature. It seems that the initial usage of program budgeting is by hard-pressed city districts, and these officials may be the most impotent and dissatisfied with a lack of "complete success."

Local school districts do not possess some of the advantages that the federal government did when it initiated PPBS: (1) a highly developed budget-making capacity and vast experience in budget administration; (2) information systems of varying quality and analytical procedures; and (3) some experience in program analysis, planning, and development. These conditions do not prevail in most local schools, or in most municipalities for that matter.

> There are many reasons for this. The centralization of budget control, the line-item basis for budget construction and administration, the predominance of established practice in key municipal programs (e.g., police, fire, sanitation), and the lack of funds for innovation or experimentation have all contributed to the limited capacity of most operating agencies in planning, programming, budgeting, and data handling.[20]

Compounding the problem of local planning shortcomings is the fact that state planning capacities are less than ideal. Greater coordination is needed in most states in the planning of education from preschool through the university level. As more states gradually adopt the PPBS format, greater assistance in systems procedures for local schools is likely to result. Refinements and debugging of technical operational elements will then be needed to foster the convergence of curricular planning with budget planning.

Activities and programs may not be mutually exclusive

In addition to program structure variance, a difficult aspect of budgetary formulation is the determination of how to allocate resources among unlike programs with unique objectives. There are as many ways to conceive of programs as there are of organizing human activities, and the activities of one program may be part of another program. In the federal government, under an ideal PPBS structure, a school lunch program should not simultaneously be part of both a Health Program and an Education Program. Such ideal program structures do not exist, as is suggested by the fact that more than fifty federal agencies dispense funds for educational programs of some sort. Programs are not mutually exclusive in local schools either. A science activity may be part of an independent study program, of a college advanced-placement program, and of

[20] Frederick O'R. Hayes, "PPBS in New York," Statement by Director of the Budget, City of New York, September 19, 1967, Mimeograph, p. 2.

the general secondary schools program, depending on how the particular school district classifies its programs. It is probably desirable to have program categories cut across organizational lines.

Success of PPBS has not been measured

More definitive verificational research evidence is needed to determine whether PPBS has, in actual experience, fulfilled its promise. Most of the literature describing this concept deals with its potential value, but does not validate it. After carefully following the progress of program budgeting in the Department of Defense, Wildvasky concluded that to the best of his knowledge, ". . . not a single study of this important experiment was undertaken (or at least published) before the decision was made to spread it around the land."[21] Furthermore, he provided an insightful, critical analysis of some shortcomings of PPBS in the Department of Defense and suggested that a good operational test would be to discover whether the systems analysts of DOD actually use the figures from the vaunted five-year plans or whether they go to the military services for the "real stuff." Schools will have the distinct advantage of being able to assess the performance of program budgeting in a number of kinds of organizations prior to adopting it.

Research Needs: Technical Operational Elements

Before PPBS is implemented in a school system, research at the local level is needed in order to determine the best possible features to adopt. This research should begin with a reasonably thorough review of the literature which leads to the preparation of procedural manuals appropriate for the local staff. The research activities should be time-phased to allow for maximum citizenry and staff participation. Phase One might begin with a consideration of explicitly stated objectives of the school, including community involvement, and the final phase would probably pertain to refinements of basic models and analytical systems. These would be used

[21] Aaron Wildavsky, "The Political Economy of Efficiency," *The Public Interest*, No. 8 (Summer, 1967), p. 42.

in making instructional and financial (fiscocurricular) projections and testing alternative administrative choices. As a suggestive guideline, the ten areas of research activities outlined below could be placed on a PERT network.

Areas of research needed and possible products of local school research

1. *Systems analysis application.* Examine the many uses of the term *systems analysis,* and consider the systematic approaches to planning contributed by both the exact and inexact sciences. Review disciplinary literature, determine constraints, outline the range of options, and choose the preferred mix. The result of this research could be a descriptive handbook and an up-to-date basic bibliography for the use of local school personnel.

2. *Curricular program identification.* Based upon operational instructional objectives, formulate program structures appropriate for PPBS. Priorities are developed along with flow charts for individual subject areas. The structure and process of education are considered in the light of contemporary curriculum efforts. The product of research in this area should be a program structure for grades K-12, and might include curriculum manuals for teachers and department chairmen, five-year priority plans, and a guide for teacher conferences, workshops and other inservice programs.

3. *Organization structural design.* No single form of organization is prescribed by PPBS, so an optimal structure should be designed. Degree of centralization is assessed, anatomy of the system reviewed, and organizational theory literature considered. The traditional pyramidal organization is neither the only system nor necessarily the best. New patterns of organization may, for example, replace hierarchical norms and command relationships with a model that emphasizes the administrator's support function. By replacing hierarchy, this so-called "lowerarchy" depicts the instructors at the topmost levels with administrators at the bottom.[22] From many alternatives, the district should be able to devise a suitable organization chart. Basic program categories may cut across certain organi-

[22] Gordon Lippitt, "Don't Be a Prisoner of Your Organization," *Nation's Cities,* V, No. 8 (August, 1967), 23.

zation elements, so that the program structure need not completely reflect organization structure.

4. *Administrative Planning and Programming Procedures.* Planning, programming, and budgeting are all essential elements of administration. Planning is the production of the range of meaningful potentials for selection of courses of action through a systematic consideration of the alternatives. Programming is the more specific assignment of the needed personnel, supplies, and facilities. Support services are specified, management reports and program memoranda prepared, and a management information system may be devised. A decision matrix could be one research product. Long-range planning is needed, along with both a format for outlining PPBS procedures to teachers and manuals for central office and building-level administrators.

5. *Instructional Methodology.* Intensive research is needed into recent curricular-instructional projects and proposed innovations. Topics include instructional media, materials, methods, staffing patterns, services to be rendered, programs of the future, and the like. Products of research may include guidelines for making departmental reports, program summaries, performance appraisals, and experimental programs.

6. *Time Sequence Design.* The operations of the system are time-phased on the basis of a master plan. This extended time horizon encourages long-range planning and determination of immediate and long term needs. Critical path methods such as PERT are advisable. The products of research might include annual planning cycles, Gantt charts, and time schedules for individual programs.

7. *Computer Applications.* Investigation of the feasibility of using electronic data processing is suggested. Many of the routine aspects of school planning can be assigned to the domain of data processing. Of major concern are cost and available personnel trained in this field. Many of the elements of financial administration and certain instructional methods can be handled by computers, but discretion is needed so as not to upset those who fear the potentially dehumanizing and impersonal facets of education. Research results could include student data banks, computational assistance for teachers, suggestions for possible computer uses, and technical manuals to meet PPBS requirements.

8. *Economic Analysis and Cost Accounting Procedures.* Research is needed in the broad area of the economics of education and into specific types of quantitatively measured techniques. Cost accounting procedures are developed in the light of recent cost analysis research. Comparative costs of program elements are presented along with cost schedules and manuals of accounting procedures.

9. *Budgetary Procedures.* On the basis of the newly designed program structure, specific resources are transformed into budget dollars and the budget is projected for several years ahead. The financial administrator is provided with data on fiscal resources, capital facilities, personnel requirements and the reward system, pupil enrollment projections, and other information relevant to program cost tabulation. He should study modern budget theory in addition to state and federal requirements prior to developing operating and capital budgets. Manuals describing new budget codes, procedures, and policies will be the research products.

10. *Review and Evaluation Policies.* The final recommended category of research that a local district may wish to include pertains to assessing and revising the PPBS format. After a feasibility study or pilot project, the district should have a better notion of how to improve the implementation. Performance measures, criteria of accomplishments, work-load measures, and system renewal devices can be developed. Debugging of the original systems design helps to make this approach a dynamic one. Change and innovation are sought, and some bases for evaluation are the results of the research in this area.

Conclusion

It is easy to exaggerate the extent to which PPBS can assist schools, and so the purpose of this chapter was to expose some of the shortcomings and research needs of this systematic planning concept. It is imperative that a high degree of collaboration and dialogue among the various educational specialists take place when a school chooses to develop a program budgeting structure. Unless planning comes from within the profession, the potential risk is that outsiders, including impatient economists and operations analysts, will design and impose programs that may be at odds with the existing general objectives of the schools. Education is more than mission-oriented departments whose aims are strictly measured by technical proficiency. As a public service, it is the target of perpetual criticism, much of which is directed toward policy makers who have had relatively poor means for assessing implications of choosing one alternative over another. Program budgeting procedures will aid the policy maker, but will not eliminate uncertainties, risks, and errors of judgment that are inherent in complex situations of choice. Perhaps the greatest danger in PPBS or ". . . in all planning is the threat that unimaginative minds will accept plans as rigid commitments."[23] Some of the limitations surrounding PPBS are summarized below:

1. Program budgeting does not eliminate organizational conflicts.
2. It is subject to political considerations.
3. It does not prescribe a particular form of organization.
4. The United States Office of Education program structure is not suitable for local schools.
5. Every systems analysis has defects.
6. Long-range projections are subject to miscalculations.
7. There is opposition to planned change in education.
8. Public incapacity to understand the merits of program budgeting may result in a lack of financial support for implementation.
9. Evaluative criteria need refinements.
10. Program structures will not be uniform.
11. Programs may not be mutually exclusive.
12. Local schools have inadequate staffs for planning.
13. Conclusive evidence of the success of PPBS is not abundant.
14. Planning has its limits, and schoolmen should not be promised too much too soon after PPBS installation.
15. There exist a number of research needs into such technical operational elements as: systems analysis application and structural design; curricular program identification and instructional methodology; administrative procedures and evaluative methods; time sequence design and computer applications; and economic analysis and budgetary design.

The limitations of PPBS are outweighed by the potential advantages gained by this concept. The virtues are described through-

[23] Melvin Anshen, "The Program Budget in Operation," in *Program Budgeting,* David Novick, editor (Cambridge: Harvard University Press, 1965), p. 362.

out the text, and it is possible that many of the present defects of this system can be overcome eventually.

It is apparent in systems analysis that the best way to control the quality of output is to control the quality of input. However, public schools have no such intake value; they must serve all. Program budgeting in education merely sets the proper stage (for systemic planning) but does not guarantee that the play will be a success. For the time being at least, there remains the possibility that PPBS may not be widely adopted by local school districts. Such inaction would be rather tragic, but then the subject of all tragedy is, after all, the conquest of the ideal by the real.

Suggestion for Discussion

Summarize the advantages gained by PPBS over conventional school planning procedures; analyze the shortcomings and research needs for PPBS; and discuss the pro and con positions regarding implementation in a local school district.

Selected References

Drew, Elizabeth B., *et al.*, "PPBS: Its Scope and Limits," *The Public Interest,* No. 8 (Summer, 1967). Pp. 3–48.

Exton, Elaine, "State Legislators Urged to Install PPBS," *American School Board Journal,* CLIV, No. 2 (February, 1967). 13–16.

Fisher, G. H., *The World of Program Budgeting.* P-3361. Santa Monica, Calif.: RAND Corporation, May, 1966. 30 pp.

Novick, David, editor. *Program Budgeting: Program Analysis and the Federal Government.* Cambridge: Harvard University Press, 1965, Chapters 10 to 12.

Wildavsky, Aaron, *The Politics of the Budgetary Process.* Boston: Little, Brown and Company, 1964, Chapters 4 and 5.

GLOSSARY

Account Class: a descriptive heading or numeric code used to categorize similar financial transactions according to program, function, object, or source; contained in a chart of accounts.

Annual Planning Calendar: phases of current organizational activities are integrated with long-range planning on scheduled annual cycles to coordinate procedures for all agencies or program centers; time schedules may be designed.

Appropriation: an allocation of funds made by a governing authority for specified purposes and often restricted as to the time when it may be expended.

Benefit-Cost Analysis: a means of assessing the worth of existing and proposed projects; it involves the enumeration and evaluation of all relevant costs and benefits over a period of time; ideally, benefits should exceed costs, or $\frac{B}{C} > 1$; measurement criteria for the benefits should be specified.

Budget Document: a written statement of an estimate or plan describing expenditures and revenues for financing an organization's entire program for a specified time period, usually one year; the most common fiscal year begins July 1 and ends June 30; at the termination of the defined period, the budget technically no longer exists, other than as an historical document.

Budgetary Process: continuous activity comprised of planning, formulation of a budget document, interpretation, presentation to the approving authority, formal adoption, fiscal administration, and appraisal.

Component: level of program subordinate to element level and above task level.

Cost-Effectiveness Analysis: a means of relating the cost of a particular activity or project to effective performance or goal attainment; the decision maker may choose from among feasible alternatives on a basis of least cost and greatest effectiveness.

Crosswalk: the expression of the relationship between the program structure and the appropriation–budget structure; the translation of multiyear program and financial plans into annual budgets; a simple table vertically listing program categories and horizontally listing appropriations and budget activities; based upon the program budget code.

Direct Costs: actual or budgetary costs that may be charged directly to, or prorated as a part of, the cost of a program, service, function, or department. They are eliminated if a program is eliminated or added if a program is added.

Element: level of program subordinate to program level and above component level; cost elements include personal services, contracted services, equipment, materials, supplies, and fixed charges.

Evaluation: comparison of desired outcomes or objectives with actual accomplishments; based upon educational performance indicators, such as indices that measure changes in pupil cognitive development.

Function-Object Budget: widely used presently by local public schools to identify costs under a number of broadly defined function and object categories, such as administration, instruction, debt service, and plant maintenance; emphasis is upon objects of expense rather than programs of the school.

General Systems Theory: an interdisciplinary, holistic, integrative approach that includes logicomethodological investigations of the empirical; the philosophical basis for systems analysis and related procedural strategies.

Indirect Costs: actual or budgetary costs that are not readily identified with a specific program, service, function, or department and that are seldom completely eliminated if a program is eliminated.

Input-Output Analysis: an economic technique designed to examine the effect of changes in certain input variables to the outcome or output variables of the system under study; a form of systems analysis; inputs are the resources employed to achieve objectives and outputs are the products of a program, often expressed numerically.

Management Information System (MIS): integrates the dynamic functions of an organization, such as instruction, personnel and finance, and provides computer-aided systems of information control for administrators; it may be a reporting system or a decision making system, depending on level of application.

Multiyear Program Summary: concise description in numerical, dollar, and other values for the past year, current year, and future year projections, the authorized program output, input, personnel and material needs, and proposed program changes.

Needs Research: formalized studies and problem solving steps designed to specify the most appropriate level of systems analysis to be used.

Operations Analysis: term used by United States Office of Education to describe quantitative, analytical studies in education; it combines operations research and systems analysis.

Operating Budget: that part of the total budget of a school system which contains instructional and related costs; it does not include capital outlay, debt service, transportation, and other similar costs; it is defined differently from state to state.

Operations Research (OR): a process for simulating the complexities of reality through mathematical equations; developed shortly before World War II in England and applied first to radar problems; usually restricted to problems that may be stated in terms of quantitative analysis.

Performance Budget: used to evaluate work-cost data in terms of unit work measures; the forerunner of the program budget; led to the introduction of activity classifications; evolved in the era of scientific management; provided numerous workload statistics, but did not aid greatly in planning future courses of action.

Planning: relating means to ends; formulating rationally feasible courses of action through a systematic consideration of alternatives; planning may be unilateral or participatory in nature; it also applies to settings where objectives and ends are not predetermined.

Planning-Programming-Budgeting System (PPBS): a conceptual approach to decision making developed by RAND Corporation and installed in the Department of Defense in 1961; a structured procedure for policy determination; introduced into the entire federal establishment in 1965; emphasizes outputs, program activities, and accomplishments; long-range planning, analytic evaluative tools, and economic rationality are basic ingredients.

Program: a group of interdependent, closely related services or activities possessing, or contributing to, a common objective or set of allied objectives; a package of subprograms, elements, components, tasks, and activities.

Program Budget: relates resources, financial and otherwise, to an organization's activities, outputs, services, missions, or programs; the financial expression of value priorities; helps to achieve cost-effectiveness if not cost-reduction; based upon a program structure classification; the budget is a statement of policy that relates cost to differentialed programs; sometimes used in a broad sense to denote the entire process of PPBS.

Program Evaluation and Review Technique (PERT): a method for planning, controlling, monitoring, and evaluating complex projects that have been divided into component parts, time elements, and cost factors; involves a critical path network to identify overruns and underruns and to eliminate potential bottlenecks.

Program Memorandum: an internal planning document that records analyzed programs and lists alternatives and recommendations.

Programming: the determination of the manpower, materials, and facilities required to support a program; inputs are related to outputs by lines of action through an information system.

Program Statement: a formal, recorded description of multiyear program needs, objectives, authority, inputs, outputs, and supportive information.

Program Structure: organization of the general program areas, subprograms, elements, components, and tasks; it facilitates analytic comparisons of the costs and effectiveness of alternative programs; programs may cut across existing departments and agencies.

Proration of Costs: the distribution of costs to two or more program areas in proportion to the benefits provided; the basis for proration may be a formula or some other arbitrarily determined procedure.

Quantification: the numerical expression of variables.

Scenario: a statement of assumptions about the operating environment of the organization to be studied; it is a helpful aid in making projections of different future conditions.

Synergism: cooperative action of discrete units or agencies which results in a total effect that is greater than the sum of those effects taken independently.

Systems Analysis: formulation of a problem within the environment of uncertainty; objectives may or may not be given; determination of structural-analytical specifications; provision of comparative benefits for a multiplicity of options; not limited to quantitative data; its aim is to provide decision makers with a more complete basis for rational choice.

Unassigned Support: a budget category containing items that are not assigned to more direct program, service, or function-object categories; a kind of residual budgetary item.

APPENDIX A

CONVENTIONAL, LINE-ITEM BREAKDOWN OF
AVERAGE U.S. PUBLIC SCHOOL TOTAL EXPENDITURES
PER PUPIL FOR 1967-1968

OBJECT OF EXPENDITURE	PER CENT OF TOTAL
Administration	3.3
Instructional Salaries	62.2
Instructional Materials	4.3
Operating Costs	8.1
Health Services	0.6
Transportation	3.8
Maintenance	2.6
Capital Outlay	2.4
Debt Service	9.3
Fixed Charges	3.4
	100.0

APPENDIX B

PROGRAM BUDGET SUMMARY OF
EXPENDITURES FOR SACRAMENTO PUBLIC SCHOOLS

DESCRIPTION	1965–1966 ACTUAL EXPENDITURES No. of Employees	Amount
ADMINISTRATIVE SERVICES		
Board of Education		$ 33,667.94
Office of Superintendent	6.00	68,102.48
Personnel Services	11.00	111,336.68
Planning and Research	6.00	71,520.98
Business Services	46.00	403,061,31
TOTAL ADMINISTRATIVE SERVICES	69.00	$ 687,689.39
INSTRUCTIONAL PROGRAMS AND SERVICES		
Administration Instructional Services	6.00	$ 84,170.24
Curriculum Development	31.00	393,176.67
Special Services	66.00	663,558.09
Special Programs	13.50	178,494.00
Elementary Schools	1,052.48	8,803,678.36
Junior High Schools	559.50	4,901,236.07
Senior High Schools	519.10	4,872,523.23
Schools for Adults	33.50	477,936.87
Continuation High School		6,126.19
Summer School Programs	1.00	237,131.50
Staff Training and Summer Demonstration School	1.00	36,626.42
Special Projects Department		
Special Projects		1,386,198.33
TOTAL INSTRUCTIONAL PROGRAMS AND SERVICES	2,283.08	$22,040,855.97
SUPPORTING SERVICES		
Transportation	19.86	$ 243,540.29
Maintenance and Operations	366.50	3,313,269.86
Fixed Charges		1,376,157.69
Food Services		8,273.11
Community Services	21.50	480,177.12
General Capital Improvements		331,189.44
TOTAL SUPPORTING SERVICES	407.86	$ 5,752,609.51
TOTAL EXPENDITURES	2,759.94	$28,481,154.87
STATE BUILDING LOANS REPAYMENTS		373,197.68
TRANSFERS		161,848.24
UNDISTRIBUTED RESERVE		
Uncommitted		
TOTAL EXPENDITURES & DISBURSEMENTS		$29,016,200.79
ACTUAL ENDING BALANCE JUNE 30, 1966		1,504,339.28
ACTUAL ENDING BALANCE JUNE 30, 1967		
BUDGETED ENDING BALANCE JUNE 30, 1968		
TOTAL BUDGET		$30,520,540.07

1966–1967 ACTUAL EXPENDITURES		1967–1968 ADOPTED BUDGET APPROPRIATIONS	
No. of Employees	Amount	No. of Employees	Amount
	$ 23,768.97		$ 41,660.77
4.00	74,721.74	4.00	67,110.72
11.00	114,808.41	12.00	125,712.05
6.00	73,017.41	5.00	71,710.60
46.50	432,181.50	46.70	517,404.54
67.50	$ 718,498.03	67.70	$ 823,598.68
6.00	$ 85,106.80	6.00	$ 88,483.83
31.00	430,495.44	28.50	444,521.05
67.50	738,525.05	60.50	692,473.59
16.50	207,315,86	16.50	228,073.40
1,094.88	9,473,023.16	1,121.50	10,509,798.32
579.59	5,363,799.65	582.42	5,816,209.76
528.82	5,212,914.08	549.42	5,891,419.90
41.50	573,010.46	41.00	651,819.62
15.00	119,805.02	16.50	144,516.05
1.25	324,737.79	1.50	453,789.06
2.00	41,664.98	2.00	48,208.35
		.40	3,972.35
	2,266,569.89		2,753,689.00
2,384.04	$24,836.968.18	2,426.24	$27,726,974.28
27.63	$ 258,835.99	39.63	$ 311,606.00
381.10	3,647,623.93	387.00	3,967,194.04
	1,559,441.77		1,942,364.00
	21,503.97		25,000.00
27.50	455,698.59	27.50	626,064.00
	402,630.84		415,937.00
436.23	$ 6,345,735.09	454.13	$ 7,288,165.04
2,887.77	$31,901,201.30	2,948.07	$35,838,738.00
	355,005.98		377,536.00
	4,200.00		6,206.00
			642,755.00
	$32,260,407.28		$36,865,235.00
....	1,110,466.83		
....	....	....	225,000.00
	$33,370,874.11		$37,090,235.00

APPENDIX C

CONVENTIONAL BUDGET SUMMARY BY
STATE CLASSIFICATION OF EXPENDITURES FOR
SACRAMENTO CITY UNIFIED SCHOOL DISTRICT*

DESCRIPTION	1965–1966 ACTUAL EXPENDITURES		
	No. of Employees	Amount	% of Total Expenses
100 Administration	76.50	$ 831,938.23	2.94
200 Instruction			
Certificated Salaries	2,048.60	18,620,523.10	65.37
Classified Salaries	195.98	1,359,050.17	4.77
Other Expenses		1,169,055.87	4.10
Total Instruction		($21,148,629.14)	(74.24)
400 Health Services	32.00	$ 341,501.62	1.19
500 Transportation	19.86	262,655.41	.92
600 Operation	303.50	2,513,202.29	8.82
700 Maintenance	62.00	802,595.68	2.81
800 Fixed Charges		1,415,198.84	4.98
TOTAL CURRENT EXPENSE OF EDUCATION		($27,315,721.21)	(95.90)
900 Food Services		$ 47,193.94	.16
1100 Community Services	21.50	568,241.48	2.00
1200 Capital Outlay General		549,998.24	1.94
TOTAL EXPENDITURES		($28,481,154.87)	(100.00)
1300 State Loan Repayments		$ 373,197.68	
1400 Transfers		161,848.24	
Undistributed Reserve			
Committed for Special Projects			
Uncommitted			
TOTAL EXPENDITURES & DISBURSEMENTS		$29,016,200.79	
ACTUAL ENDING BALANCE JUNE 30, 1966		1,504,339.28	
ACTUAL ENDING BALANCE JUNE 30, 1967			
BUDGETED ENDING BALANCE JUNE 30, 1968			
TOTAL BUDGET	2,759.94	$30,520,540.07	

* Permission to reproduce program budgeting materials for the Sacramento Public Schools was granted by Henry J. Moeller, Director of Budget Services.

1966–1967 ACTUAL EXPENDITURES			1967–1968 ADOPTED BUDGET APPROPRIATIONS		
No. of Employees	Amount	% of Total Expenses	No. of Employees	Amount	% of Total Expenses
75.00	$ 892,530.76	2.80	75.60	$ 910,571.00	2.75
2,136.29	20,667,952.09	64.79	2,163.25	22,069,766.00	66.70
208.25	1,467,356.17	4.59	228.09	1,274,764.00	3.85
	1,284,534.44	4.03		1,263,733.00	3.82
	($23,419,842.70)	(73.41)		($24,608,263.00)	(74.37)
32.50	$ 351,753.65	1.10	27.50	$ 292,658.00	.88
27.63	373,213.71	1.17	39.63	312,411.00	.94
316.60	2,769,735.17	8.68	322.50	2,962,942.00	8.96
64.00	924,840.37	2.90	64.00	988,839.00	2.99
	1,617,504.88	5.07		1,942,364.00	5.87
	($30,349,421.24)	(95.13)		($32,018,048.00)	(96.76)
	$ 77,723.16	.24		$ 25,000.00	.08
27.50	502,676.90	1.58	27.50	626,064.00	1.90
	971,380.00	3.05		415,937.00	1.26
	($31,901,201.30)	(100.00)		($33,085,049.00)	(100.00)
	$ 355,005.98			$ 377,536.00	
	4,200.00			6,206.00	
				2,753,689.00	
				642,755.00	
	$32,260,407.28			$36,865,235.00	
....	1,110,466.83				
				225,000.00	
2,887.77	$33,370,874.11		2,948.07	$37,090,235.00	

APPENDIX D

NEW YORK CITY BOARD OF EDUCATION

FORM PPB 100
REV. 9-67

PPB PLANNING PROGRAMMING BUDGETING

P.E. ADMINISTRATOR (NAME & TITLE)

DATE OF PREPARATION

PROGRAM ELEMENT

SUMMARY DATA

PROGRAM TITLE | NO.

PROGRAM ELEMENT TITLE | NO.

MAJOR AGGREGATION TITLE | NO.

DISTRICT | BORO | NO.

P.E. ADMINISTRATOR REPORTS TO (NAME & TITLE)

OBJECTIVE (S)

DESCRIPTION

OUTPUT MEASURES

COST AND PERSONNEL DATA	/	/	/	/	/	/	/
TOTAL OPERATING COSTS							
TOTAL R&D COSTS							
TOTAL INVESTMENT COSTS							
TOTAL OBLIGATIONAL AUTHORITY							
TOTAL PERSONNEL							
ENROLLMENT (AS APPLICABLE)							

REMARKS

NEW YORK CITY BOARD OF EDUCATION

FORM PPB 100
REV. 9-67

PPB PLANNING PROGRAMMING BUDGETING

P.E. ADMINISTRATOR (NAME & TITLE)

DATE OF PREPARATION

PROGRAM ELEMENT
SUMMARY DATA

PROGRAM TITLE	NO.	PROGRAM ELEMENT TITLE	NO.
MAJOR AGGREGATION TITLE	NO.	DISTRICT BORO NO.	P.E. ADMINISTRATOR REPORTS TO (NAME & TITLE)

COST DATA - BY SCHOOL YEAR ($)

CATEGORIES	/	/	/	/	/	/	/
OPERATING COSTS							
ACTIVITY DIRECTION							
INSTRUCTIONAL SERVICES							
PERSONAL SERVICE							
OTHER THAN PERSONAL SERVICE							
PUPIL PERSONNEL SERVICES							
NON-INSTRUCTIONAL SERVICES							
PERSONAL SERVICE							
OTHER THAN PERSONAL SERVICE							
SUPPORT SERVICES							
PERSONAL SERVICE							
OTHER THAN PERSONAL SERVICE							
PLANT OPERATION & MAINTENANCE							
PERSONAL SERVICE							
OTHER THAN PERSONAL SERVICE							
OTHER THAN PERSONAL SERVICES - ALL OTHER							
TOTAL OPERATING COSTS							
RESEARCH & DEVELOPMENT COSTS							
ACTIVITY DIRECTION							
NON-INSTRUCTIONAL SERVICES							
PERSONAL SERVICE							
OTHER THAN PERSONAL SERVICE							
SUPPORT SERVICES							
PERSONAL SERVICE							
OTHER THAN PERSONAL SERVICE							
OTHER THAN PERSONAL SERVICES - ALL OTHER							
TOTAL R & D COSTS							
CAPITAL INVESTMENT COSTS							
CONSTRUCTION							
MODERNIZATION							
TOTAL INVESTMENT COST							
TOTAL OBLIGATIONAL AUTHORITY							

PERSONNEL DATA - BY SCHOOL YEAR (NO. OF PEOPLE)

ACTIVITY DIRECTION							
INSTRUCTIONAL SERVICES							
PUPIL PERSONNEL SERVICES							
NON-INSTRUCTIONAL SERVICES							
SUPPORT SERVICES							
PLANT OPERATION & MAINTENANCE							
TOTAL PERSONNEL							

PUPIL DATA - BY SCHOOL YEAR (NOS. AS APPLICABLE)

ENROLLMENT							
CLASSROOM SEATS							
AVERAGE CLASS SIZE							
AVERAGE DAILY ATTENDANCE							
AVERAGE DAILY ENROLLMENT							

REMARKS

APPENDIX E

SACRAMENTO CITY UNIFIED SCHOOL DISTRICT

SUMMARY BUDGET REPORT

LOCATION ESEA READING ELEM/JR IDENTIFICATION CODE 15808 PERIOD COVERED 06/30/67 PAGE NO. 76

ACCOUNT CODE	ACCOUNT TITLE	TOTALS TO DATE: ABATEMENTS (MEMO ONLY)	APPROPRIATION	ENCUMBRANCES	NET EXPENDITURES	UNENCUMBERED BALANCE
3430870	TEMP PRNCP SAL		2,199.00		108.00	2,091.00
3430968	SUPERVISOR SAL		16,361.00		13,634.20	2,726.80
3431068	TEACHERS SAL		165,844.00		149,243.33	16,600.67
3431070	TEACH TEMP SAL		2,500.00		2,662.22	162.22-
3431168	OTHER CERT SAL		7,500.00		8,630.50	1,130.50-
3431170	TEMP CERT SAL		1,500.00		410.60	1,089.40
3431368	CLASS SAL OF INST		10,850.00		8,698.58	2,151.42
3431370	CLASS TEMP SAL		8,550.00		1,344.52	7,205.48
3431654	OTHER BOOKS		28,840.00		10,615.11	18,224.89
3431706	AUDIO-VISUAL		14,500.00		11,452.05	3,047.95
3431745	MAGAZINES				4.00	4.00-
3431759	PUBLICATIONS		3,000.00		2,017.43	982.57
3431778	SUPPLIES / EXP		8,200.00		11,984.97	3,784.97-
3431780	TESTS-STUDENTS		2,306.00		2,306.81	.81-
3431788	TRAVEL EXP-DIST		600.00		514.20	85.80
3431789	TRAVEL EXP-O.D.		600.00		465.53	134.47
3432070	TEMP CERT SAL		1,000.00			1,000.00
3432278	SUPPLIES/EXP		77.00		76.28	.72
3432678	SUPPLIES / EXP					.00
3432687	FIELD TRIPS		1,500.00		1,686.73	186.73-
3432968	CLASSIFIED SAL		4,500.00		3,204.04	1,295.96
3432970	TEMP CLASS SAL	80.39	12,001.00		11,092.30	908.70
3433027	GASOLINE					.00
3433093	TELEPHONE/TELEG		2,400.00		1,530.98	869.02
3433522	EQUIP REPAIRS		1,450.00		1,158.50	291.50
3433878	SUPPLIES / EXP.		4,785.00		3,337.56	1,447.44
3433978	SUPPLIES / EXP.		270.00		138.00	132.00
3434178	SUPPLIES / EXP.		886.00		505.37	380.63
3434278	SUPPLIES / EXP.		597.00		336.38	260.62
3434330	INSURANCE COMP		1,160.00		774.06	385.94
3434331	INSURANCE GROUP		2,610.00		1,724.14	885.86
3434968	CERTIFICATED SAL		17,200.00		16,961.62	238.38
3435178	SUPPLIES/EXPENSE		60.00		58.58	1.42
3436660	RENOVATIONS		1,405.36		1,405.36	.00
3437021	EQUIPMENT		41,345.00		18,427.31	22,917.69
	DEPARTMENT TOTAL	80.39	366,596.36		286,509.26	80,087.10

MIS. FORM NO. 83-6 (REV. 10-62 - 10M)

APPENDIX F

SACRAMENTO CITY UNIFIED SCHOOL DISTRICT

SUMMARY BUDGET REPORT

LOCATION MARK TWAIN ELEMENTARY SCHOOL IDENTIFICATION CODE 11235 PERIOD COVERED 06/30/67 PAGE NO. 187

ACCOUNT CODE	ACCOUNT TITLE	TOTALS TO DATE: ABATEMENTS (MEMO ONLY)	APPROPRIATION	ENCUMBRANCES	NET EXPENDITURES	UNENCUMBERED BALANCE
	INSTRUCTION					
6621654	OTHER BOOKS		1,376.80		1,376.80	.00
	SUB TOTAL		1,376.80		1,376.80	.00
	BUDGET ALLOCATION		4,971.80			4,971.80
	GENERAL SERVICES					
5501778	OFFICE SUPPL OR EX					
5501780	TESTS STUDENTS					
5531778	SUPPLIES OR EXPENS					
6101778	AUDIO VISUAL				6.96	
6341778	GENERAL CLASSROOM				5,020.36	
6621745	LIBRARY MAGAZINES					
6621778	LIBRARY SUPPLIES					
6621779	MAPS AND GLOBES					
6741778	MUSIC INSTRUMENTAL					
6761778	MUSIC VOCAL					
6831778	PHYSICAL EDUCATION					
	SUB TOTAL		4,971.80		5,027.32	55.52-
	INSTRUCTION TOTAL		6,348.60		6,404.12	55.52-
	HEALTH SERVICES					
	BUDGET ALLOCATION		216.00			216.00
5502247	MEDICAL SUPPLIES					
5502248	SUPPLIES/EXPENSES				222.58	
	HEALTH SVCS TOTAL		216.00		222.58	6.58-
	OPERATION SERVICES					
5493078	SUPPLIES OR EXPENS					
5503078	SUPPLIES/EXPENSES	1.70	1,122.00		1,088.43	33.57
	OPERATION TOTAL	1.70	1,122.00		1,088.43	33.57

MIS. FORM NO. 83-6 (REV. 10-62 - 10M) ®

APPENDIX G

EXAMPLE OF BUDGET CLASSIFICATION CODES USED IN THE PROGRAM BUDGET FORMAT OF SACRAMENTO PUBLIC SCHOOLS

GENERAL INFORMATION

An explanation of the function and use of this "Budget Classification Codes" is presented here to assist those who make requisitions against budgeted allotments.

Responsibility for budget control is being assigned to Administrators. Therefore, responsibility for determining the initial budget classification for each expenditure is being shifted to the Administrator. The Budget Director is responsible for overall budget control and will review all budget classifications.

The "Budget Classification" code consists of two parts, the "Identification Code" and the "Account Code."

A. Identification Code

This code makes use of a series of five digits to identify the fund to be charged, the instructional level and the location of the school or facility making the request, as follows:

Fund	1 digit
Level	2 digit
Location	3 digits

Using the codes in the following sections, the code number for California Junior High School would be 1-2-415, or General Fund, Junior High School, California Junior High.

B. Account Code

Here also another series of seven digits makes it possible to classify a requested expenditure into the proper department, State classification, and specific expense account, as follows:

Department	3 digits
State Classification	2 digits
Expense Account	2 digits

To illustrate the application of the "Account Code," assume that a request from California Junior High School is for instructional supplies for Home Economics. This would be a number 638-17-78. The 638 coded the request to "Home Economics", the 17 to the State Classification of "Other Expense of Instruction"; and the 78 classifies the expense as "Supplies."

Combining the two series of numbers 1-2-415 and 638-17-78, produces the Budget Classification Code for the request which is 1-2-415 638-17-78.

The Budget Classification Code shall be used for all Purchase, Stores, Maintenance and Repair, and Capital Improvement requisitions.

APPENDIX H

FLOW CHART FOR AN INSTRUCTIONAL PROGRAM: MATHEMATICS

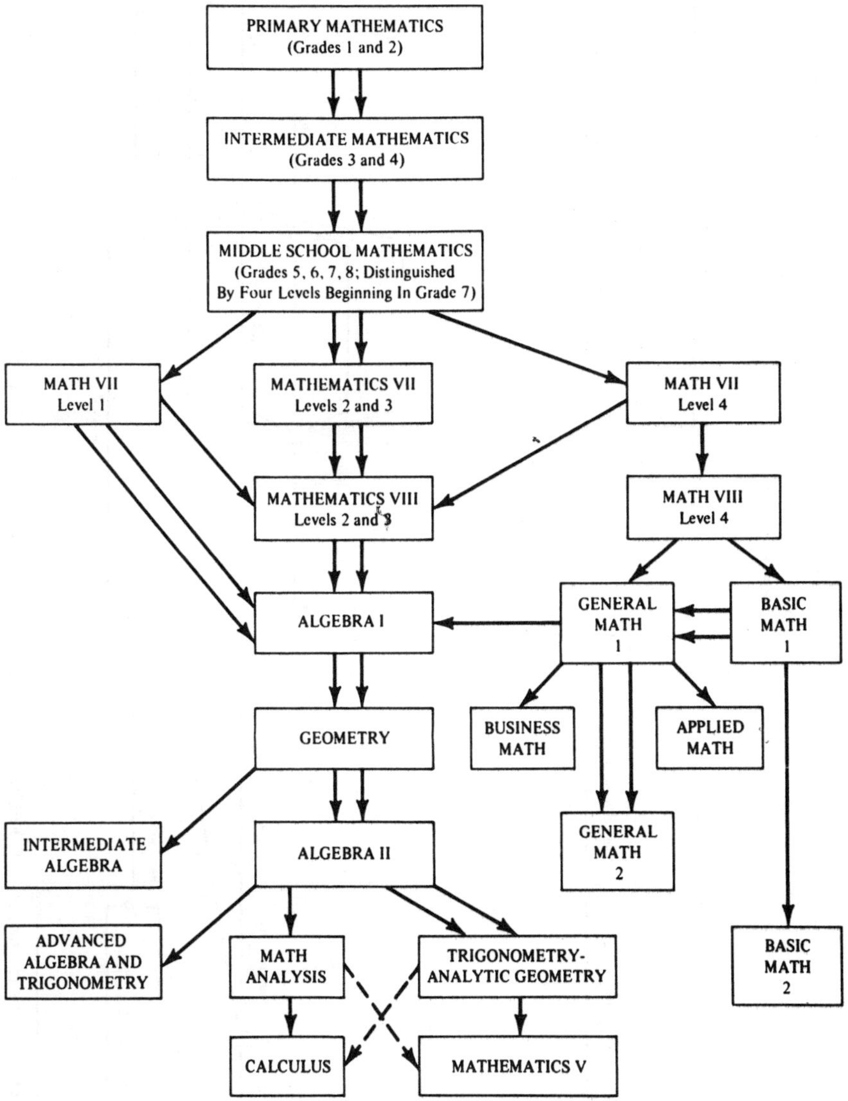

Note:
Double lines = sequence followed by most students continuing to study mathematics
Single lines = alternative possibilities
Dotted lines = optional sequences

APPENDIX I

FLOW CHART FOR INSTRUCTIONAL
PROGRAM INNOVATION PROPOSALS
FOR SEATTLE PUBLIC SCHOOLS

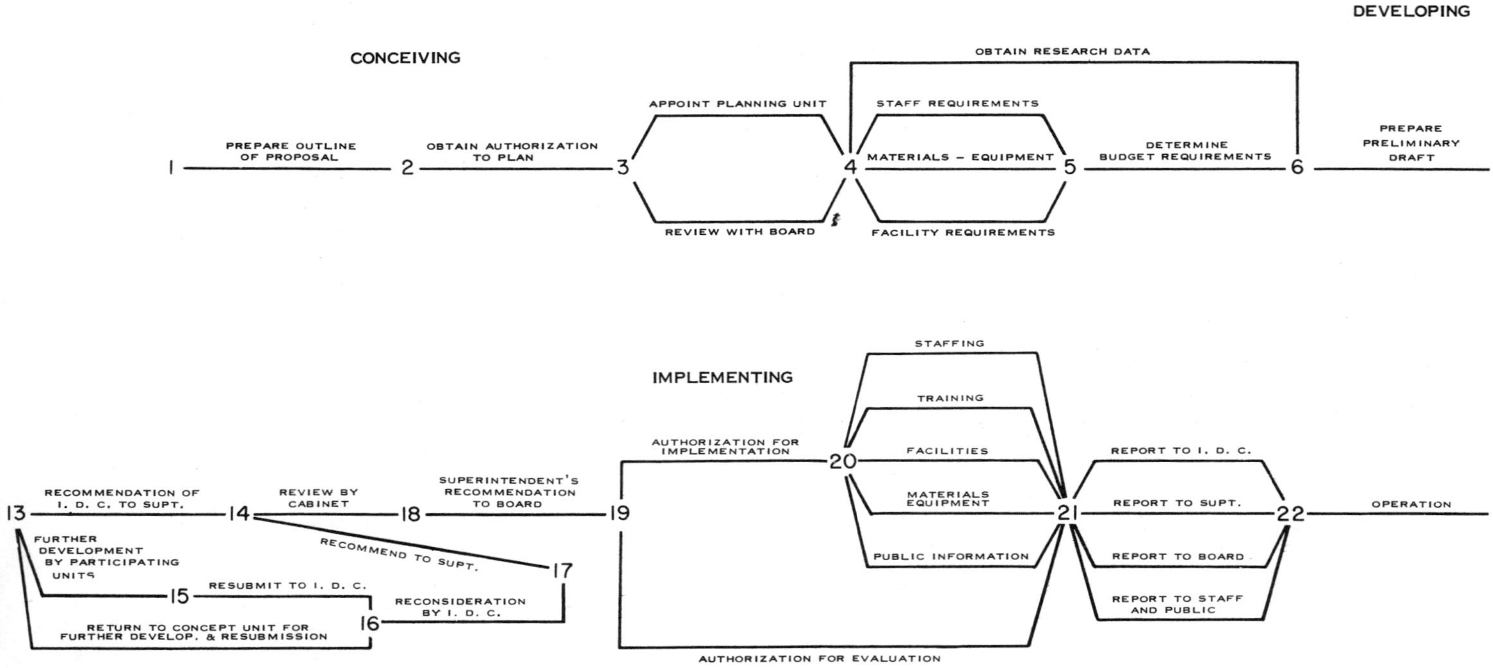

Reproduced with the permission of Forbes Bottomly, Superintendent, Seattle Public Schools.

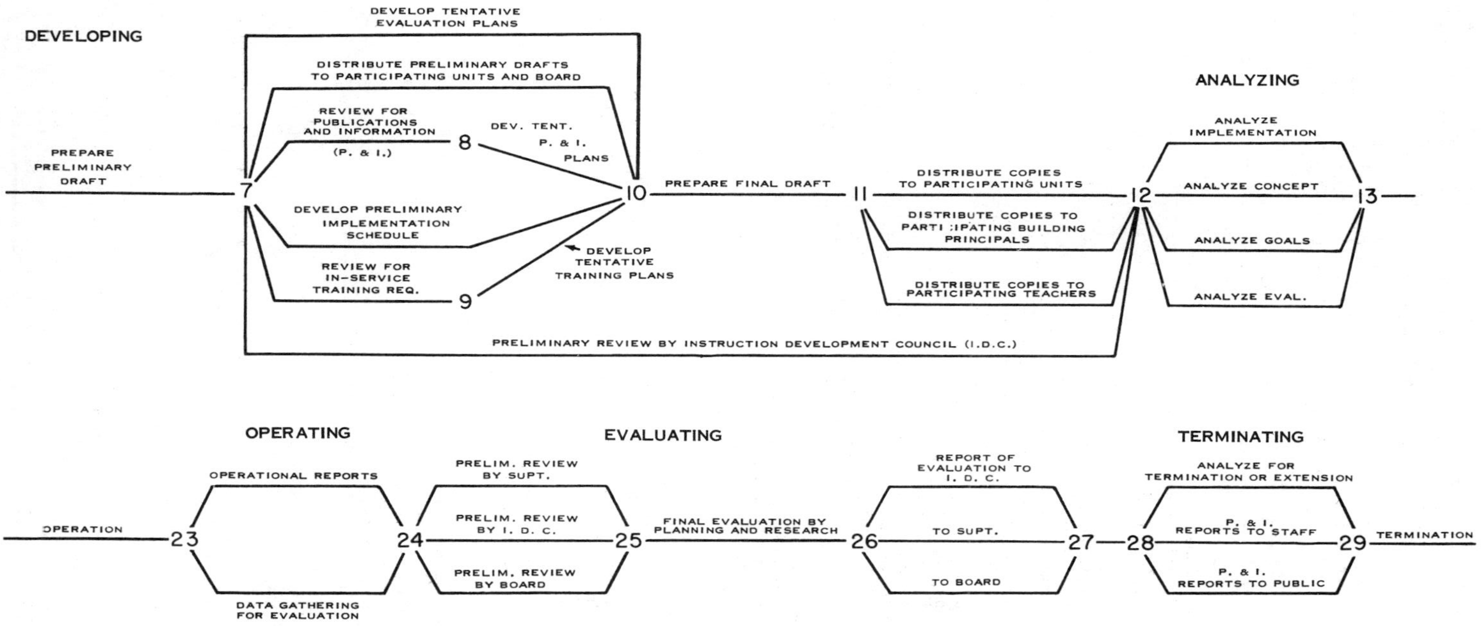

SYSTEMS DEVELOPMENT PATH

APPENDIX J

EXAMPLE OF A TYPICALLY SMALL, LOCAL SCHOOL DISTRICT WHOSE EXPENDITURES MAY BE REPORTED TWO WAYS? (1) WITH A FUNCTION-OBJECT BUDGET FORMAT, AND (2) WITH A PROGRAM-BUDGET FORMAT [a]

Part 1
FUNCTION-OBJECT BUDGET FORMAT

Object Category		Amount	Share
Board of Education			
Personal Services	$ 2,650		
Supplies	3,810		
Other Expenses	13,725		
SUBTOTAL		$ 20,185	0.6%
Central Administration			
Personal Services	78,300		
Equipment	100		
Supplies	2,500		
Other Expenses	7,450		
Services from other districts	11,900		
SUBTOTAL		100,250	3.0%
Instruction, Regular Day School			
Personal Services	1,765,920		
Equipment	32,525		
Supplies	97,585		
Other Expenses	61,460		
Services from other districts	150,830		
SUBTOTAL		2,108,320	62.4%
Instruction, Special Schools			
Personal Services	25,500		
Equipment	650		
Supplies	650		
Other Expenses	770		
SUBTOTAL		27,570	0.8%
Community Services			
Personal Services	34,700		
Equipment	500		
Supplies	3,000		
Other Expenses	1,500		
SUBTOTAL		39,700	1.2%
Transportation			
Personal Services	34,180		
Supplies	950		
Other Expenses	66,675		
SUBTOTAL		101,805	3.0%
Operation and Maintenance			
Personal Services	130,300		
Equipment	4,105		
Supplies	16,845		
Other Expenses	76,950		
SUBTOTAL		228,200	6.8%
Undistributed Expenses			
Employee Benefits	391,985		
Insurance	13,150		
Unclassified	6,400		
SUBTOTAL		441,535	12.2%
Debt Service			
Principal Payments	195,000		
Interest Payments	136,755		
SUBTOTAL		331,755	9.8%
Transfers	9,450	9,450	0.2%
TOTALS		$3,378,770	100.0%

[a] The New York State school district whose data were used for this illustration is in a suburban setting and possesses about average wealth for the State. It has a K-12 enrollment of approximately 2,500 pupils with a professional staff of 130. Although its expenditures per pupil may exceed many districts, the general characteristics of the district are quite similar to many of the 20,000 local school districts in the United States. The function-object budget is state-mandated, whereas the program budget is optional.

Part 2
PROGRAM-BUDGET FORMAT

Program Category		Amount	Share
Classroom Instruction: Elementary Level			
General Classroom Programs	622,011		
Subject Area Teachers Specializations	89,577		
Library Services	18,300		
Cooperative Teacher-aide programs	6,000		
Prekindergarten Recognition Program	1,000		
Special Education	24,300		
Television Instruction Project	2,880		
SUBTOTAL		764,068	22.6%
Classroom Instruction: Intermediate Level			
General Classroom Programs	587,095		
Library Services	20,920		
Special Education	23,400		
Summer School Program	6,950		
Television Instruction Project	1,600		
SUBTOTAL		639,965	18.9%
Classroom Instruction: Secondary Level			
General Classroom Programs	602,252		
Vocational-Technical Programs	40,500		
Library Services	24,456		
Special Education	15,700		
Television Instruction Project	13,900		
Summer School Programs	10,250		
Athletic Programs	27,730		
Cocurricular Programs	4,000		
SUBTOTAL		738,788	21.8%
Classroom Supporting Programs			
Curriculum Research & Development	35,675		
Administration of School Buildings	119,919		
Pupil Personnel Programs	161,615		
Teacher Personnel Programs	51,725		
Custodial Care of the Buildings	204,700		
Pupil Transportation Services	84,580		
Food Service Programs[b]	9,450		
SUBTOTAL		667,664	19.7%
Community Benefits & Involvements			
Youth Recreation Programs[b]	39,700		
Adult Education Programs[b]	9,370		
Public Meetings & Information	5,050		
Census & Populations Projections	3,825		
Benefits to Nonpublic School Students	29,050		
SUBTOTAL		86,995	2.6%
Property Acquisition, Preservation & Management			
Building Debt Service Payments	331,755		
Building Maintenance Services	37,560		
Equipment Maintenance Services	5,785		
Property Insurance	4,715		
SUBTOTAL		379,815	11.3%
Business & Fiscal Management			
Business Office Operations	29,160		
Tax Collection & Control	1,500		
Independent Auditors	1,500		
SUBTOTAL		32,160	1.0%
System Wide Administration			
Board of Education Commitments	865		
Central Administration Expenses	44,350		
Legal & Liability Protection	1,200		
Assessments to Cooperative Educational Districts & Organizations	22,900		
SUBTOTAL		69,315	2.1%
TOTALS		$3,378,770	100.0%

[b]Excess of expenditures over receipts

APPENDIX K

SUMMARY OF A PROGRAM-BUDGET RESEARCH PROJECT

	Function 1 Research of Overall System Design	Function 2 Cost Analysis Research	Function 3 Program Identification Research
OBJECTIVES	The preliminary design of organizational system conducive to the successful operation of the budget techniques	To establish cost schedules of direct and indirect costs of instructional programs	To identify present instructional programs as they relate to (1) Strategy of Education (2) cost accounting (3) program budget
PROCEDURES	1-Identify goals 2-Determine support requirements 3-Synthesize organization 4-Design data flow and analysis system 5-Design evaluation procedures	1-Analyze instructional support function costs in terms of direct and indirect costs 2-Establish formulas for periodic revision of costs 3-Compose and publish initial cost schedules	1-Establish program definitions that accommodate goals, support organization cost, cost accounting, and program budgeting in terms of present instructional programs 2-Identify present programs for budgeting 3-Analyze future program objectives 4-Continued refinement of goal and program design
PRODUCTS OF RESEARCH	Preliminary report for establishing guidance for Steps 2 through 7	A manual of cost schedules appliable to programs with revision procedures	A list of programs which is adaptable to cost accounting budgeting and EDP

[a] Permission to reproduce the summary was granted by E.L. Whigham, Superintendent, Dade County Public Schools.

FOR DADE COUNTY PUBLIC SCHOOLS (MIAMI, FLORIDA)[a]

Function 4	Function 5	Function 6	Function 7
Accounting Procedures Research	Budget Procedures Research	Data Processing Applications Research	Planning & Evaluation Procedures Research
To design accounting procedures to accommodate cost accounting and the program budget for federal, state & local funds, and management requirements	To design budgeting procedures which accommodate the program budget and exercise the best financial planning techniques	To design an EDP sub-system which best satisfies the requirements of the Strategy of Education	To design a planning and evaluation function under the superintendent
1-Determine all functions requiring accounting services and reports, internal and external 2-Determine accounting, personnel, payroll, purchasing and other interrelated functional procedures 3-Establish accounting procedures to satisfy all requirements	1-Determine the report requirements for federal, state and local agencies 2-Determine financial planning procedures for revenues and appropriations 3-Determine best procedures for budgeting programs 4-Design coordination procedures with planning and support functions 5-Establish budget presentation and review procedures	1-Analyze guidance from senior consultants, reference Step 1 2-Observe and analyze old and new organization to determine interim and planned CDP requirements 3-Design and develop EPD procedures which accommodate data flow plan of the senior consultant	1-Design procedures for goal revision and policy formation and dissemination 2-Design planning function based on goal, policy, priority and resource allocation 3-Design an overall supporting system evaluation function including statistical analysis
A manual of accounting procedures which accommodate the Strategy of Education	A manual of budget policies and procedures	A manual of optimum procedure description for data processing to meet all system requirements	A manual of goal and policy formulation planning and evaluation procedures

APPENDIX L

TAXONOMY FOR A THIRD GRADE READING PROGRAM ILLUSTRATING THE SEQUENCE FROM BROAD LANGUAGE ARTS GOALS TO SPECIFIC READING SKILLS[a]

PROGRAM CATEGORIES	PROGRAM OBJECTIVES	PERFORMANCE MEASURES AND OPERATIONAL OBJECTIVES
Language Arts	develop proficiency in communications skills: reading, writing, speaking, and listening	achieve a mean rate of advancement for pupils equivalent to one full year (providing mean I.Q. for pupils in the building is 100) on the language, vocabulary, and reading comprehension sections of the Iowa Tests of Educational Development.
Reading	cultivate the ability to decode, comprehend, and evaluate printed materials (developmental), establish work-study skills (functional); and promote taste and appreciation for literature (recreational)	achieve a mean rate of advancement equivalent to one full year on the reading subtests of the Iowa Tests of Basic Skills.
Developmental Reading	enhance the ability to decode, comprehend, and evaluate printed materials	achieve a mean grade equivalent score of 3.9 on Metropolitan Reading Tests
Reading Comprehension	develop the ability to detect the main ideas of a paragraph	achieve a mean grade equivalent score of 3.9 on the paragraph meaning section of the Metropolitan Reading Tests
Critical Reading	foster the ability to analyze and evaluate both the content and style of printed argumentative, informational, or literary materials	achieve a mean grade equivalent score of 3.9 on the Ohio State University Critical Reading Test
Authenticity	develop the ability to judge the relevancy and validity of information derived from printed materials	achieve a mean grade equivalent score of 3.9 on the sub-test of the Ohio State University Critical Reading Test

[a] An extensive statement of qualifications and limitations might accompany this example so that one would not misinterpret these operational definitions. It is recognized that achievement is multi-dimensional, and that test scores can be misleading. One might establish grade norms, percentile norms within grades, and individual pupil profile charts to plot the growth in skills for each child.

AUTHOR INDEX

GENERAL INDEX